THE ART OF MARGARET ATWOOD
Essays in Criticism

The Art of Margaret Atwood

Essays in Criticism

Edited by
Arnold E. Davidson &
Cathy N. Davidson

Anansi   Toronto

Cover design: Peggy Heath

Published with the assistance of the Canada Council and the Ontario Arts Council, and printed in Canada for

House of Anansi Press Limited
35 Britain Street
Toronto, Ontario M5A 1R7

Canadian Cataloguing in Publication Data

Main entry under title:

The Art of Margaret Atwood

Bibliography: p.
Includes index.

ISBN 0-88784-080-9

1. Atwood, Margaret, 1939-   — Criticism and interpretation. I. Davidson, Arnold E., 1936-
II. Davidson, Cathy N., 1949-

PS8501.T86Z57   C813'.54   C80-094136-5
PR9199.3.A87Z57

---

1 2 3 4 5 / 87 86 85 84 83 82 81

THE ART OF MARGARET ATWOOD

Contents

Introduction

"Canadian literature? Isn't Margaret Atwood a Canadian?" That question in various forms has often been put to us during the year that we have spent in Japan teaching and lecturing on Canadian literature. Even though she has not yet been translated into Japanese, Margaret Atwood is still widely read on this far side of the Pacific, read in English, which is a definite tribute to her very broad appeal. It is that same broad appeal that prompts the present volume. In the subsequent essays, thirteen critics and scholars seek to illuminate different aspects of Atwood's work. Their baker's dozen of critical commentaries should offer the reader — the specialist as well as the literate "generalist" who is most responsible for Atwood's success — different perspectives on a writer who refuses to be pinned down, labelled, or dismissed. The final item in the book, Alan J. Horne's comprehensive bibliography of scholarship up to 1980, can also refer any interested reader, generalist or specialist, to still other assessments of Atwood and her work.

Margaret Atwood — poet, short story writer, novelist, and critic — is at least four authors in one. We say at least four in one because, as the subsequent essays demonstrate, the author of *The Edible Woman* is not identical to the author of *Surfacing* or *Lady Oracle* or, for that matter, *Life Before Man*. What characterizes Atwood as a novelist is both her talent and her diversity. She is not one of those authors who rewrites, attempting to refine in the process, the same basic book. Nor does she, in the great tradition of

William Faulkner or Margaret Laurence, rework and thereby work out the past and present of one representative fictive location — the heritage of Yoknapatawpha County or Manawaka, Manitoba. Atwood did not follow the apprentice social and sexual comedy of her first novel, *The Edible Woman*, with a more finished exercise in the same vein. Even more to her credit, although her second novel, *Surfacing*, was almost immediately recognized as a contemporary classic, she did not attempt to duplicate that early accomplishment with further studies of lost women mythically found. Instead, she has adhered to her own course, a course that has allowed each of the novels to speak with a different voice and to set forth a different vision.

Neither is she the same poet in the various volumes of poetry, even though the journey from *Double Persephone* to *Two-Headed Poems* is not, as even those two titles suggest, the same far journey as the road taken between the first novel and the recently published fourth one. Nevertheless, Atwood is a major poet too, one of Canada's best. Perhaps her best poetic work is *The Journals of Susanna Moodie*, a book in which she conjoins her voice and sensibility with the evoked words and imagined awareness of her famous predecessor from whom the book takes its title. And neither has she gone unnoted as a critic. Atwood herself has observed that the approximately 75,000 copies of *Survival* so far sold in Canada must represent some kind of a record for Canadian criticism.

Margaret Atwood is a writer of many facets. So the method of this book is — appropriately, we think — its multiplicity of approaches. Different critics hold different works up to their individual critical lights. If the resultant observations and insights do not give us a real-life portrait of the complete artist at work, they do, like the scattered but calculated observations in the early poem, "This is a Photograph of Me," suggest how other perusers of the face that is and is not there might proceed to develop their own picture. Certainly much of the necessary background is provided, starting with the first essay in the volume, Sandra Djwa's "The Where of Here: Margaret Atwood and a Canadian Tradition." That first essay assesses Atwood's poetry within the larger context of Canadian poetry especially as it developed in the Fifties and Sixties, two decades during which a Canadian poetic renaissance was substantially shaped by Northrop Frye's criticism, by emerging Canadian nationalism, and by a new feminism. As

Professor Djwa observes: "It is almost as if [Atwood] consciously sets herself down right in the middle of the Canadian literary landscape and tries to make sense of it all by filtering archetypal Canadian experience through her poetic sensibility." She also suggests that it is Atwood's central position in this poetic land-scape — a Canadian landscape which naturally gives rise to "questions of identity" as well as to a "Darwinian habit of seeing and placing the human animal" in the natural world — that has "uniquely equipped Atwood to be a spokeswoman for today's world." Readers well-versed in Canadian poetic traditions as well as more general readers should appreciate Professor Djwa's discussion of the context that provides the inspiration for much of Atwood's poetic accomplishment. General readers especially interested in Atwood's poetry are also introduced, through the opening essay, to Atwood's literary antecedents and compatriots.

The second essay in the collection provides a complementary voice to the first one and gives a poetic assessment of matters not included in Professor Djwa's scholarly study of Atwood's heritage as a poet. Because of Atwood's singular success in the United States, we have asked, for our second essay, an American poet and critic, Judith McCombs, to discuss the international (as opposed to the national) literary traditions that she perceives in Atwood's poetic corpus. Professor McCombs, incidentally, lives in Detroit, barely across the international border, and has published a good deal of her own poetry in Canadian literary magazines. So she comes to Atwood's texts with a double sensitivity: to Canada but also to a non-Canadian tradition of women's Gothic literature and nature writing. She hears in Atwood's work the resonances and refrains of a nineteenth-century British Gothic tradition. She also demonstrates how Atwood utilizes the more distant tradition by giving a contemporary habitation to the conventional sexual tropes of the nineteenth-century Gothic.

From that joint beginning, the other essays move on to discuss the different styles, images, themes, and forms of all of Atwood's major writings, exploring, by extension, manifestations of a Canadian poetic and fictional tradition even as they assess aspects of a writer now known to many readers who know little about Canada or Canadian literature (and who often do not even realize that Atwood is a Canadian). The progression of these essays requires only a little commentary. After the two "background" studies already mentioned, Sherrill E. Grace analyzes the duplici-

tous voice in Atwood's poetry and remarks on the particular
success of the double vision in *The Journals of Susanna Moodie*.
Professor Grace also suggests that a structuralist or phenomeno-
logical model might best illuminate the intricacies of that book.
Lorraine Weir provides just such an essay. Her "Meridians of
Perception: A Reading of *The Journals of Susanna Moodie*"
focuses on the merging of collage and poem, the resonances between visual and verbal images which give one of Atwood's most
sustained poetic sequences its structure and depth.

Professor Weir's essay is complex, specialized, not designed
for the casual reader. In contrast, the final two essays on the poetry
proceed more generally and more broadly. The first of these is by a
distinguished American scholar, Linda W. Wagner. Professor
Wagner assesses theme, style, and evolving sexual politics as the
implicit criteria which determined the contents of *Selected Poems*.
Wagner argues that the process of producing a "selected" volume
constitutes a landmark in the developing sensibility of any writer.
That same landmark also attests to Atwood's arrival as a major
voice in twentieth-century North American poetry. The final essay
in the poetry section of this volume examines still a different kind
of selection. Professor Lorna Irvine shows the way in which the
female voice becomes more controlled and controlling with each
successive volume of poetry and the ways in which the primary
emphasis shifts, especially with *Two-Headed Poems,* from a man-
versus-woman dichotomy to a woman-to-woman pairing.

Canadian critics have tended to credit Atwood more for her
poetry than for her fiction, while in the United States the balance
of praise definitely tips the other way. So Lee Briscoe Thompson, a
Canadian currently teaching in the U.S., has set out to harmonize
these differences. In "Minuets and Madness: Margaret Atwood's
Dancing Girls," Professor Thompson traces the relationships
between the poetry and the fiction and suggests that the short
stories, collectively published as *Dancing Girls,* provide thematic
and stylistic bridges between the poems and the novels. The next
three essays in the collection — by Catherine McLay, Annis Pratt,
and Clara Thomas — focus, in succession, on the first three novels.
Employing as their starting points the theories of Northrop Frye,
C.G. Jung, and Ellen Moers, these three essays examine image
patterns, narrative movements, and plot structures to chart the
evolution of the female protagonist in each work. These essays
also postulate an essentially positive pattern of growth. Thus

Professor McLay argues that *The Edible Woman* — a novel often discussed and too often dismissed as an apprentice feminist satire — can best be read as a "romance" in the Frygian sense, and a surprisingly finished romance at that. The well-known literary critic and biographer, Professor Clara Thomas, similarly maintains that Atwood's second comic novel, *Lady Oracle,* has also been underestimated. Professor Thomas explores the essential seriousness that underpins the comic episodes and also demonstrates the subtlety and even profundity of Atwood's most maligned novel.

Lady Oracle was especially condemned by critics who expected another *Surfacing.* Atwood's second novel did receive the extravagant praise that could have turned the head of a less clearheaded writer. Immediately hailed as one of the great novels of the twentieth century by more than one enthusiastic commentator, *Surfacing* is already accepted as a feminist quest classic. But instead of documenting again the mythic elements in *Surfacing,* Professor Pratt takes Atwood's feminized quest as her starting point. She argues that Atwood's pathways are ancient and modern, archetypal and idiosyncratic. Pratt's archetypal generalizations extend considerably beyond Atwood. Yet we would also note that Professor Pratt, the third American commentator in this volume, is the one critic who especially employs the kind of "synthetic" criticism that Atwood sees as essentially "Canadian." Atwood has argued that the American writer typically asks "how does it work?" whereas the Canadian tries to find "where does it fit in?" "Where does *Surfacing* fit in?" is, for Professor Pratt, the crucial question.

It is Robert Lecker, a Canadian, who in "Janus through the Looking Glass," poses the knotty question of "how does it work?" By so doing he also assails the popular mythic approach to Atwood's fiction and documents the ways in which the first three novels deliberately parody "search for identity" literature. In contrast to the three essays before it, Professor Lecker's essay gives us another side of Atwood and another side of Atwood criticism. Together these four essays constitute a literary debate. Such debate reveals the ways in which Atwood's work — like any serious artistic endeavour — sustains different interpretations, even contradictory ones. Nor could we permit that contradiction to stand uncontradicted. Our own discussion of Atwood's fourth novel shows how this most recent fiction both does and does not fit the mythic patterns established by the earlier novels and argued by the preceding critics. *Life Before Man* mythicizes the mundane even as it banalizes the mythic. Reality and its imagined opposites, romances of escape and countering inescapable realities, are all mixed and merged.

Finally, George Woodcock's essay discusses Atwood's critical assumptions and practice as well as what Atwood's criticism reveals about her as a poet and a novelist. He takes *Survival* just seriously enough — recognizing its importance, enjoying its idiosyncratic lack of self-importance, its sense of *play* (a noun or verb that supposedly has no place in a serious work of criticism). And just as Sandra Djwa provided an appropriate beginning, George Woodcock gives us the note on which we prefer to end. A sense of play characterizes all of Atwood's work, alleviating even the somber tone of *Life Before Man* and making it much more than a study in despair. Collectively, the essays in this collection also play — in the sense that they come in contact with each other, make connections, interact, contradict, but do not pretend to resolve. There is no final word. Nor should there be. If Atwood is a writer worth reading, it is because she is complex enough to sustain varied interpretative approaches which can elucidate but not finally delimit the free play — the work — of the poet, novelist, short story writer, and critic to whom this volume is devoted.

A.E.D.
C.N.D.
Kobe, Japan

SANDRA DJWA

The Where of Here:
Margaret Atwood and a Canadian Tradition

Margaret Atwood and I belong to the same generation. We were born in the same year, 1939; we attended Canadian universities in the fifties and went on to graduate school in the sixties. Her first poetry chapbook, mythic, ironic, erudite, was *Double Persephone,* published in 1961; my first graduate essay of 1964 was a long heavily footnoted study of the Persephone myth. As a poet Atwood is often consciously Canadian; the nature that appears in her poetry, often as primal myth, draws strongly from Canadian poetry and criticism of the last four decades. As a critic, the focus of my work has been the attempt to chart the nature of a Canadian poetic tradition. Our paths crossed briefly at two conferences on Canadian literature on the prairies in the mid and late sixties. At the second, in 1969, Ronald Sutherland gave a paper in which he characterized the Mrs. Moodie of *Roughing It in the Bush* as an imperialist Englishwoman, an argument which I countered during the question period with the suggestion that she had become a Canadian by the end of the book. After the paper, several of us, including Margaret Atwood, walked across the University of Alberta campus to lunch, still speaking of Mrs. Moodie and her attitude to Canada, a question already explored by Atwood in some poems of *The Journals of Susanna Moodie* published in 1970.

I draw these parallels simply to remark that for younger Canadian women who were also poets or critics there were certain cultural 'givens' which modified the inherited literary tradition. Tradition, the product of a cultural inheritance influenced by the contemporary, is both the same and a little different for each succeeding generation. And for our generation, those who came to maturity in the late fifties, the literary tradition had broadened to include the Canadian. Up to the middle fifties the tradition was the English (and male) tradition of Milton, Wordsworth and Arnold rendered slightly more palatable by a sprinkling of the Americans, Hawthorne, James, Poe and Eliot. But by the time our generation was studying English literature at Canadian universities there were certain new elements to be considered. There was now a body of Canadian writing. We fell heir to several good poetry anthologies: the Klinck and Watters *Canadian Anthology* of 1955 and A.J.M. Smith's *The Oxford Book of Canadian Verse* of 1960, an enlarged version of his pioneer anthology of 1943. There was the prestige of the myth-centered criticism of Northrop Frye which found in Canadian poetry a national archetype. There was the new nationalism of the early sixties. Finally, there was a barely perceptible, but growing, feminine consciousness. Two of the more important women poets in Canada, Jay Macpherson and Margaret Avison, were associated with the University of Toronto when Atwood enrolled as an undergraduate at Victoria College. It was an exceptionally good time to be at Victoria: Pratt would sometimes come in for lunch, Frye was very much a presence, Atwood was taught by Macpherson.

Not surprisingly, Atwood was the first of her generation to acknowledge that she was writing from within a continuum of Canadian poetry. This was not the case for earlier poets. A.J.M. Smith, Dorothy Livesay and Al Purdy, all of whom had come under the influence of Bliss Carman, tended to remark upon this fact *sotto voce*. Atwood, reading her poems on the Canadian Broadcasting Corporation early in the seventies, stated matter-of-factly that she had, of course, read and learned from her predecessors.

There was now a recognizable Canadian poetic canon. It included E.J. Pratt's *The Titanic* and "Silences," Earle Birney's *David* and "Bushed," F.R. Scott's "Laurentian Shield" and "Lakeshore," A.M. Klein's "Portrait of the Poet as Landscape," Jay Macpherson's "The Boatman" and Margaret Avison's "New Year's Poem." Atwood absorbed all of these poems early in the sixties when she read Smith's Oxford anthology and the Klinck and Watters anthology. About the same time, she read the *Collec-*

ted Poems of Pratt and books of poetry by Jay Macpherson, Margaret Avison and P.K. Page. She also read some of the younger poets in the newly founded *Tamarack Review* and began to keep up with contemporary criticism. Northrop Frye was writing the annual review of Canadian poetry for "Letters in Canada" of the *University of Toronto Quarterly* from 1950 to 1959, reviews which Atwood followed with interest. She was impressed by "Klein's Drowned Poet: Canadian Variations on an Old Theme," an article written by Milton Wilson, Frye's successor at the *University of Toronto Quarterly*, for the recently founded *Canadian Literature.* Wilson's article pointed out the incidence of the figure of the drowned poet in Canadian poetry, focussing on the final verse of Klein's "Portrait of the Poet as Landscape":

> . . . he
> makes of his status as zero a rich garland,
> a halo of his anonymity,
> and lives alone, and in his secret shines
> like phosphorus. At the bottom of the sea.

Klein, the drowned poet, is both nth Adam and decomposing corpse. As Adam, he takes "a green inventory," listing the world by naming it, thus achieving "a single camera view." By the end of the poem in Wilson's rendering, the poet has "resurrected his own drowned body as well as the world's."[1] Hovering above Wilson's Blakean analysis is the implication that the "drowned poet" is a Canadian archetype, a concept suggestive of Frye's criticism.

As a critic and teacher Frye had a far reaching effect on Canadian writing. Not the least of his importance to our generation was the fact that Frye, a critic with a growing international reputation, remained *here* (in Canada) as opposed to *there* (in the United States) — a choice that Douglas Bush, A.J.M. Smith, Leon Edel, Hugh Kenner and E.K. Brown were unable to make. In the simplest sense, Frye's example encouraged an interest in archetype as psychological truth and shaping form; an interest that radiated out from his lectures and writings on Blake to the myth-centred poetry of Eli Mandel, James Reaney and Jay Macpherson. In a larger sense, Frye helped to make us aware of the place of myth in interpreting and shaping cultural consciousness; in essays and reviews like "Canada and Its Poetry" (1943) and "The Narrative Tradition of English-Canadian Literature" (1946), in epigraphs and stray remarks in *The Educated Imagination* (1963) and, above all, in his "Conclusion" to *The Literary History of Canada* (1965).

In this last essay Frye describes Canada as an alien continent, remarking that "the traveller from Europe edges into it like a tiny Jonah entering an inconceivably large whale." Canadian nature was a fearful one against which man fought by erecting his physical and psychological garrisons. This conquest of nature by shutting it out, he goes on,

> has its own perils for the imagination. . . . I have long been impressed in Canadian poetry by a tone of deep terror in regard to nature. . . . It is not a terror of the dangers of discomforts or even of the mysteries of nature, but a terror of the soul at something that these things manifest. The human mind has nothing but human and moral values to cling to if it is to preserve its integrity or even its sanity, yet the vast unconsciousness of nature in front of it seems an unanswerable denial of those values.[2]

In the same essay Frye writes half-humourously that Canada's Centenary, the celebration of its first one hundred years as a Dominion was then (in 1964) looming up "with all the urgency of a Day of Atonement." The literary nationalism of the early sixties, an off-shoot of the national feeling generated by World War II, accelerated in the early sixties. And, as Frye's last review of the year's poetry in 1959 demonstrates, the cultural nationalism of the period had an important shaping influence on some aspects of his criticism:

> Poetry is of major importance in the culture and therefore in the history of a country, especially of a country that is still struggling for articulateness. The appearance of a fine new book of poems in Canada is a historical event, and its readers should be aware that they are participating in history. To develop such awareness it is an advantage to have a relatively limited cultural horizon. *Ubi bene, ibi patria;* the centre of reality is wherever one happens to be, and its circumference is whatever one's imagination can make sense of.[3]

This perspective on Canada's poetry owes something to E.J. Pratt, whose major poems were directed towards the creation of a national mythology (and who taught Frye to judge poetry while both sorted manuscripts for the *Canadian Poetry Magazine* which Pratt began in 1935). Frye's perspective also owes something to E.K. Brown, his predecessor of "Letters in Canada" at *University of Toronto Quarterly* and the author of *On Canadian Poetry* (1943), a classic exposition of the problems of a Canadian literature within the context of a national culture. Frye's criticism, in turn, was to encourage a new generation of younger poets, notably Reaney, Eli Mandel and Atwood, towards making Canada the mythic centre of their imaginative reality. In time, this process of influence and acknowledgement went full circle. Frye, when issuing a collection of his essays on Canadian literature, entitled them *The Bush Garden* (1971) — echoing the title of a poem from Atwood's *The Journals of Susanna Moodie*.

Generally speaking, poets and critics of the late fifties and early sixties were far more optimistic about Canada and its poetry than their predecessors. For some of the poets of the forties, Canada was, in Douglas LePan's depressing phrase, "A Country Without a Mythology." By extension, it lacked the imaginative ground for a national literature. The attitude that Canada had no literature and was not likely to produce one continued through the fifties and sixties (even in some cases to the early seventies) in semi-official circles such as the English Departments of some Canadian universities. In fact, the tide had begun to turn about 1943 although this was not to become manifest for nearly three decades. The Second World War had sparked a new poetry, four little magazines, and two critically significant anthologies, those of Ralph Gustafson and A.J.M. Smith. The second of these, Smith's judiciously edited *The Book of Canadian Poetry* (1943), demonstrated, perhaps for the first time, a respectable body of native poetry stretching back over a hundred years. Northrop Frye, in "Canada and Its Poetry," a review of Smith's selections, discerned "the existence of a definable Canadian genius . . . which is neither British nor American. According to Mr. Smith's book," he went on, "the outstanding achievement of Canadian poetry is the evocation of stark terror . . . The immediate source of this terror is obviously the frightening loneliness of a huge and thinly settled country."[4] In effect, Frye was to create a Canadian myth by articulating a new "primal" sense of Canadian nature, a nature already implicit in the poetry of Pratt, F.R. Scott and Birney. It was Frye's threatening, unexplored nature, a uniquely Canadian strain of Romanticism infused by Darwinism, that was to be further developed by younger poets like Purdy and Atwood.

Finally, the generation of the late fifties and early sixties was influenced by a new feminine consciousness. Roy Daniells in 1964, when he came to write on Isabella Valency Crawford for the *Literary History of Canada*, hovered over the adjective "lady" as descriptive of a female poet and then abandoned it. Crawford was far too good a poet, he judged, to be called a "lady poet." No Canadian critic before this time would have shown this distinction. The status of Canadian women poets — and of poetry itself — had begun to change. Margaret Avison's *Winter Sun* (1960), reviewed by Atwood in 1961, contributed to this reassessment. Quite simply, it was one of our very best books of Canadian poetry. Like P.K. Page, Avison brought to poetry a remarkable capacity for psychological introspection and a brilliant command of form and metaphor. Jay Macpherson's Blakean poetic cycle, *The Boatman* (1957), also contributed directly. Her witty and iconoclastic variations on the white goddess, one of which is apparent in the verse epigraph to this collection — "Sir, no man's nightingale, your foolish bird" — effectively demolished previously held renditions of the Philomela myth and asserted a new and tougher female muse.[5] Because the book is structured through cycles of innocence and experience it is the 'doubleness' of the female experience which strikes the reader; there is a despairing Sibylla and a jaunty Sibylla; a vulnerable Persephone, "the lost girl under water," and a powerful "Hell's Queen."

Margaret Atwood's first book, *Double Persephone*, owes a great deal to Macpherson, primarily the play of intelligence on various archetypes of the female, and a new authoritative, astringent tone. It was a tone new to Canadian poetry although Edith Sitwell had earlier exemplified it in English poetry. Like many of our generation Atwood gravitated to the myth of Persephone, the archetypal patriarchal version of feminine experience; certainly, Blake in *The Book of Thel* and Lawrence in *The Lost Girl* treat it as such. The tendency in the fifties was to opt in rather than out. In its classical versions, the myth tells of the rape of Persephone by Pluto: her abduction while picking flowers on the fields of Enna, the descent into Hades through the waters near Sicily, the eating of pomegranate seeds followed by a long winter of confinement and spring rebirth. The symbolic context of the myth is obviously powerful: the descent through the waters as sexual initiation, longed for and dreaded; the connection between eating, sexual experience and gestation; the organic relationship between Persephone (flower and corn maiden, the Kore) and the land itself. In the old Eleusinian mysteries she is the fertility principle: corn grains and pig bones dropped into a furrow of earth generated the new life of flower and grain.

Nonetheless, for contemporary women poets, Persephone may represent one of the anterooms to the feminist movement. For once women begin to explore the received archetype, as did Kathleen Raine, they also begin to register their acceptances and rejections of specific aspects of the myth as do Carolyn Kizer and Margaret Atwood. Women in the late fifties wanting to explore the feminine invariably turned to the literary archetype — the received image of woman — rather than to society itself. In *Double Persephone* Atwood begins with the traditional myth but like Macpherson she tends to invert the received image to emphasize a more resilient female. The book begins with the fruitful Persephone of classical myth. "From her all springs arise/To her all falls return/ The articulate flesh . . ./Root flower and fern." Like Macpherson, Atwood emphasizes her double aspect: "The dancing girl's a withered crone. . . ." In "Her Song" (suggestive both of A.J.M. Smith's and Edith Sitwell's "Metamorphosis") and in the title poem, "Double Persephone" Atwood adds to the traditional fertility complex the creation of art as well. In this last poem Persephone is associated with the flower as art and artifact (icon): "Where letters grown from branch and stem/Have no green leaves enclosing them . . ." Moreover, she shares with her lovers complicity for her own descent, a descent which is closely related to the creation of her art: she gathers "words as cruel as thorns" while "the black horses of her breath/Stamp impatient for her death. . . ."

> And when word thorn leaf letter blossom fall
> These woods loves hooves will trample all.

Atwood's myth incorporates all aspects of the triple goddess; it also reflects the changing emphasis of an emerging feminist movement which tends to present the female as the agent of her own destiny. In effect, the poem creates another "Iconic Landscape" which celebrates the descent of Persephone as woman and poet.

The new feminism, a myth-centred poetry, Frye's criticism and the growing nationalism of the early sixties all helped to shape Atwood's literary inheritance: together they produced a particular sensibility, a mythic imagination reflected in her treatment of the male-female relationship and Canadian nature. Atwood's first four books of poetry, *The Circle Game* (1966), *The*

Animals in That Country (1968), *The Journals of Susanna Moodie* (1970) and *Procedures for Underground* (1970) are informed by a reworking of myth, especially fertility myth, and by the desire to explore, as in the archetypes of *Power Politics* (1971), the position of woman in today's society.

The circumference of Margaret Atwood's imagination — a world of explorers, drowned poets, humans that merge into landscape, and oddly metamorphosed birds and animals — is often contained by Canada's national and literary boundaries. It is almost as if she consciously sets herself down, right in the middle of the Canadian literary landscape, and tries to orient herself by filtering Canadian experience through archetypes of her poetic sensibility. She employs a variety of personae; the trapper, the pioneer, the settler (Frye calls Mrs. Moodie the archetypal Canadian pioneer, "a one-woman garrison . . . individualized by accident"[6]), Indian shaman, contemporary diver, today's woman, man and child in Alliston, Ontario. The poem is often a journey across the continent, through the wilderness, underground, or down into water. Many of these journeys are seen as a descent, ultimately a journey down into the psychological self.[7]

As such the mythic descent is related to questions of identity — sexual, aesthetic, national. In the Canadian critical tradition landscape has always been closely associated with identity. Frye has remarked that for Canadians the question is not so much "Who am I?" but rather a variant such as "Where is here?,"a point which Atwood emphasizes in *Survival,* her commentary on Canadian writing. Frye's remark can be related to Carl Berger's exposition of the dominant 19th century Canadian political myth, "The True North Strong and Free," which assimilated Canadian identity to the northern landscape. In the Canadian cultural tradition the process of coming to terms with self and with country has historically required a coming to terms with landscape. It was the sense of a rugged northern nature, a nature of struggle, that provided a mythic basis for the strong, bold canvasses of the Group of Seven in the early twenties. The new art of the Group, in turn, encouraged a new landscape poetry in the years between the wars: Pratt's *The Titanic,* Birney's *David,* Scott's "Laurentian Shield" — a strain that culminates in the sixties in books such as Al Purdy's *North of Summer.*

It is the need to centre oneself in a tradition that is answered in part by a Canadian literary nationalism. In Atwood's poem,

"Comic Book Vs. History (1949, 1969)," the literary maps of the United States and Canada are contrasted. To the child in 1949, America was rich in imaginative possibilities, a land to be filled in with dramatic, comic book heroes in swinging capes: "from their fists came beautiful/orange collisions." Our side of the map, Canada, was disappointingly drab: "it held only/real-sized explorers, confined/to animal skin coats. . . ." However, for the adult travelling in America in 1969 reality displaces myth: she finds "space contracted, the/red and silver/heroes had collapsed. . . ." And so she turns back again to her own country Canada: its reality becomes the basis of a new mythology.

> I turn back, search
> for the actual, collect lost
> bones, burnt logs
> of campfires, pieces of fur.

In this search the artifact has potentially numinous meaning as it is the basis on which one pieces together a civilization, a mythology, a nation.

The Circle Game, like any poet's first book, is both derivative and original. Every now and again we hear what is to become Atwood's mature poetic voice; aware, a little dry, reporting the comedy (or tragedy) of the sexes:

> You have nothing
> that serves the function of a sceptre
> and I have
> certainly
> no flowers.

The allusion is to the King and Queen on the backs of playing cards but it could well be Pluto and Persephone: such figures are ultimately You and I, the archetypal male and female of the poem. One of the most attractive poems in this book is the sequence, "Letters Towards and Away" with its wonderfully complex emotion. Keep away, says the female persona to her lover, don't invade me: a command promptly followed by a wondering recognition of all that he offers and a brusque, grudging, half-surprised, acceptance:

> I don't wear gratitude
> well. Or hats.

> What would I do with
> veils and silly feathers
> or a cloth rose
> growing from the top of my head?
>
> What should I do with this
> peculiar furred emotion?

The ending of this poem is entirely predictable, entirely human, "Quickly,/send me some more letters."

Much of the charm of Atwood's first poetry is her gift for flamboyant metaphor. The line, "this/peculiar furred emotion" strikes us as exactly right although it takes some puzzling to see why. Superficially, the persona might want to reject a fur coat along with a silly hat — both belong to the category of trivia. But here the line seems to be working at a deeper level. This ridiculous emotion called love and its accompanying warmth, we are led to see, is ultimately sexual in origin; it tends to blur/fur back into the animal itself and its primary needs. Atwood's metaphors, her sense of the human as animal in an evolutionary (more specifically, devolutionary) context, are quite unique in contemporary British and American poetry. This is one of the reasons that her poetic metaphors seem so fresh and new although her poetic concerns, centring on questions of female/male identity and relationships, are quite familiar. The Canadian tradition, in which questions of identity have always been stressed and where a Darwinian habit of seeing and placing the human as animal has already been established, may have uniquely equipped Atwood to describe the contemporary battle of the sexes.

In her first books Margaret Atwood is exploring relationships through what ultimately becomes her own version of a primal fertility myth. *The Circle Game* begins with an archetypal drowning, a poem which embodies the generic myth of Atwood's early poetry, the myth of the descent. The book concludes with two poems, "Pioneers" and "Settlers," which embody her characteristic metaphor, that of body-into-landscape. The first poem, "This is a Photograph of Me," bears the same relation to *The Circle Game* as does Leonard Cohen's "Elegy" to his *Let Us Compare Mythologies*, although it describes not Orpheus but a feminine variant, a "Me" who has affinities with the drowned poet which Milton Wilson had implied was a Canadian archetype. The second poem, "After the Flood, We," offers a new myth of origins; the biblical myths of the Fall and the flood are united with the classical myth of Cadmus and the dragon's teeth. There are two survivors after the flood, the "I" and the "You." The "I," presumably the woman, gathers the bones of the "drowned mothers" while the "You," presumably the man, tosses pebbles not hearing

> the first stumbling
> footsteps of the almost-born
> coming (slowly) behind us,
> not seeing
> the almost-human
> brutal faces forming
> (slowly)
> out of stone.

Adam engenders the Fall and Darwin has already entered this new Eden. As the last image shows, Atwood, like Pratt and Scott before her, is fascinated by the metamorphosis from inanimate to animate (and back again) within an evolutionary context. In "Towards The Last Spike" Pratt's labourers are metamorphosed into Laurentian rock. Scott, in his own origins poem, "Old Song," emphasizes the inhuman strangeness of the inanimate/animate transformation. He speaks of "a quiet calling/of no mind/out of long aeons/when dust was blind/and ice hid sound:"

> only a moving
> with no note
> granite lips
> a stone throat

Similarly, what we fear at the conclusion of Atwood's "After the Flood, We" is the "stone" and "almost-human quality" of this new life. Again, in Atwood's striking "Pre-Amphibian" we are brought (as often with Scott and Pratt) to the world before man. What Atwood's myth of descent here emphasizes is fulfilled sexuality, natural process, "this warm rotting/of vegetable flesh/ this quiet spawning of roots. . . ."

> but here I blur
> into you   our breathing sinking
> to green milleniums
> and   sluggish   in our blood
> all ancestors
> are warm fish moving

This fascination with devolution appears again in her later novel, *Life Before Man* (1979). There, Atwood sets the familiar Prattian scene,[8] the prehistoric arena in which two women (one meta-phorically identified as a carnivorous dinosaur and the other as herbivorous) struggle for a mate/Nate. In the last two poems of her first book of poetry, *The Circle Game*, Atwood offers an evolutionary variant on the fertility cycle — bone becomes land. In "The Explorers" and "The Settlers" the skeletons of the two lovers intermixed are dug down into solid granite, "where our bones grew flesh again,/came up trees and/grass."

> children run, with green
> smiles, (not knowing
> where) across
> the fields of our open hands.

Like Scott in the conclusion of "Laurentian Shield" Atwood has turned rock into children.

The voices of Atwood's poetic ancestors resound in *The Circle Game*. The title poem picks up the association of two lovers and the "circle"-"crystal"-"island"-"water" imagery from "The Island" section of Macpherson's *The Boatman*. We hear P.K. Page's "Perennial Tourists" in Atwood's line, "perennial watchers,/tourists of another kind." F.R. Scott's "Laurentian Shield" is heard in the association of "language" and "law" in Atwood's poem "Migration: C.P.R." and also in the line "the prairies were so nearly/empty as prehistory. . . ." Pratt's imagery also echoes in this poem in the association of "ancient oceans/first flood" and "blood." Of all Atwood's borrowings, I find most interesting the fact that she evokes Pratt and Scott in collocation, largely, I suspect, because their poetry embodies some of the same evolutionary structures. They appear together not only in "Migration: C.P.R." but also in "A Descent Through the Carpet," and in "Notes from Various Pasts."

"A Descent Through the Carpet" embodies Atwood's characteristic poetic journey, the myth of the descent, and shows her connection to one aspect of a Canadian poetic tradition. This poem describes an imaginary descent into the evolutionary sea, a sea which is both womb and battleground. Part I describes the descent, Part II defines the world at the bottom of the sea, and Part III describes the return. In the first section, the narrator stares outside through a window at the Vancouver harbour, its surface reflected "depthless on the glass." Inside there is a patterned carpet on the floor. As she stretches out at eye level, window and carpet merge and she finds herself in imagination drifting down through

"fronds" and "green half-light" past "marginal orchards" to the
long ice age of winter at the bottom of the sea. The descent, then, is
a journey back into evolutionary time.

In Part II this underwater world is described as "not/rocked/
not cradled not forgetful/there are no/sunken kingdoms no/edens:
in the waste ocean. . . ." It is not, as we are led to recognize, like
Whitman's ocean, "out of the cradle endlessly rocking;" nor are
there sunken kingdoms like those of Poe in "The City in the Sea."
Nor do we find as in Scott's "Lakeshore" a forgetful underwater
Eden where the swimmers, amphibians, return to their prehistoric
womb. What we do find is ferocity: "battles . . . the voracious eater/
the voracious eaten. . . ." For Canadian readers this is recognizably
the underworld of Pratt's "Silences": we are away back, down deep
where "the sharks kill the barracudas,/And the giant mollusks
rend the sharks." Atwood's rhetorical reiteration of the same terms
for victor and victim, "the voracious eater/the voracious eaten",
verbally emphasizes the connection between her sea creatures and
Pratt's who "slay in silence and/are as silently slain."

In Part III the narrator is brought back to the surface by the
reverberation of the Vancouver nine o'clock gun. Her return,
"breaking the membrane of water," is a return from water as
womb, as primeval past and as unconscious. Once more breathing
the air, she stares at "the sackful of scales" at "fisted/hand" and
"fossil bones and fangs." What she recognizes is that she too (like
the underwater creatures "all/gaping jaws and famine") is a fish, is
an animal. She too, in terms of the poem's opening metaphor, is a
battleship: "dredged up from time/and harboured/the night these
wars began." That Atwood concludes by specifying her own
birthdate in association with war — suggests that she speaks not
only as an individual but as a member of the war generation.

Because Atwood defines her vision of the undersea world by
allusion and negation (it is not Poe's world, not Whitman's) a
Harold Bloom might want to make the point that she is clearly
arguing with some of her poetic predecessors. And one can understand why Atwood, a product of the Canadian stream, would take
issue with the Romanticism of a Poe or a Whitman by rebutting it
with a version of the 'real' — the survival of the fittest found in
Pratt's "Silences." This is not a new strain in Canadian poetry.
There is a similar antagonism of a Romantic idealism and a
Darwinian 'real' in Earle Birney's *David*. Moreover, Atwood's
poetic 'moral' in "A Descent Through the Carpet" is as explicit in
its own way —

> and here
> to be aware is
> to know total
>   fear.

— as is Frye's pronouncement on "the deep tone of terror in regard to nature" which characterizes Canadian poetry.

One of the curiosities of this poem is that although it explicitly rejects a beneficent nature, its informing myth and poetic metaphors are clearly drawn from F.R. Scott's "Lakeshore," a poem expressing just the view that Atwood rejects. The development of each poem is strikingly similar. Each begins with a narrator staring through a glassy surface, "windows" at reflected objects. Scott sees stones, fish, planes, "floating upon their broken sky;" Atwood sees mountains, sailboats and destroyers, "depthless on the glass." Scott, the swimmer, is a tall "frond," seeking the "light" that leads "down" to "the forest floors." In fantasy, Atwood drifts through the carpeted "floor" with its "fronds" "down" in "the green half light" past "marginal orchards." For Scott, the experience is a return to the amphibian past, to the water as womb where the swimmers ". . . lie, diagonal,/Within the cool and sheltered grove/Stroked by the fingertips of love" until forced by their bursting lungs, they return to the "prison" of their land. Scott's wit, apparent in his description of man's amphibian nature, "This is our talent, to have grown/Upright in posture, false-erect,/A landed gentry," lapses into nostalgia for a prelapsarian Eden when all mankind were fish. In fantasy he stands on Mount Ararat "watching the whole creation drown. . . ."

The setting of Atwood's "A Descent Through the Carpet," the manner of ordering experiences and finally the evolutionary return — the human as fish/amphibian/animal — all suggest Scott's "Lakeshore" but the informing view of nature is ultimately that found in Pratt's "Silences": the Darwinian struggle for survival. That both strains, a beneficent and a frightening evolutionary view have shaped the same poem suggests to me that they are equally part of the Canadian tradition in poetry. That Atwood has chosen to emphasize (here as in *Survival*) one aspect rather than the other might imply that she has opted for that view of the tradition found most strongly in the poetry of Pratt and the criticism of Frye.

This aspect of the Canadian poetic tradition is perhaps best approached through the concluding lines of "Progressive Insanities of a Pioneer":

On his beaches, his clearings,
by the surf of under-
growth breaking
at his feet, he foresaw
disintegration
                and in the end
through eyes
made ragged by his
effort, the tension
between subject and object,

the green
vision, the unnamed
whale invaded.

Atwood's phrase, "the surf of under-/growth breaking," calls up a
line from Birney's *David* where the narrator, Bob, found at his feet
"a long green surf of juniper flowing;" in both cases, images of the
sea are transposed to the land.[9] But here, the "under-/growth
breaking" is representative of psychological eruption as it is in
"Bushed." The sense of nature as a "green/vision, the unnamed/
whale" owes something to Frye's conception of the Canadian
continent as a threatening wilderness, a "whale" entered by the
European traveller. In this poem — as in Pratt's *The Titanic* and
in Birney's *David* and "Bushed" — nature invades and destroys.
When we find, as we do here, evidences of a transmission of a
poetic myth (a particular view of nature as embodied in verbal and
thematic allusions) it is possible to speak, perhaps for the first
time, of the continuity of a Canadian tradition.

The emergence of this tradition can be traced largely to Pratt's
epic *The Titanic* (1935), a Hardyesque reworking of an encounter
between an iceberg and an English liner off the coast of Newfoundland in 1912. Although Pratt animates both ship and berg it
is the berg that animates the poem. Initially a sea-cathedral
("facade and columns with their hint/Of inward altars and of
steepled bells/Ringing the passage of the parallels") it is soon
acted upon by sun and storm, which begin "to fret/The arches . . .
deform/The features," demolishing "the last temple touch of
grace."

Another month, and nothing but the brute
And palaeolithic outline of a face
Fronted the transatlantic shipping route.
A sloping spur that tapered to a claw

In the context of the poem, the iceberg's descent from shining spire to hidden claw is analogous to the 'fall' of the *Titanic*. Initially representative of twentieth-century man in all his pride of achievement, it is "the greatest ship the world has ever known." However, when the captain of the *Titanic* allows the ship to steam too fast through berg-infested waters and neglects to post a watch, man relinquishes the one quality that distinguishes him from other animals: "the judgement stood in little need/Of reason." Subsequently, the ship is described in animal terms as a "whippet" and a "mastiff." Symbolically the collision of ship and berg becomes the tooth-and-claw struggle of one animal against another.

To understand Pratt's influence on later poetry, particularly in terms of the transmission of a particular form of Romanticism — a modified Darwinism which asserts a dual view of man and nature — we must turn to Earle Birney's *David*. Like *The Titanic* Birney's poem centres on the struggle of man against nature, a struggle which takes place in a Darwinian framework; in fact, images of Pratt's evolutionary sea are transposed to the height of Birney's mountain.[10] Two young climbers, David and Bob, climb to get away from "the ruck of the camp." They find:

> . . . peaks to the sun. The ice in the morning thaw

> Was a gurgling world of crystal and cold blue chasms,
> And seracs that shone like frozen slatgreen waves.

Bob, the novice, initially sees nature as idyllically supportive — "I jumped a long green surf of juniper flowing" — but the underlying menace of nature is soon manifested by the first sight of the mountain which is to become their goal. Like Pratt's iceberg, it embodies the metaphoric opposites of shining cathedral and threatening claw: it is "remote,/And unmapped, a sunlit spire on Sawback, an overhang/Crooked like a talon."

The transition from a beneficent to a fearful nature is explicit in the description of the last ascent. Reaching the peak, the two young climbers carelessly unrope to build a cairn. It is then that Bob succumbs to a foolishly Romantic view of nature, and leans out to admire the landscape: "the glistening wedge of giant Assiniboine." Swaying, he is steadied by his partner David, who, as a consequence, loses his own foothold and falls six hundred feet to the ice below, "a cruel fang/Of the ledge thrust in his back." The metaphoric progression of Birney's peak from "sunlit spire" to the "cruel fang" which pierces David is precisely the same as the movement from the "crystal peaks" of Pratt's iceberg to the "claw" which rips through the *Titanic*.

In *David*, the Romantic, benevolent nature first perceived by the narrator Bob ("The woods were alive/With the vaulting of muledeer") soon gives way to the Darwinian struggle for survival evidenced by goat bones sprinkled with "the silken feathers of hawks," and by "the beetle-seal in the shale of ghostly trilobites,/ Letters delivered to man from the Cambrian waves." At first, Bob cannot accept this view of life and nature.

> That day returning we found a robin gyrating
> In grass, wing-broken. I caught it to tame but David
> Took and killed it, and said, 'Could you teach it to fly?'

But at the end of the narrative, he has adopted David's perspective:

> A hawk was buoying
>
> Blackly its wings over the wrinkled ice.
> The purr of a waterfall rose and sank with the wind.
> Above us climbed the last joint of the Finger
> Beckoning bleakly the wide indifferent sky.

Nature, the "indifferent sky," the poem implies, always has this potential if man succumbs to carelessness and a falsely romantic view of nature.

Similarly, the old trapper of Birney's much anthologized "Bushed" romanticizes nature by projecting human meaning upon it: he "invented a rainbow but lightning struck it." His own fears magnified soon rebound upon him from the landscape, "he found the mountain was clearly alive/sent messages whizzing down every hot morning."

> But the moon carved unknown totems
> out of the lakeshore
> owls in the beardusky woods derided him
> moosehorned cedars circled his swamps and tossed
> their antlers up to the stars
> Then he knew though the mountain slept the winds
> were shaping its peak to an arrowhead
> poised
>
> And now he could only
> bar himself in and wait
> for the great flint to come singing into his heart

The great flint, the peak of the mountain poised, like Pratt's "corundum" berg destroys all who attempt to meet nature on any terms but her own. In "Bushed," however, the destruction of the human is not physical but psychological. There is a curious pleasure, almost a consummation, generated by the lyric quality of the last line describing nature's invasion: the great flint comes "singing" into the old trapper's heart.

Atwood's "Progressive Insanities of a Pioneer," is a contemporary version of Birney's "Bushed." The pioneer, who "stood, a point/on a green sheet of paper/proclaiming himself the centre," is analogous to the old trapper who attempts to impose his own order on nature; both are destroyed by this stance for neither can accept nature on its own terms. Each attempts to fence it out with psychological garrisons: the old trapper by a Romantic vision of nature; the pioneer by a mistaken belief in the superiority of human reason to nature's order. The trapper finds that his Romanticized nature is soon overpowered by the 'real' world of natural struggle: "When he tried his eyes on the lake ospreys/ would fall like valkyries/choosing the cut-throat." The economy of this last noun, depicting both the captured trout and the old trapper, emphasizes his identification with the victim. Hiding in his cabin by day, he attempts to keep himself separate from the reality outside. When the struggle proves overpowering, his mind snaps: "Then he knew though the mountain slept the winds/were shaping its peak to an arrowhead/poised."

Atwood's pioneer, attempting to assert his order on fields, finds that the land replies with "aphorisms:/a tree-sprout, a nameless/weed, words/he couldn't understand." For many years he fished fruitlessly for a great vision, but came to the conclusion "in that country/only the worms [cutworms?] were biting." At night, in his cabin in the middle of nowhere, external reality begins to invade: "the idea of an animal/patters across the roof./ . . . everything/is getting in." Unlike Birney, Atwood articulates the moral:

> If he had known unstructured
> space is a deluge
> and stocked his log house-
> boat with all the animals
>
> even the wolves,
>
> he might have floated.

The formulation in which unstructured wilderness is seen as a deluge suggests not only a response to Birney's "Bushed" but also a fairly self-conscious response to Frye's theory that Canadian poetry is dominated by the "garrison mentality," by the tendency to form small communities or garrisons, psychological as well as physical, for the purpose of shutting out the overpowering Canadian wilderness.

Atwood borrows a complex of biblical metaphors, very probably by way of the playful "ark"-"deluge"-"leviathan" metaphors from Macpherson's *The Boatman,* to suggest that the pioneer could have survived if only he could accept the wilderness — signified by the animals — inside him. Macpherson, whose persona aims to survive the flood, wants to convert her "gentle reader to an Ark."

> After me when comes the deluge
> And you're looking round for refuge
> From God's anger pouring down in gush and spout,
> Then you take the tender creature
> — You remember, that's the reader —
> And you pull him through his navel inside out.
>
> That's to get his beasts outside him,
> For they've got to come aboard him. . . .

In a more serious vein, Purdy in poems like "After the Rats" speaks of the beasts entering and taking up residence in the human. Frye in his "Conclusion" to the *Literary History* has spoken of the curious tendency in the Canadian animal story to assimilate the animal to the human consciousness, a theme which recurs in Atwood's *The Journals of Susanna Moodie.* Here in "Progressive Insanities of a Pioneer" Atwood's "wolves" (like Birney's "osprey," or the battling undersea creatures of Pratt's "Silences," or Atwood's "A Descent Through the Carpet") represent that primal aspect of nature both external to man and within him, which cannot be denied without destruction to the organism:

> The wolves hunted
> outside.
>
> On his beaches, his clearings,
> by the surf of under-
> growth breaking
> at his feet, he foresaw
> disintegration

> and in the end
> through eyes
> made ragged by his
> effort, the tension
> between subject and object,
>
> the green
> vision, the unnamed
> whale invaded

To open a book of Canadian poetry at random is to find a nature poem. To read this poem is often to discover a double perspective on nature in which a traditionally Romantic approach to nature is ironically undercut by a Darwinian "real." Because our Romantic movement came so late in time — our first poetic movement did not come until 1880 — Canadian Romanticism was tinged from the start by Darwin's *Origin of the Species*. In modern Canadian poetry the typical romantic myth of aspiration is replaced by the myth of descent. Whether it is defined in primarily evolutionary terms (the journey into the waters of the evolutionary past as in E.J. Pratt's "Silences" or in F.R. Scott's "Lakeshore") or whether it is the journey into the psychological self (Earle Birney's "Bushed" or Margaret Atwood's "Progressive Insanities of a Pioneer") the result is a curiously unmodern modernism, a kind of new Romanticism in which the climactic moment comes not through union with the infinite but rather through devolution. Because man is now seen as an animal, as part of the physical cycle and composed of the same elements as earth itself, images of metamorphosis from animate to inanimate predominate.

The new *frisson* is generated by man's penetration by nature; in effect it is an inversion of the old Romantic myth — the 'claw' that rips through the *Titanic*, the 'fang' that impales Birney's *David*, the great 'flint' that aims toward the heart of the old trapper in "Bushed." In Canadian criticism it is the Canadian continent as an overpowering "whale" in Northrop Frye's "Conclusion" to the *Literary History of Canada*. It is this same irrational and threatening nature, "the green/vision, the unnamed/whale" that overpowers Margaret Atwood's archetypal pioneer and informs her early vision of Canadian nature.[11]

JUDITH McCOMBS

Atwood's Haunted Sequences:
The Circle Game, The Journals of Susanna Moodie, and *Power Politics*

> *It was the addiction*
> *to stories . . .*
> *Stories that could be told*
> *on nights like these to account for the losses,*
> *litanies of escapes, bad novels, thrillers*
> *deficient in villains . . .*
> *Who knows what stories*
> *would ever satisfy her*
> *who knows what savageries*
> *have been inflicted on her*
> *and others by herself and others. . . .*
> — Margaret Atwood, "Gothic Letter on a Hot Night,"
>   *You Are Happy*[1]

Return of the Gothic: Atwood's Ghosts

In Margaret Atwood's work generally, but especially in her three long poetry sequences, the neglected and long outcast stepchild of literature, the Gothic, comes to life again. An obviously Gothic terror haunts *The Circle Game* (1966), *The Journals of Susanna Moodie* (1970), and *Power Politics* (1971).[2] Although this Gothic inheritance was spelled out in 1968, in Atwood's "Speeches for Dr. Frankenstein" and in the Gothic "Revenant" poem, which complains of the ghosts from *Wuthering Heights* that inhabit "the skull's noplace, where in me/refusing to be buried, cured,/the trite dead walk," still Atwood's Gothic voices were not widely recognized until her satiric, anti-Gothic novel, *Lady Oracle* (1976), brought the old tradition into daylight focus.[3] Nor was this Gothic inheritance much valued by contemporary critics until Robert D. Hume, Peter Haining, Ellen Moers, and others began to reclaim the Gothic and the female Gothic tradition for serious literature.

The original Gothic inhabits that body of British literature which begins in 1765 with Horace Walpole's *The Castle of Otranto*, and flourishes in William Beckford, Ann Radcliffe, Matthew Lewis, Charles Maturin; in the nineteenth century, in *Frankenstein, Wuthering Heights, Jane Eyre, Dracula;* and, crossing the Atlantic water, in certain Poe tales, etc.[4] The Gothic aims at terror or horror as a dominant effect; it customarily invokes the feudal past and the weird supernatural. The usual elements of the Gothic were the haunted setting — customarily a castle or forest — whose supernatural powers, be they real or deceptive, menaced and dwarfed the human characters; the hero-villain, who often goes back to the demon-lover of the ballads; the female victim or, in Radcliffe especially, the female hero-victim; and an overall reality that is either negative or, at best, deeply split between good and evil.[5] In the twentieth century, the Gothic comes to life in (for example) certain works of William Faulkner and Flannery O'Connor, in Jean Rhys' *Wide Sargasso Sea*, Sylvia Plath's *Bell Jar* and death poems — and in much of Atwood's lyric poetry, in many of the interior monologues of her fiction, and especially in her first three poetry sequences, *The Circle Game, The Journals of Susanna Moodie*, and *Power Politics*.

These three sequences resurrect the Gothic spirit of terror in the female hero-victim, a terror emanating from the major elements of the original British Gothic literature — or from their direct descendants. Beginning with *The Circle Game*, this terror inhabits a female *I* who is, like Ann Radcliffe's heroines, "simultaneously persecuted victim and courageous heroine."[6] As the earlier Gothic heroine (Walpole's Maddalena, Radcliffe's Emily) was trapped in chamber and cell, so Atwood's *I* is trapped in a chamber of horrors inside her skull.[7] As the traditional female hero-victims confronted a haunted, menacing castle or a monstrous, threatening forest, so Atwood's *I*'s are menaced by an inhuman universe, grim and icy wastes, entangled and haunted wilderness. As the elder female heroes were tempted by what Atwood's recent creator of costume Gothics calls "the hero in the mask of a villain, the villain in the mask of a hero,"[8] a man who offers an exciting but threatening escape from the boredom and constraints of ordinary female life, and who might reveal himself as demon, killer, monster; so Atwood's female *I*'s are tempted by male Others whose power animates and captivates, whose guises enthrall, whose love spells death. As Mary Shelley's unique Gothic, *Frankenstein*, divides and links the creator-villain to his monster-creature, so Atwood's creating *I* is author-victim to her lover-Other. Lastly, as the elder Gothic terror fed on divided and doubled realities — the hero-victim, the escape-trap, the villain-hero, the Frankensteinian monster-creature, the demonic or vampirish love-death — so Atwood's divided and redoubled images, lies in the mask of truth and truth in the mask of lies, permute and magnify the Gothic terror that her work creates.

This essay will focus first on the interior Gothic that dominates *The Circle Game*; next on the wilderness Gothic of *The Journals of Susanna Moodie*; and finally on the Frankensteinian mirrored and remirrored Other of *Power Politics*. Because, in all three books, this Gothic terror emanates from female *I*'s who are both hero and victim — and behind these *I*'s, from a female author — Atwood's work belongs to the genre Moers calls female Gothic; this essay will consider, as Moers does in *Literary Women*, how femaleness feeds or shapes this Gothic.

Interior Gothic: The Circling *I*

The Circle Game is apparently the least sequential of Atwood's first three sequences, and yet its effect is the most claustrophobically and terrifyingly Gothic. It lacks the signposts of place and time that segment Moodie's *Journals*, the epigraphs that categorize *Power Politics*. But it has a centre — the short title sequence — and framing poems at start and end; it has concurrent and encircling images, and a recurring flight from man to nature, self to Other, threat to death.

Most important, the *Circle* has throughout a single *I* and single setting in which the Gothic terrors gather. The female *I* is herself the setting of this Gothic; the chamber of horrors is interior to her consciousness. Though the horrors she sees are always possible — in nature, myth, or man — still no other character confirms her terror; no other agent sets loose the menaces. What is visible to other characters is ordinary and harmless; only her vision opens into horror. She is simultaneously the hero and the victim of the Gothic horrors that unreel inside her skull; the author who conceives these torments and their imperiled sufferer. Like a witch or sibyl, a Faust or Dr. Frankenstein, she summons up the menaces, the villains and the shambling monster-shapes: and yet she is the corpse, the prisoner, the target in the stories that she tells.

Like a stoic hero — or a greedy adventurer — in the midst of terrors, this *I* will not cry out; like a helpless victim — or enthralled addict — she dare not voice her terror. In *The Circle Game* as in the *Journals* and in *Power Politics*, only the reader and the *I* witness the terror. Literally or psychically, the *I* is isolated, a silenced scream, a paralyzed Cassandra. If an Other is present, he seems oblivious to the cause or fact of terror; at best he ignores it; at worst, he may *be* the cause. Even in *Power Politics*, which is ostensibly addressed to an Other, there are hardly any poems in which the *I* really speaks so that the *you* really hears. For to tell an Other (where he is present) would be to test the spell, to risk his confirming and thereby aggravating the terror — or to risk his denying and thereby aggravating the isolation.

Thus, in the opening poem, only the *I* can see her body lost in nature, invisible, distorted, drowned beneath the lake. In the second poem (which reruns Ovid's Flood), only the *I* perceives, as they stroll through an apparent mist, the underlying Diluvian Flood and slowly forming brutal faces. In "A Descent through the Carpet," only this Alice adventures below the surface harbours, descending in her mind's eye to the icy, voracious, prehistoric depths that bred her mammal life, the Darwinian seas of starved dream creatures where

> to be aware is
> to know total
> > fear (22).

In the title poem, only the *I* senses the prisoning rhythms of nature and myth, children and lover, *I* and *you*. In the following camera man poem, only the *I* sees how nature shifts and dissolves, beyond his lense's range. Only the *I* witnesses her own flight from him into nature, her dissolution into a hurricane speck. In the northern ice poems, only the *I* sees how glaciers, winter, and breakup menace self and Other. In the paired ending poems, only the *I* witnesses their future skeletons, gone back to nature, cannibalized by one of them, now fields where children play.

The natural universe, then, is in *The Circle Game* a modern version of the Gothic setting that surrounds and menaces the hero-victim *I*; here nature, in her mind's eye, drowns, obliterates, shocks, freezes, buries the self, and sometimes the Other as well. The traditional claustrophobic cells and passageways have narrowed to the smaller circle of the *I*'s skull; but have simultaneously metamorphosed into a modern, northern, and inhuman universe, where floe and flood, shifting time and expanding space, conspire against the *I*. The fictions of this universe are scientific rather than literary. The terms are modern rather than romantic or sacred. The scene is cold and vast Canadian (overlaying Frankenstein's final Arctic flight) rather than the picturesque Mediterranean landscape of much Gothic of the eighteenth and nineteenth centuries. But the effect of this universe, this nature — where to be aware is to know total fear — is the same pervasive and animating terror that galvanized the elder Gothics.

This deadly nature in a deadly universe is the coldest, vastest, and least human of the three concurrent horrors that encircle the summoning *I*. The second sort of horrors are the monster-ghosts from myth and history that come alive inside her skull; and the third sort are her menacing familiars, the joyless circling children and the imprisoning lover of the title sequence.

These second, specific monsters are still interior Gothic, and they haunt the *I*'s vision in the midst of ordinary, harmless scenes: walking beside him, only she can see beneath apparent mist the Diluvian Flood and shambling, brutal life; outside her window, the random face of the Hanged Man (her Muse?) disintegrates,

> shouting at me
> (specific) me
> desperate messages with his
> obliterated mouth
>
> in a silent language   (14).

As she pauses between trains, the scream-toppled lady and the razor man who travel like voodoo dolls in her suitcase come to life. Her powers summon them even as her emptiness attracts their forms, and their terror is the edge that she inhabits:

> I move
> and live on the edges
> (what edges)
> I live
> on all the edges there are   (16).

Only the *I* sees that the billboard lady is a vampire, and the grey flannel man is food for ghouls; and that the *you* and *I* may also be those Frankensteinian "scraps glued together/waiting for a chance/to come to life" (p. 30).

The same interior emptiness that attracts and feeds these smaller Gothic monsters is what binds the hero to the villain-lover, the empty *you* of the central title sequence:

> You refuse to be
> (and I)
> an exact reflection, yet
> will not walk from the glass,
> be separate   (36).

Like a clinging double, an empty Alice or a science-fiction pod, she looks to him, and he to others, in a travesty of Victorian sex roles: he for images alone, she for images in him:

> You look past me, listening
> to them, perhaps, or
> watching
> your own reflection somewhere   (37).

It is he who commands the tranced and joyless children who play at circling: "You make them/turn and turn, according to/the closed rules of your games" (p. 43). The power is his, the dependency hers; it is she who is caught in his indifferent gaze, "transfixed/by your eyes'/cold blue thumbtacks" (p. 40). Lover and double, villain and fellow victim and Muse, his incarnations are multiple, and his powers therefore inescapable. Like an evil wizard or magician he rings her with his spells: "your observations change me/to a spineless woman in/a cage of bones" (p. 43).

But does the real danger come from Gothic spell or outer world, from him or them?

> (of course there is always
> danger but where
> would you locate it)   (43).

Sheltered by his dangerous games, caught in female dependency and female powerlessness, she crumples in his eyes. At the end of the sequence, she is still half-paralyzed and half-enthralled, able only to want "the circle/broken" (p. 44).

After this nadir the whole book is transformed: the *I* breaks out and flees to nature; a male Other alternately pursues or accompanies her. Though these continuing flights, escapes, and deaths are her metaphors and her nightmares — therefore an interior

Gothic still — yet in overview these repeated escapes and deaths, this continuing flight of the female *I* to/from/with a male Other, to/from a nature that is both refuge and death, evoke the fleeing Isabellas and Maddalenas of the elder Gothics. Or the Arctic ice chase of wretched creator and wretched being that ends Shelley's *Frankenstein:* for after the central sequence, nature becomes far vaster and far icier; deaths are constantly foreseen; the hero-villain lover-Other is skull and skeletal; rescuer or not, he brings death. At book's end, deadly nature and deadly man have triumphed: the *you* and *I* are buried, and her bones gnawed, apparently by him.

The Circle Game, then, creates a spell of female Gothic terror, centered in a hero-victim *I* who flees from man to nature, from self to Other, from threat to death. Remove the spell, and what would be left? A plot where nothing happens: a flat enclosing circle, inside which a modern female *I* languishes, discontent and bored. Passive, she passes for normal — i.e., normal for a female. Powerless, she feels herself surrounded by powers that she cannot control or become — powers that belong to men, her sexual Others. Childless, she fears and avoids children. Menaced, she does not venture on her own; she follows or goes escorted — or else becomes a target. Dependent, she divides herself between herself and her sexual Other, and assigns to him the stronger role. Empty, circling and encircled, she is her victim and her jailor, bored with her own plight.

Return the Gothic terror, and this plot, this character, come to life. Like a vampire lover, this terror calls forth the wilder powers of the *I,* and rescues her from stagnant female "normalcy." Because this Gothic terror stays hidden, silent and interior, it is with her everywhere; it animates and inwardly subverts — but does not overtly challenge — the patriarchial status quo. Like a vampire lover, this terror carries its own punishment; for she is victim, target, paralyzed and drained.

Wilderness Gothic: The Victim and the Witch

The Journals of Susanna Moodie, Atwood's dream-conceived[9] account of what the actual nineteenth-century Ontario pioneer and commercial writer, Susanna Moodie, witnessed but did not in her lifetime reveal, is the most Gothic of the poetry sequences to date. *The Circle Game,* as we have seen, creates the spirit of female Gothic terror, but reruns tradition in another century, another universe; *Power Politics* has a wealth of Gothic elements and exemplifies the Gothic doubleness of Atwood's thought; but in *Power Politics* the female Gothic terror is undercut by other, non-Gothic politics. Only in the *Journals* do the original Gothic spirit and elements prevail.

These three journals, which begin in the nineteenth-century backwoods of Ontario, reveal a wilderness Gothic of old patterns imported to the new continent: here the forest is menacing, invading, breeds monsters. Its inhabitants are either alien and jeering villains, or else its victims. Surrounded by its undergrowth, the hero loses her body's image and her soul's identity. The shadowy husband turns wereman; the children die and come back as brier-fingered haunts; in the last journal Moodie herself turns ghostly revenant. Like the dark woods of our foremothers' tales in Grimm and the haunted forests and castles of eighteenth- and nineteenth-century Gothic, this wilderness setting casts a spell that overpowers the humans, breaks down their civil Christian souls, and drags them deathward.

Furthermore, although this wilderness is not personified, it nonetheless tempts the hero as the Gothic Heathcliff lover tempts: for it offers Moodie an escape from the proper menfolk's rule: it provides a savage kingdom that, like a demon-lover, compels her surrender to its power. Against the forest power the menfolk dwindle, impotent as Lintons; the hero escapes from their "legitimate" order to a savagery that, as in the demon-lover ballads and Julia Anne Curtis' "Knight of the Blood-Red Plume,"[10] first excites, then takes her life. But Atwood's *Journals* does not end there: Moodie's death initiates her into a wilderness kingdom that she makes her own: at the end, like a triumphant witch or an immortal Catherine, she becomes the voice of the wilderness, the prophet of her own wild, eternal realm.

This vision of the wilderness as menace and temptor may have one other source as powerful as the Gothic, Grimm, and ballad literature: I mean the Northern forests themselves — or rather, the Northern forests as "universally" experienced by carriers of Western European culture. Moodie's terror of the wilderness, then, would not be confined to Moodie, nor to Atwood, nor to literature, nor to the literate. Fear of bodily death and spiritual disintegration may well be *the* (Western European) human response to a nature that is dark, unpeopled forest and harsh winters. Atwood was raised in such terrain, and may know. In *Survival* she argues that Canadian literature — including the historic Moodie's work — is haunted by Nature as Monster, inhuman, anti-human, freezing, and deadly.[11] Certainly a lot of non-literary nineteenth-century settlers and trappers were panicked, threatened, crazed, and quite literally killed by the North American wilderness.

In the *Journals*, as in *The Circle Game*, the vision of nature as monster-villain stays interior to the female *I:* no other character notices or confirms the danger. Even though the horrors that Atwood's Moodie endures in the wilderness — isolation, disintegration, death — seem genderless; and even though her first-person narration, using the generic pronoun, *I*, implies a universal human voice — still it is only the female *I* who admits — and magnifies — the danger.

Like all Atwood's female Gothic heroes, Moodie is both author and character, egotist and victim:

> I take this picture of myself
> and with my sewing scissors
> cut out the face.
>
> Now it is more accurate:
>
> where my eyes were,
> every-
> thing appears   (7).

The double portrait-frame ovals that follow this self-scissoring epigraph (and introduce each of Moodie's three journals) are empty, save for dates. Atwood's accompanying collages are scissored-out images of the hero, dead or alive, surrounded by emptiness, stuck like an encapsuled cyst into a wilderness she does not touch.

From epigraph on through the first of the three journals — the one which covers her seven years' trials in the wilderness — Moodie attacks her own vision, assumes guilt for distorting, sides with the non-human wilderness but against her species and herself. Disembarking at Quebec with book, knitting, and shawl, she seems outwardly a mirror image of Moers' Traveling Heroines of the Gothic — one of those "British ladies who in point of fact did set sail for Canada and India and Africa, with their bonnets, veils, and gloves, their teacups and tea cozies — ill-equipped for vicissitudes of travel, climate, and native mutiny, but well-equipped to preserve their identity as proper Englishwomen."[12] But the heirloom image cracks as, disembarking, Moodie blames her "own lack/of conviction which makes/these vistas of desolation,/. . . omens of winter" (11). When the water refuses to reveal her image and the rocks ignore her, she becomes in her own eyes invisible, untranslatable.

Trapped on the backwoods farm, Moodie sees the wilderness as a large darkness: "It was our own/ignorance we entered./I have not come out yet" (12). A stranded Red Riding Hood, she needs wolf's eyes — not her human eyes — to see true: "Whether the wilderness is/real or not/depends on who lives there" (13). If it depends on the men, it only seems real, for as planters they impose their own illusions of progress, force the tangled forest to become the straight Cartesian rows of their futile dream. If the wilderness depends on her, it may be real, but then she is not: her opened eyes are "surrounded, stormed, broken/in upon by branches, roots, tendrils" (17).

With heroic courage, alone and unaided, Moodie faces the terror of her own disintegration. When she is finally able to look in a mirror, at the end of the first journal, she sees a body gone back to nature, an exhumed corpse, the proper lace and black rotted off, the skin "thickened/with bark and the white hairs of roots," the eyes bewildered, almost blind, budlike. The "heirloom face" she brought with her is a "crushed eggshell/among other debris" (24) of shattered china, decayed shawl, pieces of letters — all those artifacts and emblems of the English gentlewoman she once was. Helpless, invaded — a female Gothic plight — she has been taken over by the wilderness as by an evil spell: she is the living but unrecognizable dead:

> (you find only
> the shape you already are
> but what
> if you have forgotten that
> or discover you
> have never known)   (25).

In the tradition of female Gothic, this facing of the empty self is heroic courage: but it is also a female lack of identity, a female dependency on the image to *be* the self.[13]

Throughout the journals, while men impose their civil power on the wilderness, Moodie lets the wilderness impose its savage, Gothic power on her. The first journal, with Moodie as Gothic matron invaded by monstrous lair, builds a climactic Gothic terror. But when Moodie is unexpectedly rescued from those seven years of captive terror and is hauled back to civilization on her husband's sleigh, then she suddenly finds herself dispossessed of the wild eyes that had begun to glow within her; she feels relief but also "unlived in: they had gone" (27).

The middle journal, of Moodie's first thirty years in Belleville, shows her recollecting in tranquillity her experiences of savagery. (You can take the woman out of the wilderness, but you can't take the wilderness out of the woman.) Outwardly rescued, inwardly she rejects civilization, and dwells among danger, death, and horror. She sees her children die (literally) back into the land and return as clutching, brier-fingered ghosts. She sees the painfully built homesteads that were her composite self revert to forest. She sees the land itself as icy river and unknown ocean on which the living float; only the dead can enter its depths. Inside her head history breaks down to gibberish. The 1837 War she witnessed unravels into "those tiny ancestral figures/flickering dull white through the back of your skull,/confused, anxious" (35), idiot faces and banana-clustered hands holding flags or guns, their advances through trees and fire no more actual than a child's crayon-scribbled fort.

Gothic victim turned celebrant of Gothic chaos and death, Moodie shows us the universal savagery beneath our civil selves:

> (Note: Never pretend this isn't
> part of the soil too, teadrinkers, and inadvertent
> victims and murderers, when we come this way
>
> again in other forms, take care
> to look behind, within
> where the skeleton face beneath
>
> the face puts on its feather mask, the arm
> within the arm lifts up the spear: (37).

Her dreams are nightmare ghosts that claim her waking life: she is haunted by the wet and surging horror of the long-past bush garden where anything planted came up blood; by the suicidal and scar-throated hunter, Brian, who killed and felt his skin grow fur, his soul run innocent as hooves. Her dream-imagined, fear-furred night bear

>   is real, heavier
> than real   I know
> even by daylight here
> in this visible kitchen
>
> it absorbs all terror

as it moves inside her skull towards her family in the lighted cabin.

By the end of the middle journal, Moodie comes to see herself not as the captive of exterior Gothic powers, but instead as the source of an interior Gothic wisdom: there are two voices inside her head, dividing reality between convention and horror. The truths she chooses are "jubilant with maggots" (42). Atwood's accompanying collage shows Moodie scissored out, aged, hooded, staring witch-like from one baleful, deeply shrouded eye; a thin emptiness divides her, not from wilderness, but from civil, steepled Belleville.

In the last, death journal (which ranges up to the present), Moodie transcends her Gothic horrors of decay and death by joining them as, aging, she lets slip her human shapes and consciousness. In the "Daguerreotype Taken in Old Age" she accepts her image as pitted, cratered, eroded, a moon-face in the garden, a dead "being/eaten away by light" (48). In the "Wish: Metamorphosis" she welcomes her shrinking, furred, and feather-wrinkled body, her puckered, burrowing mind, and exults at last in the animal eyes that may glow within her later, underground.

Dying, Moodie renounces flesh and custom, teacup and history. With a hero's — or a witch's — spirit of adventure, she crosses over into the wilderness and becomes its voice. Dead and underground, she prophesies against the bulldozer's silver paradise. Atwood's collage shows her buried body curving with the strata, completely touching, blending in at last, her limbs drifting or dancing with the earth. In a resurrection that is both Christian and pagan, she joins "those who have become the stone/voices of the land" (59).

At the last Moodie appears as a ghostly old lady on a modern bus, unbanishable: "this is my kingdom still." Allied with snow and storm, she threatens her twentieth-century audience — us — with her wild, Gothic powers:

> I am the old woman
> sitting across from you on the bus,
> her shoulders drawn up like a shawl;
> out of her eyes come secret
> hatpins, destroying
> the walls, the ceiling
>
> Turn, look down:
> there is no city;
> this is the centre of a forest
>
> your place is empty   (61).

Like a triumphant witch, or a science-fiction time traveller, or a medieval revenant, this hero haunts us with the Grimm and Gothic terrors of the elder, wilder realm that she has made her own.

Double or Nothing: The Victor and the Being

Power Politics is Atwood's most doubled and dividing sequence: even its Gothic structure is dual, for its victor/victim games (Atwood's critical terms, from *Survival*)[14] reenact not only the invaded hero-victim *I* vs. the monstrous hero-villain *you* of *The Circle Game* and elsewhere; but also, concurrently, the Gothic nightmare of that early victor who dared create a monster being — Mary Shelley's Victor, surnamed Frankenstein.

These two sets of Gothic antagonists overlap, contrast, juxtapose, and superimpose upon each other, so that the victim of one set may simultaneously be the victor of the other pair: "How can I stop you/Why did I create you"[15] asks the female *I*, shifting from imperilled victim to guilty author of her torments — and she is truly both. Each of these Gothic antagonists is paired to an external Other who is its double, shadow, outcast self — as Shelley's Victor and "being" (her term) were each other's alter images.[16] Each of Atwood's antagonists is also self-split within, for evil or good, power or suffering: female and male compete for victory and victimhood; creator and created vie like Shelley's pair in enmity and wretchedness. The Gothic terror and the Gothic horror, so divided and redoubled, take place as in a hall of mirrors, where reality is instantly evaded and yet reflected, distorted and yet magnified.

Even the cover of *Power Politics* (conceived by Atwood and executed by William Kimber)[17] forewarns us of reality within reality: for the warrior and his captive woman are sadomasochism in Gothic dress. (See Illus.) But they are simultaneously the burdened male tied to dependent female, for his extended arm, tied to her dangling weight, would suffer excruciating pain. They are simultaneously a suit of rigid, empty armor (he has no flesh, no eyes) which props the female seer whose pose is the Hanged One of the Tarot, signifying "life in suspension," real bodily "life and not death."[18]

Throughout *Power Politics* reality is thus triple: the Gothic sadomasochistic pair are true — so true that the book is usually read as sexist realism, women readers confirming it and men

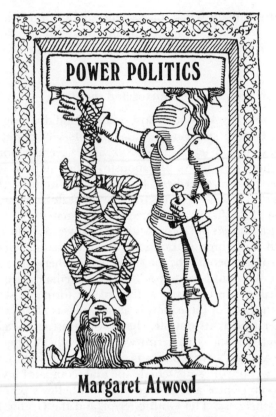

readers protesting, as Atwood has observed.[19] But the pair are also
true reversed, he victim and she heartless. And always they are
characters within a third, Frankensteinian Gothic where as
creator-seer she is Victor, he the hapless being.

Thus, in the first of the three sections, he enters as a cruel
hook; then a three-headed monster, rising like Victor's being or a
Canadian Indian monster from a snowbank, shivering
"cunningly" (2). Farcically stabbed, he inflates to a dirigible-sized
Superman. Drunk, he plays Christ. Beautiful wooden General, he
promises bronze rescues but delivers her blind, paralyzed, one of a
slavish horde of female followers who casts flowers under his
hooves. Strange and repellent growth, he thrives in darkness. A
body with head attached, he collides and they both shatter. A dead
starfish, he floats belly up on her. And when towards the end of the
section he escapes, "nothing/remembers you but the bruises/on
my thighs and the inside of my skull" (13).

As the above litany makes clear, his role of monstrous Gothic villain alternates with his role as pathetic Gothic monster. The Superman gets stabbed; the beautiful wooden General fixes it so he almost wins and longs to be bandaged before he is cut; the bruiser makes *his* escape. But even his sufferings smack of romantic male egotism, a demand for female sympathy as well as female submission.

Though her role of victim alternates with, and is compounded by snarl, threat, and self-denunciation, her rebellion is all an interior female Gothic, a victim's fantasy: the restaurant stabbing is farce and wish, an act that doesn't happen, unreal as his apotheosis into Superman dirigible. The next poems show him alive and dominant, fake Christ who gets her succour, fake General who literally overrides his female followers. Her perception that he is fake is but interior female hatred, a victim's curse, silent or unheard. The double victim/villain roles of each confuse and paralyze the female *I;* her horror and her guilt confound escape, for she would escape his menace and cannot escape his suffering or her guilt.

But the above litany also reveals the *you* as a projection made monstrous by the creating *I,* a Gothic Other drawn from Shelley's *Frankenstein.* As the first wretch (Shelley's term) was made outwardly hideous but inwardly humane; as he sought love from his horrified creator, fled in rain, wandered suffering and unpitied, then reappeared to his heartless creator in an Alpine sea of ice, so this monster in the opening poem "reappears" (2) in a snowbank with needs and "cunning;" shivers, seeks love, and flees from his unloving creator, and dissolves in rain at the end of the first section. But this Victor has read *Frankenstein,* and coldly proclaims her guilt:

> I approach this love
> like a biologist
> pulling on my rubber
> gloves & white labcoat
>
> You flee from it
> like an escaped political
> prisoner, and no wonder   (10).

As in *Frankenstein,* this creator repudiates the "body with head/attached" that is the complement to her own divided self, the "head with/body attached" (11). The being's flight reveals the creator's monstrous and unloving egotism. As in Shelley, the two compete for power and victimhood. When one waxes, the Other wanes. But unlike Shelley's being, this Other is a sexual Other, and yet so close a mirror-double that his external reality is never sure. Throughout the first section, the creating *I* shapes him cruel, hideous, fake, evil, multiform; at the end she forgets his vanished, rain-dissolved shape, which, like the Cheshire Cat or Watchbird haunts her bed:

> My walls absorb
> you, breathe you forth
> again, you resume
> yourself, I do not recognize you   (14).

Read as a Frankensteinian Gothic, then, the first section of *Power Politics* covers creation and flight of the wretch. The victor *I* projects an outwardly monstrous Other, and monstrously recoils from it. The second, central section corresponds roughly to the wretch's unsuccessful attempts to join humanity. In Atwood as in Shelley, humanity is revealed as murderous persecuters, and the wretch begins to imitate them. In this section the real monster is what the legend of Frankenstein has become for the whole world in the twentieth century: the atomic nightmare given life, the monster system that may destroy us all.[20] Against the gigantic horrors of the war machine, the private Gothic costumes recede, quaint fakeries; the *I* and *you* struggle simply to stay alive and innocent. What does appear of private victor-victim games here is mostly defrocked; the *you* could be anyone generic and faceless, merely alive, ordinary, and "growing older, of course you'll/die but not yet, you'll outlive/even my distortions of you" (16). At the end of the second section, she preaches mutual flight from power games, but there is no reply, perhaps no listener.

The third and final section turns from global horrors back to the personal Gothic duel where the *I* and *you* contend in sterile sadomasochism. She would go back to nature, but fears creation and refuses children; nature thereafter threatens her with death, and the literary horrors "fertilize each other/in the cold and with bulging eyes" (41). This final section corresponds roughly to the last parts of Shelley's novel; in both books the hideous being turns from man to nature, and turns to hideous killer. The creating *I* is racked by the monster's persecutions and by guilt. Like Victor's being, Atwood's Other crosses over into nature, and flourishes there as bestial god or noble, godlike beast. The original Victor followed but died in pursuit; Atwood's creator starts to follow but, fearing death, turns back.

In Atwood's third section the Gothic sadomasochism breaks out unchecked: as in the first section, but far worse, it is she who dies, gets broken, blames herself; she who waits, dependent, for his revelation or torment; she who gets trampled in his escape; she who is the imperilled and tortured female victim; and, at the end, the human target stalked by natural monster him. The beautiful wooden General of the first section seems naive and playful compared to this monster-villain loosed from horror film, from *Frankenstein*, from sadomasochistic tales. Now he is simultaneously the evil Rochester (see Jean Rhys' female Gothic novel, *Wide Sargasso Sea*, for how Rochester changed from lover to villain, and drove his first wife mad),[21] King Kong, and Frankensteinian monster of the film.

Now her victim's alliance *with* her tormentor is grotesque terror and masochism:

> catastrophe, I see you
> blind and one-handed, flashing
> in the dark, trees breaking
> under your feet, you demand,
> you demand
>
> I lie mutilated beside
> you; beneath us there are
> sirens, fires, the people run
> squealing, the city
> is crushed and gutted,
> the ends of your fingers bleed
> from 1000 murders
>
> Putting on my clothes
> again, retreating, closing doors
> I am amazed/I can continue
> to think, eat, anything
>
> How can I stop you
>
> Why did I create you   (47).

The terror is real, the sadism is real, only the Gothic costumes are false. In the next poem, as she hesitates outside the door, telling the wrong lies, she sees him as bleeding Christ and slain God, and warns him to escape her costumes. Yet the door leads to his Bluebeard's castle stairs, his Fichter's room of bloodied, dismembered wives.[22] But the last alternative — sans costumes, sans lies — is the worse: "In the room we will find nothing/In the room we will find each other" (51).

Now he escapes again to nature; she briefly follows, but soon pulls back to the human side of the window. Like Victor's being in the Alpine heights and Arctic wastes he goes on, allied with earth, sea, and death, lost in water and moving shadow. In the penultimate poem the *I* repudiates all costumes; the bronze man, the fragile man, the scaling fanged Dracula she made "were all inaccurate" (55). But were they? She is still inside a mirrored and remirrored Gothic horror chamber where the victim cannot know who is victim and cannot flee: the last poem shows him scaled again, and Frankenstein's monster again, rising from "the pits and starless/deep nights of the sea," unstoppable, bearing towards her "a new death/which is mine and no-one else's" (56).

Power Politics, then, creates a mirrored Gothic of the Other where a male who is both wretch and victim, monster and villain, stalks a female who is both distorter and creator, adventurer and victim. Inside this doubly Gothic structure the horror and the terror redouble, divide, and multiply. Atwood's sequence thus reflects not only Gothic literature and modern, fragmented reality, but also the particular power politics of a society where men have outward power and women have inward pain: the female *I* is alienated from her body and her head, even from her terror; addict, she comes alive only in relation to a sexual Other who is a series of oppressive masculine poses. His power threatens her, his sufferings milk her; either way, she is his victim and yet guilty of her victimization. That she prefers the Gothic horrors to reality is not only her private addiction, but also the politics of how the dominated endure, and the aesthetics of how the bored escape. That the Gothic stays interior, and that the *I* creates only by seeing — not by speaking, leading, acting — is not only a Gothic addiction/vision, but is also the silence of the politically isolated and disabled.

Atwood's Frankensteinian *Politics,* then, brings to static climax the Other-centered and interior Gothic of the first two sequences.[23] Here, as in *The Circle Game,* the female *I* flees in static and recurrent terror the shifting, deadly, vulnerable, monstrous lover-Other. Here, as in *The Circle Game,* the *I* is locked into a polarized victor-victim duel with her sexual Other and/or with an inhuman, icy, post-Darwinian universe that promises her death. In *Power Politics,* the terror swings inward to the mirrored and remirrored Frankensteinian Gothic; in the nineteenth-century *Journals,* the terror swings outward to the inhuman natural universe, which becomes a monstrous, haunted lair, tempting as a demon-lover, luring the hero-victim into its deadly, savage realm.

But, whether the worst danger come from sexual Other or from inhuman Other, in all three sequences the target is the same: the female *I.* And the outward power and danger, for good or evil, is the same: the Other, be it inhuman or masculine. And, in all three sequences, the Gothic stays interior to the female *I* who is its secret author, its silenced victim: no character, but only the reader can (perhaps) be trusted to share this animating and addicting terror. The politics of this terror, invisible to patriarchs yet everywhere for those who share and identify, are female-centered: for this interior terror releases, diverts, and dangerously, narrowly channels the limits and burdens and nightmares common to the ordinary, daylit female life.

This essay, having followed the Gothic terror and its elements through Atwood's first three poetic sequences, book-by-book and theme-by-theme; having pursued the more visible ghosts of Grimm and British Gothic therein; having then, like a traveller at journey's end, gathered its memories and souvenirs into a summary display (a simple one, but with a dangerous two-way metaphor of female Gothic life and literature saved for the last) — this essay could well stop here. But that summary display, which appears complete but gathers only some parts into a convenient and deceptive whole, misrepresents the protean nature and effects of Atwood's Gothic: these sequences, these Gothic elements and terrors, should not be left to fall by default into such a whole.

For Atwood's poetic work, here and elsewhere, is multi-faceted as the fly's eye: to fix one aspect in one light is to turn away to darkness the other facets. These three poetic sequences reflect, refract, and like a lens distill from/to reality (whatever that appears to be) and Atwood's other work, made and not yet made; from Grimm, *Frankenstein,* the Brontës; from science fiction, comic books, horror films; from the *Bible,* scientific fictions, modern politics and sexist realism, Canadian literature and North American Indian myth; from the Lord Knows What. Though Atwood's best work, in these sequences and elsewhere, is as compellingly original as Coleridge's Xanadu, in one (misleading) sense it is not original at all, but a place in which the shapes of her culture come to life, metamorphosing[24] like Proteus, like ghosts, like caterpillars: and among these shifting forms the Gothic is one obvious yet transient shape, one kind of voice, not simple, not stable, but resonant, echoing, drifting back and forth and sideways with the other voices that it has become and will become in other readings, other sequences.

SHERRILL E. GRACE

Margaret Atwood and the Poetics of Duplicity

Two-thirds of the way through the story of her lives Joan Foster, the "Lady Oracle," née Delacourt, alias Louisa K. Delacourt, summarizes her existence for us:

> This was the beginning of my double life. But hadn't my life always been double? There was always that shadowy twin, thin when I was fat, fat when I was thin.... But not twin even, for I was more than double, I was triple, multiple.... [1]

The men in her life, she realizes, have also had "two selves" — her father, healer/killer; the ravine man, rescuer/pervert (*LO*, 292); the Royal Porcupine is also Chuck Brewer; Paul is Mavis Quilp; and Arthur has as many selves as Joan does (*LO*, 211). From *Double Persephone* (1961) to the recent *Two-Headed Poems* (1978), duplicity — deceit and doubleness — is a familiar Atwood subject and a fundamental Atwood concern. It informs her vision of this world, is at the root of her poetics, and is, indeed, the systemic model for her work.

When Atwood writes in "The Woman Who Could Not Live With Her Faulty Heart" that

> . . . most hearts say, I want, I want,
> I want, I want. My heart
> is more duplicitous,
> though no twin as I once thought.
> It says, I want, I don't want, I
> want, and then a pause. [2]

she is speaking, not only metaphorically, but physiologically. This heart is not a candy or a valentine, but a "lump of muscle," "purple blue" with a "skin of gristle." Duplicity is the state of being double or two-fold as, of course, most organic forms are. "Duplicity principle" itself refers to the doubleness of the retina in vertebrates which accounts for our ability to see. Duplicity, in a metaphorical sense, describes a doubleness of intention or purpose in order to deceive. Language is duplistic in its structure and organization, as well as in its use, for example, in irony.[3] Atwood, a poet but also the daughter of an entomologist, consciously and deliberately explores duplicity in life and art, as state of being and as ironic deception.

For Atwood, duplicity is a natural state that should be viewed positively. It is not, therefore, to be confused with polarity or opposition. By reducing relationships to polar opposites — subject/object, mind/body, male/female, or culture/nature — we set up adversary positions, the power politics of victims and victors that lead us to "attempt merely power/. . . accomplish merely suffering" (PP, 32). Atwood has said that as long as we insist upon binary opposition we shall remain locked into victor/victim positions or "the tension between subject and object" (AC, 39). What we need is a third way of being that allows us to live in a natural "creative harmony with the world."[4] Instead of defining ourselves over against our surroundings and each other like the progressively insane pioneer, we must learn to accept our place within a duplistic system which we mirror and in which we are mirrored.

Atwood's view of perception and of the self is consistent with this ethical position for, according to her, we are not self-enclosed egos looking out at alien objects nor solipsists creating all we see, but places where things happen, places that are co-extensive with environment.[5] It is our duplicity that forcibly relates us to our environment —

> Not above or behind
> or within it, but one
> with it
> (CG, 76)

Even a cursory look at Atwood's work, especially the poetry, reveals her interest in duplicity (or duality) as well as the destructive forms of opposition. This interest is thematically explicit in

titles such as *Double Persephone* and *Two-Headed Poems.*
Implicit in *The Animals in That Country* is *this* country — a
point I have discussed in *Violent Duality*[6] — while *Procedures for
Underground* assumes the existence of its opposite. In *Power
Politics* and *The Circle Game*, Atwood is primarily concerned
with themes of opposition: lovers who "are opposite" and "touch
as though attacking" (*PP*, 37), cameramen who replace movement
with an "organized instant" (*CG*, 45).

The artist in *Double Persephone*, trapped between opposites
of life and art, must necessarily transform life into an art of "Hard
marble, carven word," while in each of the subsequent books
Atwood strives for a constructive reconciliation of various polarities. Frequently, the books conclude on one side or the other of a
given set of opposites. For example, where *The Circle Game* ends
with an affirmation of natural forms, *Procedures for Underground* withdraws into the safety of artifice. Implicit throughout,
of course, is the need to overcome a one-sided adversary position,
but it is in relatively few poems that Atwood offers us this vision —
"A Place: Fragments" and "The Settlers" (*CG*), "River" perhaps
and "I was reading a scientific article" (*AC*), "Procedures for
Underground" and "A Soul, Geologically" (*PU*), part III of
"They are hostile nations" (*PP*), most certainly "Book of Ancestors" (*YAH*), and in a comic vein "The Woman Makes Peace with
her Faulty Heart" (*THP*).

The Journals of Susanna Moodie is a special case. It is the best
of Atwood's works to date, for many reasons. Not the least of these
is the power with which she conveys her vision of duplicity.
Moodie is the mythic embodiment of Atwood's vision, at once an
emblem of Canada's cultural past, a model for national potential,
and a symbol of human physiological, psychological, and linguistic doubleness. In Susanna Moodie Atwood finds and recreates the
duplicity of myth (as Lévi-Strauss describes it),[7] for Canada is a
country of "violent duality" and Moodie

> finally accepts the reality of the country she is in, and at [the end of
> Journal III] she accepts also the inescapable doubleness of her
> own vision.

Ojibway and North Coast Indian mythology, both based
upon fundamental homologies that facilitate transformation,
have an important place in Atwood's work, particularly in

Procedures for Underground and *Surfacing*. Operating in an analagous fashion with native myth, Moodie can assert that burial does not "banish" her — "this is my kingdom still" (*JSM*, 60) — because "in-/formed" by "two fires" she can speak and see double; she *is* this land. Even the Bluebeard and Frankenstein legends take on something of the nature and function of myth in Atwood's work. The latter becomes a metaphor for the transformational powers of the imagination. The former, and more important of the two, figures forth the duplicity of appearance and story ("Hesitations outside the door," *PP*, 48-51), or the duplicity of the self (*Lady Oracle*, pp. 341-343). In Atwood's hands, then, myth is an effective structure for embodying her personal vision.

Under the influence of quasi-structuralists like Frye and James Reaney, Atwood views myth as a system that articulates and unites the individual and universal, indeed all the basic dualities of existence. Thus, in the early poems, we find central importance given to the figure of Persephone who is, by nature, double:

> The dancing girl's a withered crone;
> Though her deceptive smile
> Lures life from earth, rain from the sky,
> It hides a wicked sickle;
> *(DP)*

Furthermore, in *You Are Happy*, we discover that the enchantress Circe has her own story and that the mythical Siren is only an unhappy woman trapped in a "bird suit":

> I don't enjoy it here
> squatting on this island
> looking picturesque and mythical
>
> with these two feathery maniacs,
> I don't enjoy singing
> this trio, fatal and valuable.
> *(YAH, 38-39)*

Myth or woman? It all depends on which side of the "bird suit" you are on. And her cry for release from duplicity is in itself a trap for a single-minded "unique" listener — "Alas/it is a boring song/but it works every time " (*YAH*, 39).

Atwood has shown a persistent interest in the double, aural/ visual, effects of poetry; so much so that many of her poems must be seen as well as heard. She has illustrated some of her poems (e.g. early chapbooks and *Journals*), designed covers for others (e.g.

Double Persephone, Journals, and *Two-Headed Poems*), and, of course, she exploits the visual impact of poetic line on the space of the page to full effect. While her interest in duplicity is apparent in many image patterns — inside/outside, self/landscape, body/head or two heads, duplicitous hearts — her visual imagery is both more central to her poetic and to the double, aural/visual, thrust of the poems. Specifically, eye and mirror images form important loci of meaning through which Atwood explores not so much a positive duplicity, but polarity, adversary positions, or power politics. Usually this visual imagery reminds us of the alienating space between perceiving eye and object seen (whether map, lover, or poem), of the unreliability of "single reason" (what is that "bird suit" after all?), or of the need to complement the sense of sight with "another sense" (*CG*, 76) and "other knowledge" (*JSM*, 42).

For the speaker in "The Circle Game," or the woman in "Tricks With Mirrors," mirrors are terrifying because they reflect and limit the self, reducing us to objects seen, "transfixed/by your eyes'/cold blue thumbtacks" (*CG*, 40). As objects we in turn become mirrors, in which the viewer or subject sees only himself; duplication and re-duplication assert the victory of subject over object in a perpetual circle game of power politics. And yet mirrors are necessary. Both Moodie and the narrator in *Surfacing* must face the mirror in order to see who they are, while for the woman in "Marrying the Hangman," "To live in prison is to live without mirrors. To live without mirrors is to live without the self" (*THP*, 48).

Eyes, so closely related to mirrors, are equally ambivalent — limiting and destructive on one hand, yet providing occasional images for *in*sight and vision on the other. On the whole, however, Atwood creates shocking and violent eye images to reinforce a basic mistrust of visual perception. Like the "I" of ego, the eye asserts priority of subject over object, of here as opposed to there. Eyes are "cold blue thumbtacks" (*CG*, 40), you are a "Cyclops," "unable to see what is beyond/the capsule of your dim/sight" (*PU*, 42), the surveyors clear a "trail of single reason" (*AC*, 4) recalling Blake's attack on "Single vision and Newton's sleep."[8] And it is "through eyes/made ragged by his/effort, the tension/between subject and object" (*AC*, 39) that "the green vision" invades the pioneer. If this fear of the eye/I recalls Blake, it also brings McLuhan to mind, for Atwood's eye imagery illustrates the fragmentation of space and the alienation of the psyche in our obsessively visual world.

In order to overcome this reductive vision the poet prefaces the
Journals of Susanna Moodie with this preparatory act:

> I take this picture of myself
> and with my sewing scissors
> cut out the face.
>
> Now it is more accurate:
>
> where my eyes were,
> every-
> thing appears

Only now will Moodie and the reader be able to 'see'. In "Two
Gardens" (*PU*, 16-17), it is touch that enables us to understand the
presence of the other garden "in another land." While in "A Place:
Fragments" (*CG*, 76), Atwood is explicit about our need to
abandon sight in order to 'see': "An other sense tugs at us" because
our identity is "something too huge and simple for us to see " (*CG*,
76).

In "Book of Ancestors," one of her most beautiful poems to
date, Atwood offers a fully positive eye image. The lovers in this
poem are free of "the gods and their/static demands." Significantly, for them,

> History
> is over, we take place
> in a season, an undivided
> space, no necessities
>
> hold us closed, distort
> us.
> (*YAH*, 95)

Linear chronologies and enclosed spaces no longer pertain,
separating the lovers into hostile opposites. Part of the effect of the
subsequent eye image arises from its negative uses in the earlier
poetry; this time the eye is a window opening inward and outward
— inward on the offering of the lover's heart, outward towards the
speaker:

> You are intact, you turn
> towards me, your eyes opening, the eyes
> intricate and easily bruised, you open
>
> yourself to me gently . . .
>
> open yourself like this and become whole
> (*YAH*, 96)

Moving from theme, myth, and image to the duplicity of structure, language, and voice, we can perhaps understand how Atwood strives to make us see. To begin with, the eye is not only a "thumbtack"; it is also vulnerable:

> you fit into me
> like a hook into an eye
>
> a fish hook
> an open eye
> 　　　(*PP*, 1)

What is it that makes this epigramatic poemlet so violently effective, what George Woodcock calls a "poetic booby trap"?[9] The effect is a function of its poetic duplicity. Immediately apparent to the eye is the double structure of the poem, four lines in two neatly balanced pairs. The repeated sharp rhythm of three and two beats to the line together with the hard consonants reinforce aurally the semantic level of the poem. But more important, Atwood exploits a fundamental linguistic duplicity as she moves from a metaphorical relationship based on similarity — "like a hook" — to metonymy — hook: fish hook, eye: open eye.[10] This shift from metaphor to metonymy contributes to a heightened sense of defamiliarization for the reader that results from the juxtaposition of "a fish hook/an open eye" with the preceding half of the poem. Hook and eye fasteners are ordinary domestic objects; fish hooks in open eyes are another matter. Organized metaphorically — that is, in terms of analogy — this would read, "You fit into me like a fish hook fits into an open eye," which is ugly enough. But Atwood gains an extra shock of recognition as she turns something safe and familiar into something violent and unfamiliar by shifting from metaphor to metonymy. Her poems are characterized by a cool, literal language that functions syntagmatically. This type of language, relying on contiguity and synecdoche, is usually found in prose and, therefore, seems more ordinary, unobtrusive and prosaic. Obvious figurative language is less common. And yet this poem is, finally, metaphor for which we must infer meaning paradigmatically; fish hook in open eye is like sexual assault or any act of violent domination. The poem itself is the hook in the eye of the reader, violating his security and complacency, preparing him for power politics.

Metaphor and metonymy must not be viewed as opposite or mutually exclusive rhetorical figures. In his "Métonymie chez Proust," Gerard Genette points out that one must speak of "relations de 'coexistence' a l'intérieur même du rapport d'analogie: le rôle de la métonymie *dans la métaphore*."[11] Atwood, however, relies heavily upon metaphor, to the exclusion of metonymy, in her early poetry. In fact, it is chiefly the increased use of metonymy 'within metaphor' (to use Genette's phrase) that separates her mature verse from her early poems. The more lyrical language of several poems in *Two-Headed Poems* suggests that Atwood is not only exploring new subject matter and voice, but searching for a complementary style. Whatever her further developments may be, her discovery and manipulation of linguistic duplicity (metaphor/metonymy) provides the dramatic tension that makes her poems, from *The Circle Game* to the present, effective. Of course, this duplicity is often supported by a doubled structure and a double voice but, for the moment, let us examine rhetorical figures in two poems from the early 1960's. These poems, while dealing thematically with doubleness, state, rather than mirror, their subject.

Each of the following three quatrains from "The Siamese Twins" relies upon analogy to create image:

Roped in one continual skin
Their opposite bodies mingled
And bound by knotted skeins
Of blood and mangled veins,

He leans aside and listens to the crazed
Pacing of restless footsteps caged
In his green fruitless garden
And endless maze of spring. . . .

It was the serpent virtue of
Stepfather and cruel mother, since
Doubled within their ribs, to thus
Crush them in the vise of innocence.[12]

These twins are intertwined like rope or like "skeins" of wool; spring is likened to an "endless maze" and "innocence" crushes this Adam and Eve like a "vise." The theme of doubleness is presented through analogy alone. Even the heavy assonance and intermittent rhyme reinforces similarity.

In another and better poem, "The Double Nun," also published in 1964, Atwood introduces an important metonymic association as well as devices of typography and punctuation which *begin* to mirror theme. The dominant relationship, however, is still metaphoric:

Through noon and moonlight in
The strict black library
She turns the pages of the hours,
These aisles her daily habit.

Kept back by cardboard bars
And her chaste paper candles
Night with a knife waits near:
A mad monk lurking for her. . . .

She locked me out by
Opening a book; but still
We will soon change places:
Each alien face I pass may be

(Either the crafty murderer
Or) a grate through which I see
My entrance and her exit: glimpse
A possible true sky:

> inside
> outside.[13]

"Pages of the hours," "daily habit," "cardboard hours" and "paper candles" depict library and book as escapes from reality into a Gothic world. Metonymic association enters the poem with the speaker, "I", who is the other *part* of the *whole* nun, her fears or imagination, projected onto Gothic fiction. This fictionalized self wants out of her role. With the introduction of "inside/outside" "Either . . ./Or," as well the use of parenthesis, Atwood moves a step closer to the dramatic duplicities of language, structure (implied here, at least, in the position of "inside/outside"), and voice (the "I" as a part addressing a double self), so apparent in "This is a Photograph of Me."

Here the poem fully mirrors its theme:

THIS IS A PHOTOGRAPH OF ME

It was taken some time ago.
At first it seems to be
a smeared
print: blurred lines and grey flecks
blended with the paper; . . .

(The photograph was taken
the day after I drowned.

I am in the lake, in the center
of the picture, just under the surface. . . .)

> (*CG*, 11)

Metaphor is not obvious; indeed the relationship between lines or parts is one of contiguity. We *see* the print "blurred," then in focus with part of a tree "(balsam or spruce)," a slope, a house, a lake, and "some low hills." In the second half of the poem we strain to focus on the drowned speaker "in the lake"; the relationship, once again, is one of contiguity: speaker is associated with print and lake by being *in* them, a part of them. The poem develops metonymically. However, this metonymy exists within the larger metaphor of the entire poem which we have overlooked. Atwood invites us to look again with the assurance that "eventually/[we] will be able to see. . . ." "This is a photograph of me": this poem is a photograph of me, or like a photograph of me; this photograph or poem is like me. In other words, "I" am double; I have my surfaces and depths and "you" will not "see me" unless you know how to look or how to read the analogy between photograph and me.

The two part structure of the poem, emphasized by the parenthesis, repeats the duplicity of surface/depth, outside/inside, eye (of viewer or reader)/I. The relation of the second to the first part is one of perspective. Placed below the first part it suggests depth. Thus, Atwood creates a third dimension to the otherwise two-dimensional photograph (or speaker). In other poems, she uses "but" or "and" to indicate a change in perspective, but here the extended parenthetical comment carries the added irony that a seemingly casual interjection is of first importance.

Voice, another crucial element in the poem, complements language and structure. A comparison between voice in this poem and in earlier poems illustrates Atwood's developing skill. In "The Double Nun" the split speaker is addressing herself: "I" and "she" are obvious poles of the self. In two dialogue poems from 1962, "The Witch & the Nightingale" and "The Whore & the Dove," Atwood uses two clearly separate speakers to represent opposites.[14] In the first, the nightingale, or artifact, asks for freedom — "Maker, break your ice of art/release the sleeping singer/folded in my golden heart." The artist, or witch, replies that, "Your flight would shiver/the glass flowers; . . . Let me keep you here/within my hidden tower." The whore in the second poem laments that she and the dove,

> Past opposites, grasping at thin redemption
> . . . the last aspects of a scattered whole
> Must writhe in an imperfect incarnation.

Located in identifiable speakers, the voices in these poems lack subtlety or dramatic irony.

In "This is a Photograph of Me," the speaker's voice seems to come from two different places, or to be two voices. At first she is beside us showing us an album and then she tells us that she has drowned; although she is here beside us, she is still in the photograph. Because the poem appears so flat — the language is literal, specific, line and part relate metonymically, the voice is matter-of-fact — we do not expect this ventriloquism. We are not prepared for the metaphoric conjuring trick that forces us to see and *hear* double.

Double voices, then, are as important to Atwood's poetic as double structures. The challenge in "Songs of the Transformed" (*YAH*) is to locate and identify the voices who sing songs of garbage, songs we will not hear in time, songs that deceive "every time," death songs, the voices "trapped in our throats," thick red voices "muttering about life," the voices we will soon lose. It is "Corpse Song," projecting the voice within us like a ventriloquist, that explains the importance of singing and listening:

> These lanterns, my eyes
> and heart are out
>
> I bring you something
> you do not want:
>
> news of the country
> I am trapped in,
>
> news of your future:
> soon you will have no voice . . .
>
> Therefore sing now
> while you have the choice
> (*YAH*, 43)

Eyes and heart, equally untrustworthy, are useless because they cast light outwards only and because they are so easy to ignore. But voices and songs (or poems) reach us to communicate on deeper levels. Through voice we express and answer our selves. Therefore, the voice of the corpse, that rejected part of the self which exists "in two places," asks,

> Pray for me
> not as I am but as I am.
> (*YAH*, 44)

— not as "I am," a corpse, but because I exist, a disembodied voice denied by the self and thereby forced to drift, as if separate, "from head to head."

In the recent "Two-Headed Poems," Atwood portrays Canadian identity in terms of duplicity much as she did in *The Journals of Susanna Moodie*, though with less success. The two heads are our two founding cultures, French and English, and together they speak with a very double voice indeed. Atwood prefaces the poem with an advertisement for Siamese Twins, "'Joined Head to Head, and still alive,'" and then advises us that: "The heads speak sometimes singly, sometimes together, sometimes alternately within a poem. Like all Siamese twins, they dream of separation" (*THP*, 59). Who is speaking and when, however, is difficult to determine. For readers unfamiliar with Canadian politics something is lost; reference to Prime Minister Trudeau's comment, "mange de la merde," appears in poem XI: "Leave/the soul to us. Eat shit," and the voices refer to the recent debate over bilingual aviation control in poem IX: "everyone/wants to fly, whose language/is this anyway?" Stereotypes easily enough recognized by Québécois indicate who is speaking in poem III; thus, the English

> think of you as one
> big happy family, sitting around
> an old pine table, trading
> in-jokes, hospitable to strangers
> who come from far enough away.
> (*THP*, 63)

Atwood comes closest to the mythic dimension of duplicity with the description of "our leader" in poem VII; here the voices speak together:

> Our leader
> is a man of water
> with a tinfoil skin.
>
> He has two voices, . . .
>
> Who does our leader speak for?
> How can you use two languages
> and mean what you say in both?
> (*THP*, 68-69)

The voices mistrust this monstrous Siamese twin who "traps words" and is duplicitous, and yet they finally admit, "He is ours

and us,/we made him." This mistrust and grudging acknowledgement is as far as these speakers can go towards accepting their
condition or its mythic embodiment. Certainly, Atwood's attempt
to mythologize Trudeau is less compelling than the more positive
portrait of Susanna Moodie.

Perhaps more important (and more successful) than the use of
double voice to portray Canadian identity is her treatment of the
relationship between voice, language, and communication which
are problems of universal scope. In *Surfacing*, the heroine remarked that "a language is everything you do."[15] This fact is
central in "Two-Headed Poems." The English fear that separation will destroy their stockpiled French words and cause "atrophy
of the tongue." The French feel English is a language for
"counting stacks of cans." Both voices know they must hoard their
words while the Americans can afford to be "lavish/with their
syllables." To save their identity they must save their language by
finding echoes or pushing back "the other words, the coarse ones."
And yet language, "wet and living," is a burden:

> Your language hangs around your neck,
> a noose, a heavy necklace;
> each word is empire,
> each word is vampire and mother.
>
> (*THP*, 67)

In the finest poem of the sequence, poem IX, the voices, speaking
either alternately or together, though certainly not to each other,
summarize Canadian (and human) history. All the dead words of
the past are dead people; this place, even the air, signifies. Furthermore, like Susanna Moodie, "Nothing stays under/for ever." The
voices warn that, by denying realities shaped in other times by
other tongues, they will betray themselves:

> You want the air
> but not the words that come with it:
> breathe at your peril.
>
> These words are yours,
> though you never said them,
> you never heard them, history
> breeds death but if you kill
> it you kill yourself.
>
> What is a traitor?
>
> (*THP*, 71)

Ironically, these voices cannot hear each other. Although they can see and speak double, they are deaf and their dreams of linguistic freedom or of silence "settle nothing" for,

> This is not a debate
> but a duet
> with two deaf singers.
> (*THP*, 75)

These voices then are neither antiphonal nor contrapuntal. Locked in mutual isolation they babble on oblivious to each other and to the warning in "Corpse Song" (*YAH*, 43) — "sing now/ while you have the choice." Susanna Moodie is quick to realize that "this space cannot hear" her as long as she chooses to remain only "a word/in a foreign language" (*JSM*, 11), but for these two bodiless heads, harmonious duplicity cannot exist. The "choice" is left with the reader.

To see and to hear double, though difficult, is what Atwood demands of us. The strength of her poetry from *The Circle Game* to individual poems in *Two-Headed Poems*, rests in her discovery and manipulation of a poetics that mirrors theme and experience. The duplicity of the epigraph from *Power Politics* or "This is a Photograph of Me" is basic to her poetry and, furthermore, is an accurate reflection of her vision. This is not to say that every poem has this structure or that it will not be "good" if it does not. But many of the most successful poems to date do; consider "Journey to the Interior," "The Circle Game," "The Explorers," "The Settlers," "The Animals in that Country," "Backdrop Addresses Cowboy," "Projected Slide of an Unknown Soldier," "Woman Skating," most of the poems in *Power Politics*, "Tricks with Mirrors," "Songs of the Transformed," even the more subtle "Book of Ancestors," and certainly "Two-Headed Poems" where the voices are often and ironically indistinguishable.

But the integrity of this vision and the suitability of a poetics of duplicity is clearest in Atwood's *The Journals of Susanna Moodie*. In the *Journals* the poet speaks with Moodie's double voice to make us hear and see the possibilities, indeed the inevitability, of duality. In accepting, instead of polarizing our identities, we accept the self's duplication of "every-/thing." Or in Moodie's/Atwood's words —

> Two voices
> took turns using my eyes.
> (*JSM*, 42)

LORRAINE WEIR

Meridians of Perception:
A Reading of *The Journals of Susanna Moodie*

Eight collages are reproduced in *The Journals of Susanna Moodie*,[1] paradigms of the perceptual stances and operations to be presented in this volume, icons of the grammar of visual perception which structures Atwood's work. A binary system, this grammar articulates itself through the operations of enclosure and disclosure. Collage and photograph function as one code in metonymic relation to the code of eye and word, disclosing that code which is, in turn, presented in terms of the mirror world of mimetic representation and reified words. Thus mimetic disclosure within the visual code counterbalances phases of verbal enclosure in which denial of earth's language, the "green/vision" (*AC*, 39), results in amputation of the self.

Superimposition of the arbitrary convention of mimesis upon the perception of her world results in Moodie's skewed initial renderings of it. At the same time, that convention operates within collage/photograph as textual emblem of her transformation across the three journals. Accordingly, the text of the *Journals* itself exists in a state of torsion as collage and photograph, functioning as mimetic subtext, graphically present stances of semantic enclosure while — viewed synchronically — disclosing to the reader both those stances and their resolution. Present in the text from its first movement, this resolution marks the limitations of Moodie's progress through her various perceptual stances, articulates a sequential grammar for the reader, and works the intertextual balance of collage/photograph and poem. Within the larger discourse system of all of Atwood's poetry, this balance encloses the syntagmatic structures of seeing and discloses the phenomenology of visual perception which constitutes her central concerns.

* * *

First and last of the collages[2] in *The Journals of Susanna Moodie* are near-equivalent elements within the schema, with the aged Mrs. Moodie in her Belleville days first depicted in a head-and-shoulders photograph, framed by an oval which will remain as constant denotative sign within the volume. A lateral Cyclops, Mrs. Moodie gazes serenely out of an oval portrait photograph tilted onto the horizontal plane of earth, a black mass beneath her, with five abstractions of tree forms arranged on either side of her. Not only a contrast of photograph with nature, this collage signifies the equivalence of eye with self, and the triumph of the code of nature over that of mimetic representation. In the eighth collage, mimetically depicted trees, though backgrounded, serve within this reverse print to resolve the black-and-white masklike image of the poet into themselves.[3] White on black reversal dominates the visual field, absorbing specific cues of identity into landscape. It is an icon of the dance, an ironic depiction of the world of enclosure, of reified words, transcended by aqueous language.[4] Portrait has become landscape, eyes black masses within black-framed oval of face.

Reflections must be disallowed, whether in mirror or camera. The eye is a face, the face a resolution of the human code of asserted dominance. "I need wolf's eyes/to see the truth" (*JSM*, 13), where wolves are the primordial inhabitants of the land who drifted without the "networks of/roads and grids of fences" (*CG*, 79) imposed after the coming of the settlers. This is one of the "circle games" around the eye, echoed in the monocular emblem on the cover of *You are Happy* as well as in the Charles Pachter lithograph which resembles *utchat*, the eye of Horus (used on the cover of the first edition of *The Circle Game*):

> From our inarticulate
> skeleton (so
> intermixed, one
> carcass),
> they postulated wolves. (*CG*, 79)

The same postulates are found in the third of the *Susanna Moodie* collages, accompanying "The Wereman." Here the optic oval is upright within a white field, enclosing Mrs. Moodie's husband, advancing toward the wilderness in the attire of a gentleman. Wilderness is horizon, perspective thwarted by the two-dimensional quality of Moodie's image, seeming to march into the emptiness of inconceivable space, while behind him and to the right lurks an animal image, whether fox or wolf, existing in another code, blurred and inchoate. It is a paradigm of Mrs. Moodie's view:

> My husband walks in the frosted field
> an X, a concept
> defined against a blank;
> he swerves, enters the forest
> and is blotted out.   (*JSM*, 19)

"Unheld" by her sight, he may become a shape-shifter, blending with the undergrowth, camouflaged from the animals, but he will return at noon:

> . . . or it may be
> only my idea of him
> I will find returning
> with him hiding behind it.
>
> He may change me also
> with the fox eye, the owl
> eye, the eightfold
> eye of the spider   (*JSM*, 19)[5]

for he may have become a werewolf, returning to live within his wife as the animals later "moved into" her in "Departure from the Bush."

> I was frightened
> by their eyes (green or
> amber) glowing out from inside me   (*JSM*, 27)

She has become an ark, the animals inhabiting her without benefit of Noah's human intervention, though the process is incomplete for she still cannot see at night without lanterns. Wolf's eyes elude her; she has not succeeded in becoming "real" —

> There was something they almost taught me
> I came away not having learned   (*JSM*, 27)

though, by the end of Journal III, she knows at last that "the eyes produce light" (*JSM*, 52). She has been

> surrounded, stormed, broken
>
> in upon by branches, roots, tendrils, the dark
> side of light   (*JSM*, 17)

being impervious to the male "illusion" (*JSM*, 17) of civilization shared by her husband and the other planters as they work clearing the land. They are permitted to "deny the ground they stand on" (*JSM*, 16), but that choice is not available to her.

* * *

Enclosing Journal I, collages two and four present two opposed but parallel images of Mrs. Moodie, transformations of external and internal landscape. Against a rather picturesque treescape of shaded pines the youthful Mrs. Moodie is superimposed. Her arms are raised in a gesture of both despair and possession, her fingers spread wide in the manner of a child's drawing. Though shaded in, her eyes are neither the ovals of the "heirloom face" (*JSM*, 24) nor the agonized, empty spaces of the sixth collage. She is a shaded form on a piece of white paper, its border wide around her, defining her abruptly against the forest. Perspective is suggested but her form obscures the focal point. "I am a word/in a foreign language" (*JSM*, 11). Seeking to impose her language on the wilderness, she abnegates self and reflection. "I refuse to look in a mirror" (*JSM*, 13). Where the speaker of "Progressive Insanities of a Pioneer" stamps his foot in defiance and fishes for a "great vision" (*AC*, 38) of his own past, Mrs. Moodie experiences first displacement and then surrender. Where the pioneer might have become Noah, stocking his "log house- /boat with all the animals/even the wolves" (*AC*, 38), Mrs. Moodie's option is to become the ark herself and then, leaving the bush, at last to metamorphose in old age into the spirit of the forest. Asserting "I/ am not random" (*AC*, 36) as he imposes himself with shovels upon the land, the pioneer encounters earth language, "A tree-sprout, a nameless/weed" (*AC*, 36), until finally, an unwilling Jonah in reverse, he is invaded by the "unnamed whale," the "green vision,"

> through eyes
> made ragged by his
> effort, the tension
> between subject and object. . . .   (*AC*, 39)

That tension is his own doing, the language of opposition his own weapon. Mrs. Moodie, uncharacteristically using the vocabulary of the lady, takes the first step toward that "green vision" by eliminating herself:

> I take this picture of myself
> and with my sewing scissors
> cut out the face.
>
> Now it is more accurate:
>
> where my eyes were,
> every-
> thing appears   (*JSM*, 7)

Face functions as metonymy for the eyes, and eyes for language, hers and theirs, the language of "every-/thing."

    Two antinomies exist for her:

> eyes: light — transcendence;   skin: touch — limitation

There are two gardens, one a civilized garden of European flowers with their human associations of fabric, pots, imitation flowers; and the other a wilderness order of ferns, fungi, forest plants which

> . . . have their roots
> in another land
>
> they are mist
>
> if you touch them, your
> eyes go through them.   (*PU*, 17)

They are a sieve which does not hold the alien glance. Eyes speak the aqueous language of light for, after "Fishing for Eel Totems" and finally ingesting the totemic deity, the initiate learns that

> the earliest language
> was not our syntax of chained pebbles
> but liquid, made
> by the first tribes, the fish
> people.   (*PU*, 69)

To escape fear and its synonym, the city, one must become water itself so that fish and people — human predators encompassing their territory — may

> (. . . walk
> through me, not seeing
> me)

> my eyes diffused, washing
> in waves of light across the ceiling. . . .   (*PU*, 37)

To touch is to encounter the boundary of another world, to encounter it *as* boundary. It is to assert ownership.[6] This is the madness of the pioneer. Mrs. Moodie takes the photograph of herself and performs a symbolic excision of eyes and named self. She has made her face a mirror, the "ordered absence" (*AC*, 37) of the wilderness. The mirror is a *camera obscura*, inverting and projecting in darkness the image of the world of light. The eyes, "almost/blind/buds" (*JSM*, 25), must open slowly to their own light, seeing at last earth's codes.

Enclosed by the eye-lid form of skin's order, Moodie's husband is suspended in a thought-world between wilderness and wolf in the third collage. But in the fourth one, wilderness dominates. An animal form approaches the focal point of trees towering above the inset engraving of a woman at work in a log-house, with children and a cat playing around her while a visitor looks on. Concluding Journal I, the record of Mrs. Moodie's first encounter with the wilderness, the irony of this collage is complex. Having at last departed from the bush, the subject of the final poem, Mrs. Moodie is granted an image of domesticity, her anguished stance in the second collage having muted to one of transient solace. Transient, for Journal II begins with "Death of a Young Son by Drowning" and continues with dreams of earth-blood and war, "The Deaths of the Other Children," and finally a dead dog being devoured by maggots. Death crowds a world figured in the fifth collage and "The Double Voice." The land has been cleared, the log-house built, the family created. The Moodies are foregrounded — father, mother, two children, in descending order — their forms blurred on a white ground like that of the second collage, both dream visions. Forest and family assert themselves equally in terms of space but the eye is drawn to the desert of tree-stumps like wounds before the house.

> Did I spend all those years
> building up this edifice
> my composite
>   self, this crumbling hovel?   (*JSM*, 41)

And two voices, resolved into a double one, take turns using the same pair of eyes, one the voice of culture, etiquette, the lady's world; the other the voice of knowledge that

> . . . men sweat
> always and drink often,
> that pigs are pigs
> but must be eaten
> anyway, that unborn babies
> fester like wounds in the body. . . .   (*JSM*, 42)

Similarly, in "The Wereman" and collage three, Mrs. Moodie "can't think/what [her husband] . . . will see/when he opens the door" (*JSM*, 19), for he may see the results of her vision to which he is himself impervious (as the oval isolation of his figure in the collage indicates). His is the world of touch, of limitation. His vision produces the world of fences and shovels, the pioneer's notion of wilderness "absence of order," the world of "The Planters" who will be defeated if they "Open their eyes even for a moment/to these trees,/to this particular sun . . ." (*JSM*, 17). The politics of the skin, with its imposition of territory, is opaque to vision. Unless the "entire skin/[becomes] sensitive as an eye" (as it does only in "Memory" — *YAH*, 11), the encounter between the worlds of eyes and skin can only be destructive:

> you fit into me
> like a hook into an eye
>
> a fish hook
> an open eye   (*PP*, 1)

* * *

Journal III records Mrs. Moodie's descent into old age, her mutation into dying (a transitional rather than an absolute stage for her), and her resurrection into wilderness immutable. Introduced and punctuated by the last two collages within the poem cycle, it reaches to complete the optic emblem of the book, linking first and last collages through parallel inversion. In collage seven for the first time the boundary line associated with the two voices crosses the middle of the page, dividing Belleville's polite world of society and chat from the world of sight. Enearthed below the main street, the body of Mrs. Moodie young once more reclines at seeming ease, long hair rayed out around her, "opal/no/eyes glowing" (*JSM*, 49). The white border around her figure in collage one has disappeared; the blurred, oval eye-spaces have been transmuted. Where the animals had once partially inhabited her, now earth reaches to claim:

My arms, my eyes, my grieving
words, my disintegrated children

Everywhere I walk, along
the overgrowing paths, my skirt
tugged at by the spreading briers
they catch at my heels with their fingers   (*JSM*, 41)

Now at last the "heraldic emblem," the oval of face and eyes,
portrait frame and "ordered absence" of the transparent tree world
moves into place. The language of light and reflection returns:

I revolve among the vegetables,
my head ponderous
reflecting the sun
in shadows from the pocked ravines
cut in my cheeks, my eye-
sockets 2 craters

. . .

I am being
eaten away by light   (*JSM*, 48)

— both the light of nature returning her reflection rendered void
on arrival at Quebec and the light of this "Daguerreotype taken in
Old Age" reflecting a seeming solipsism which, far from denying
the world, allows its richness:

the eyes produce light the sky
            leaps at me: let there be
            the sun-
            set   (*JSM*, 52)[7]

Emptiness ("your place is empty" — *JSM*, 61) is the insistence
upon the human order, upon the hierarchical cosmology, and
thus upon the syntax of territory, ownership, expropriation. It is
the "power politics" of hook-and-eye sexual relationships, of
woman's anatomy aligned with land to be explored and exploited.
Exploration produces "thingscape":

Those who went ahead
of us in the forest
bent the early trees
so that they grew to signals:

the trail was not
among the trees but
the trees

> and there are some who have dreams
> of birds flying in the shapes
> of letters; the sky's
> codes . . .   (*JSM*, 20)[8]

Those who cannot see the wilderness must subject it to the ritual of naming, imposing a rhetoric of human analogy,[9] and gaining only a haunted universe of "ideas" (as, in "Progressive Insanities of a Pioneer," "The idea of an animal/patters across the roof" of his night-bound cabin — *AC*, 37). Landscape can only be earned, most easily by those who are themselves objects of the market economy and thus members of "underground" whose procedures include absolution. In "Fragments: Beach," it is an ablution by the sea which leaves the campers in their tents "absolved, washed/shells on the morning beach" (*PU*, 76). In *Surfacing,* it is the unforeseen result of the narrator's descent into the "multilingual" (*S*, 178) water-world and encounter with the hanged heron-god who is Christ (*S*, 140), Logos, language incarnate. "I am not an animal or a tree, I am the thing in which the trees and animals move and grow, I am a place" (*S*, 181). At first using the world's codes of power and domination, the nameless voice knows that she must "immerse [herself] in the other language" (*S*, 158) in order "to be whole" (*S*, 146), to escape the illusion of mind/body separation with its product, skin's isolationism, and to transcend "place" for earth. Initiation is first the mimesis of the animal world and then the abnegation of the mirror world of abraded touch, the refusal of status within an alien thingscape:

> I must stop being in the mirror. I look for
> the last time at my distorted glass face:
> eyes lightblue in dark red skin, hair
> standing tangled out from my head, reflection
> intruding between my eyes and vision. Not
> to see myself but to see. I reverse the mirror
> so it's toward the wall, it no longer
> traps me. . . .   (*S*, 175)

Mirror obtrudes between sight and touch, between transcendence and limitation. It is a crystal skin. Its trap is the extension of a false belonging, link between woman's body —

> Mirrors
> are the perfect lovers,
>
> that's it, carry me up the stairs
> by the edges, don't drop me,

> that would be bad luck,
> throw me on the bed
>
> reflecting side up,
> fall into me,
>
> it will be your own
> mouth you hit, firm and glassy . . .   (*YAH*, 24)

and topography, the colonized earth:

> So now you trace me
> like a country's boundary
> or a strange new wrinkle in
> your own wellknown skin
> and I am fixed, stuck
> down on the outspread map
> of this room, of your mind's continent. . . .
>   (*CG*, 39-40)[10]

* * *

Cameras operate in an analogous manner, synthesizing the light
and mirror/reflection codes in the service of the unseeing eye
Imitating only its operator's glass ambitions (its lens becomes his
"glass eye" — *CG*, 45), the camera performs its mirror tricks of
perspective, transmuting object into subject of perception — the
lover's narcissistic paradigm once again. Its vocabulary is of the
false world, the crystalline syntax of the circle game. Its product,
presented in mirror poems of reflexive structure like "This is a
Photograph of Me" (*CG*, 11),[11] is an icon of the two voices. The
mirage of time past is caught in a seemingly blurred print which,
on closer inspection, becomes a landscape of tree, lake, low hills,
and a frame house — a "syntax of chained pebbles. . . ." Like
collage seven divided across the middle by a sort of perceptual
equator, the poem turns upon itself and parentheses open on a
shifting world akin to that of the forest undergrowth in "Two
Gardens." The circle game is opposed to the luminous water-
world of "earliest language." Diffused within a transparent
matrix, voice is absolved of boundaries, even of the integument of
skin itself for

> It is difficult to say where
> precisely, or to say
> how large or small I am:
> the effect of water
> on light is a distortion. . . .

It is Susanna Moodie's vision of "union" when

> . . . each
> thing (bits
> of surface broken by my foot
> step) will without moving move
> around me
> into its place   (*JSM*, 21)

and the strife of worlds[12] (her self displaced to the margin) will at last yield to the dance.

This is the last of the procedures for underground, a poem which presents the awkward present moment of aging people practicing country dances and then, "the dance/whose patterns we could not/see almost forgotten" (*PU*, 77-9), the dance itself begins. Against "a green lawn at evening" or along a beach at sunrise, they move not in the cosmic dance whose emblem is the melothesia[13] (analogy triumphant, the world in human form), but in the dance of a lost cosmology whose emblems are wolf's eyes, the voices of birds:

> their faces turning, their changed hands
> meeting and letting go, the circle
> forming, breaking, each
> one of them the whole
> rhythm (snow on the tree
> branches)
>
>   transformed
>   for this moment/ always
> (because I say)
> the sea   the shore

LINDA W. WAGNER

The Making of
Selected Poems,
the Process of Surfacing

For Margaret Atwood, life is quest, and her writing — particularly her poetry — is the charting of that journey. Atwood's journey is seldom geographical; she may move from Canada to the States, though her antipathy for the latter is clear, but she never travels far. Unlike Charles Olson, Atwood does not dwell on location, physical presence, details of place. Her search is instead a piercing interior exploration, driving through any personal self-consciousness into regions marked by primitive responses both violent and beautiful. Atwood is interested in the human condition, a condition which exists independent of sex; and she plays a variety of games in order to explore that condition fully.

The strategies Atwood uses in her poems are similar to those of her fiction: personae described in terms of such basic biological functions as eating and sleeping; myriad patterns of disguise, whether literal or anthropomorphic; duality presented as separation, as in relationships between lovers (the hints of Jungian traits suggest that Atwood's "males" could represent the rational side of her female characters as well as their own selves); praise for life simplified, closer and closer to the natural; and a stark diction and rhythm, meant to be as far from the "literary" as Atwood's own ideal life is from the conventionally "feminine."

Whether the Atwood persona is a Circe, a Lady Oracle, a Susanna Moodie, a Marian MacAlpin, or the unnamed heroine of *Surfacing,* she is a questioning and often bitter woman, at first resisting the passions that eventually lead her to knowledge. She pits accepted roles of womanliness, with all their final ineffectuality, against those of outraged non-conformity: that Marian eats the self-caricaturing cake in *The Edible Woman* is just one image of that anger. But the final acceptance comes in Atwood's poem: "Book of Ancestors": "these brutal, with curled/beards and bulls' heads . these flattened,/slender with ritual . these contorted/ by ecstacy or pain . these bearing/knife, leaf, snake"[1]: the beginning of knowledge comes from shearing off layers of attitude, convention, falsity, the trappings of traditional female behaviour:

> A lady was what you dressed up as on Halloween when you couldn't think of anything else and didn't want to be a ghost; or it was what you said at school when they asked you what you were going to be when you grew up, you said "A lady" or "A mother," either one was safe. . . .[2]

Ironically, given the tools of the writer, Atwood finds that the most significant knowledge comes without words: "It was the language again, I couldn't use it because it wasn't mine," laments the surfacer.[3] "Useless, mouth against mouth,/lips moving in these desperate/attempts at speech. . . ./ /words we never said,/ our unborn children."[4] Atwood's poetry and fiction teem with characters who fail, consistently and harshly, in expressing themselves; and she often comments on the ineffectuality of purely rational knowledge:

> The trouble is all in the knob at the top of our bodies. I'm not against the body or the head either: only the neck, which creates the illusion that they are separate. The language is wrong, it shouldn't have different words for them.[5]

By her 1974 collection, *You Are Happy*, however, Atwood has stopped lamenting and instead shows her acceptance of the non-verbal: "History/is over, we take place/in a season . . ./ /I lean behind you, mouth touching/your spine, my arms around/you, palm above the heart,/your blood insistent under/my hand, quick and mortal."[6] One learns because one senses in the blood/heart/ hands — centers of touch and emotion rather than intellect. And one is happy, without qualification, only when she, or he, has accepted that resolution of the quest. Self-knowledge must go deeper than fragile, temporal self. It must include an other:

You are intact, you turn
towards me, your eyes opening, the eyes
intricate and easily bruised, you open

yourself to me gently, what
they tried, we
tried but could never do
before . without blood, the killed
heart . to take
that risk, to offer life and remain

alive, open yourself like this and become whole[7]

Atwood's progression to this new and apparently satisfying
resolution is clearly drawn through her first six books of poetry.
While the poems of *The Circle Game* in 1966 appeared to be direct,
cutting in their perceptions, the personae of those poems never did
make contact, never did anything but lament the human condition. As Atwood wrote in the contrived "The Islands": "There are
two of them. . . . We know they are alone/and always will be."[8]
And the cockroach in "A Meal," a poem which foreshadows the
later more effective "They Eat Out," manages to exist "on a few/
unintentional/spilled crumbs of love." The lovers, however, are
interested only in "Safety by all means," "talking/with words that
fall spare/on the ear like the metallic clink/of knife and fork" (33-
34). Relationships in these poems are sterile if not destructive:

my face flinches
under the sarcastic
tongues of your estranging
fingers,
the caustic remark of your kiss   (32)

The lovers in "Spring in the Igloo" are touching the edge of
drowning; the lover in "Winter Sleepers" has already gone down.
The female persona in "A Sibyl" admits her "bottled anguish"
and "glass despair."

Even in this first collection, however, the problem as Atwood
sees it is more than personal. There are complex reasons why love
between a man and a woman is tenuous — cultural, philosophi-
cal, anthropological reasons, many of which grow from mistaken
values in modern living. Because contemporary people judge in
terms of technology and scientific progress, they value "improve-
ments," devices, the urban over the rural, the new over the
timeless. Much of Atwood's first collection is filled with her
arguments against these attitudes: "The cities are only outposts,"

"We must move back:/there are too many foregrounds." "There is no center;/the centers/travel with us unseen" (74-75).

This dissatisfaction with the modern milieu, and the ethos it has spawned, leads Atwood first to the immediate move away from urban life. In "Migration: C.P.R." she says of her protagonists

we ran west

wanting
a place of absolute
unformed beginning   (52)

"Pre-Amphibian" reinforces that tactic, and in the three-part poem "Primitive Sources" she studies ancient beliefs about god-systems, magic, and other devices for understanding the process of life — and a sentient human being's place in it. In "A Place: Fragments" Atwood views the process as largely physical:

in order to survive
we make what we can and have to
with what we have   (73)

But in "Journey to the Interior" she has moved away from geographical exploration into the search for herself as self. In *The Circle Game* Atwood only begins this exploration — indeed, only acknowledges that it is the crucial exploration, and that the usual equipment will not suffice: "A compass is useless. . . .//Whatever I do I must/keep my head. I know/it is easier for me to lose my way/forever here, than in other landscapes" (58).

Many of these early themes come together in the title poem of the collection. "The Circle Game" — which is reminiscent of W.D. Snodgrass's "Heart's Needle" in its juxtaposition of children, love, war, and kinds of games — is a terse rendering as well of many of the themes of other poems in the book. Atwood plays again on the depravity of society, using the innocence of childhood games as one counter. The tone of the seven-part sequence is, however, clearly established in the opening poem: as the children hold hands and play their circle games, they share the constraints of Atwood's lovers; they too are separate ("They are singing, but not to each other"). The whole scene is without joy. The circles only ironically suggest unity, completion; even the innocence of the game is betrayed.

The lover too withholds. "You refuse to be," she cajoles him. Instead of loving, he observes, dissects. Once the image of war —

and the accompanying if contradictory image of *war games* — is introduced, Atwood describes him as a "tracer of maps." Her emphasis on the inferior quality of such an occupation brings to mind the root of poet, maker, creator: the artist would never be content to trace. In this interchange, the woman speaking likens herself to some object — perhaps a map — whose only role in her lover's life is to be scrutinized. She feels herself "transfixed/by your eyes'/cold blue thumbtacks" (40).

Interested only in the working out of his detailed strategies, maps, games, the lover remains apart — not because she is not trying to reach out to him, but because he wants to exist separate from her:

> You play the safe game
> the orphan game
>
> the ragged winter game
> that says, I am alone . . .   (41)

As the images of game, children, and circle merge in the concluding poem, she realizes that she can no longer be a part of this façade. For all its tact, amenity, and semblance of union, the love relationship exists only within "the closed rules of your games, but there is no joy in it." The orderly rhythms are, finally, "poisoning." Like Marian in *The Edible Woman*, the woman of the circle game escapes.

Although most of the attention in the poems of *The Circle Game* falls on personae other than the female character, the book can easily be read as her portrait. The collection opens with "This Is a Photograph of Me," which describes the landscape surrounding the lake in which the heroine has recently drowned. In Atwood's wry directions to the viewer lies her admission of the long and difficult process that "surfacing" is to be. First one must realize the need to surface. Identity comes after that, and full definition much later.

> I am in the lake, in the center
> of the picture, just under the surface.
>
> It is difficult to say where
> precisely, or to say
> how large or small I am:
> the effect of water
> on light is a distortion

> but if you look long enough,
> eventually
> you will be able to see me   (11)

As the last lines also imply, part of that full definition must also come from the viewer/reader/lover. Attention in *The Circle Game* tends to be given more regularly to the male persona — he may be disappointing but he is the authority, the determinant. Atwood is not yet able to draw her female characters as if they had distinctive qualities. They are instead mirrors, listeners, watchers:

> if I watch
> quietly enough
> and long enough
> at last, you will say. . . .
>
> all I need to know:
> tell me
> everything
> just as it was
> from the beginning   (66-67)

Atwood's eventual development from woman as pupil to the authoritative protagonist of *Lady Oracle* illustrates well the journey to self-definition.

That Atwood has excluded so many of these poems first published in *The Circle Game* from her 1976 *Selected Poems* suggests that — for all their thematic accuracy — she finds them less satisfying as poems than some later work. Perhaps the very directness and flat diction that in the sixties appeared to be strengths had grown comparatively uninteresting, for Atwood later set her direct statements in more metaphorical contexts, and often avoided making statements at all, unless they were ironic. She also began the search for poetic personae other than the woman-lover of the poems in *The Circle Game*.

In *The Animals in That Country* she wrote about anthropomorphic characters who seemed to represent the human types already drawn in her early poems. Metaphor suffuses these poems. "The Landlady" opens "This is the lair of the landlady," "a raw voice/loose in the rooms beneath me," "intrusive as the smells that bulge in under my doorsill." Not only beastlike, the landlady also dominates the tenant's life:

> From her I rent my time:
> she slams
> my days like doors.
> Nothing is mine . . .[9]

The young feminine persona remains submissive, coerced into action, dissatisfied with what choices do exist — and with her decisions about those choices. Repeatedly, she wrongs herself, whether she takes in "A Foundling" or blurs into the obliging lover ("more and more frequently the edges/of me dissolve and I become/a wish").

As if in reaction from that submission, Atwood in this collection creates many new personae, each with a distinctive and often idiosyncratic voice: Dr. Frankenstein, Captain Cook, the stage backdrop for a western, a pioneer, some unnamed voices. Her experiments here with varying rhythms and tones probably equipped her to catch the ambivalent persona of the book-length sequence of poems, *The Journals of Susanna Moodie* (1970). Her achievement in this collection is to present a protagonist believable in her conflicts. Through Moodie/Atwood, we experience hope, anguish, fear, joy, resignation, and anger. It may be more important for the thematic development of Atwood's poetry that we experience the paradox of Canadian nationalism. Like Atwood, Moodie wrote enthusiastically about life in Canada yet her journals also showed her real fear of the wild, the primitive, the untamed. As Atwood describes Moodie:

> . . . she praises the Canadian landscape but accuses it of destroying her; she dislikes the people already in Canada but finds in people her only refuge from the land itself; she preaches progress and the march of civilization while brooding elegiacally upon the destruction of the wilderness. . . . She claims to be an ardent Canadian patriot while all the time she is standing back from the country and criticizing it as though she were a detached observer, a stranger. Perhaps that is the way we still live. We are all immigrants to this place even if we were born here: the country is too big for anyone to inhabit completely, and in the parts unknown to us we move in fear, exiles and invaders.[10]

Atwood's early use of maps, explorer figures, the images of exploration and country here find more than metaphoric reality: Moodie migrated from England, traveled up the St. Lawrence, and lived in hostile Upper Canada and on a remote bush farm as well as in Belleville and Toronto. The space of Canada evokes her recognition of her own space:

> We left behind one by one
> the cities rotting with cholera,
> one by one our civilized
> distinctions

> and entered a large darkness. . . .
>
> My brain gropes nervous
> tentacles in the night, sends out
> fears hairy as bears . . .   (*SP*, 81)

The character of Susanna Moodie becomes a perfect mask for the journey to self-exploration that Atwood attempts. Her statement "Whether the wilderness is/real or not/depends on who lives there" sounds much like Atwood's later surfacer. "Looking in a Mirror" and "The Wereman" repeat this theme of unwitting metamorphosis, identity shaped by the wilderness and its arduous living. Not all changes are negative, however; and one of the results of this acrid confrontation with natural forces is an acceptance of dream knowledge. Some of the strongest poems in the collection are the descriptions of dreams, "real, heavier/than real" (*SP*, 101).

Published in the same year as the Susanna Moodie collection, Atwood's *Procedures for Underground* has as central persona a pioneer woman, whose memories seem to be given voice as she looks at old photographs. Her family, the old cabin, hard winters, her husband — she speaks with a spare wisdom, moving easily between fact and dream, myth and custom. In "Procedures for Underground" she speaks as a Persephone who has gone below, been tested, learned "wisdom and great power," but returns to live separate, feared, from her companions. Knowledge of whatever source is the prize for Atwood's persona, and many of the poems in the collection play with the definition of truth, fact, knowledge, the "search for the actual." In some of the poems Atwood moves to present-day Canada and continues the theme of search through the sexual power conflict that is to be the subject of her 1971 *Power Politics*. The poem "Habitation" draws together the images of primitive and pioneering existences, the strength of the woman's self-acceptance, and the sexual relationship:

> Marriage is not
> a house or even a tent
>
> it is before that, and colder:
>
> the edge of the forest, the edge
> of the desert . . .   (*SP*, 133)

Power Politics is Atwood's comic scenario of the themes she had treated with relative sombreness in *Susanna Moodie* and

Underground. If the former was an exploration of a sentient woman character, caught in and finally able to acknowledge "the inescapable doubleness of her own vision,"[11] then *Procedures for Underground* is a survival manual for the kind of learning that a perceptive woman would have to undertake. Handicapped as she is (with her head resting in her "gentle" husband's sack), she must make use of emotion, dream, the occult, the primitive, even the animal to find her way. In *Power Politics* the assumption that any woman's protective male *is* her handicap becomes a given, and the fun in the book comes through Atwood's myriad inventive descriptions of the power struggle — as politics, war, physical waste, innuendo, sly attack. The unusually wry tone of the collection as a whole is announced in the epigraph:

> You fit into me
> like a hook into an eye
>
> a fish hook
> an open eye
>   (*SP*, 141)

Reversing the cliché toward unexpected bitterness is a common tactic in these poems, "You take my hand and/I'm suddenly in a bad movie," "I can change my-/self more easily/than I can change you/ /I could grow bark and/become a shrub." But Atwood achieves more than verbal humour by heightening her descriptions until they are surreal. In "They Eat Out" the lover claims immortality through the poet's words and so becomes transformed, as she explains,

>   through your own split head
> you rise up glowing;
>
> the ceiling opens
> a voice sings Love Is A Many
>
> Splendoured Thing
> you hang suspended above the city
>
> in blue tights and a red cape,
> your eyes flashing in unison.
>
> The other diners regard you
> some with awe, some only with boredom:
>
> they cannot decide if you are a new weapon
> or only a new advertisement.

> As for me, I continue eating;
> I liked you better the way you were,
> but you were always ambitious.   (SP, 144-45)

Rancour has become humour, as the stereotypical description of a superman figure is used to deflate the male ego rather than that of the female.

One of the changes Atwood made in choosing work for *Selected Poems* was to omit many of the poems in *Power Politics* that were titled as if for stage directions: "He reappears," "He is a strange biological phenomenon," "He is last seen." By emphasizing instead poems about the two people in the relationship, and often the woman, she manages to reverse the expected power positions. In *Selected Poems* the male ego is less often central. The collection as represented in the 1976 book thus meshes more closely with Atwood's earlier poems, in which the female persona often moves independently on her search for self-awareness, although in her omissions Atwood has deleted some poems important to thematic strains. "Small Tactics," for example, a seven-part sequence in *Power Politics,* relates the war games described in this collection to those of "The Circle Game," but here the feminine voice laments, "Let's go back please/to the games, they were/more fun and less painful." She describes herself as an electric light, "closed and useful," shying away from the disclosures she feels imminent:

> For stones, opening
> is not easy
>
> Staying closed is
> less pain . . .[12]

More often, in this collection, the woman is wise and loving, ready to admit her own necessary anger, but not misshapen by it.

In other poems in *Power Politics* Atwood mocks various modern attitudes toward love — the intellectual, the scientific, the rational. She resumes her search for "truth" and fact, this time imaged in the act of making love; and admits that, in most cases, male and female are "hostile nations." But the recurring images are less often of warfare than of the woman's admission of her own fallibility: the male is insensitive, childlike, corrupting. Why then does she tolerate him, love him, even revere him?

> Lying here, everything in me
> brittle and pushing you away

> This is not something I
> wanted, I tell you . . .   (*SP*, 173)

"I should be doing something/other than you," she reprimands
herself; and in another poem asks, "Why did I create you?" The
key to the generally more positive tone of the later poems is the
concept of woman and poet as creator of (or at least accomplice to)
the male myth. Once the feminine persona realizes that she must
accept her lover's identity for what it is — just as honestly as she
has come to know herself through the previous poem sequences —
the serious difficulties in their love affair begin to resolve themselves.

> They were all inaccurate:
>
> the hinged bronze man, the fragile man
> built of glass pebbles,
> the fanged man with his opulent capes and boots . . .
>
> It was my fault but you helped,
> you enjoyed it.   (*SP*, 176)

This recognition — and the acceptance of the recognition —
enables Atwood to be ironically convincing at least part of the time
in her last poem collection prior to *Selected Poems*, the 1974 *You
Are Happy*. Still marked in places with the pungent anger of
Power Politics, this book stresses the difficult stages of a journey
together: if the search for self-knowledge is enough to defeat most
of us, then the complexities of making that search a dual enterprise
are almost inconceivable:

> This is a journey, not a war,
> there is no outcome,
> I renounce predictions
>
> and aspirins . . .
>
> We're stuck here
> on this side of the border
> in this country of thumbed streets and stale buildings
>
> where there is nothing spectacular
> to see and the weather is ordinary . . .
>
> where we must walk slowly,
> where we may not get anywhere
>
> or anything, where we keep going,
> fighting our ways, our way
> not out but through.   (*SP*, 226)

Spoken in the by-now recognizable voice of the spare, crisp feminist (who has moved from awareness to disappointment to anger, and now beyond, to a usually humorous skepticism), these lines are flatter, less evocative of passion than some of the poetry Atwood omitted from *Selected Poems*. In "He is last seen," the concluding poem of *Power Politics*, Atwood pictures the rounded images of death — womb and moon, snow sculptures — in lines heavy with open vowels:

> The death you bring me
> is curved, it is the shape
> of doorknobs, moons
> glass paperweights

> Inside it, snow and lethal
> flakes of gold fall endlessly
> over an ornamental scene,
> a man and woman, hands joined and running

The suggestion of Midas' touch, the patriarchal investiture of power, on the coupling (caught in a running image which could be both positive and negative) leads to the lover's ambivalence which opens Part II:

> Nothing I can do will slow you
> down, nothing
> will make you arrive any sooner

The poem, however, proceeds positively: the male lover journeys on, "serious, a gift-bearer,/through the weeks and months, across/ the rocks, up from/the pits and starless/deep nights of the sea/ towards firm ground and safety."[13]

Atwood's reasons for deleting this powerful poem with its important recognition of dual emotions remain unexplained, but the poem does picture the male as dominant — decisive, aggressive — in ways that tend to contrast with the transformation and Circe poems of *You Are Happy*. In tone, however, in the strong balance of antipathy and desire, it leads to the 1974 collection, with its somewhat richer diction and more varied rhythms.

The ironically generous central persona of *You Are Happy* is Atwood's fully-realized female — maker, poet, lover, prophet — a Circe with the power to change all men into animals, all men except Odysseus. Her capacity to control and yet give marks her as truly royal; her sometimes coy reluctance to accept praise suggests her basic awareness of the futility of bucking convention. Her

powers may be dramatic, as the poems of "Songs of the Transformed" indicate, but they are limited to the physical, and fragile
compared to the "wrecked words" Circe laments. Powerful as she
is, Circe still cannot create words, and it is words for which her
people beg. As she observes the pigs and bulls held under her
power, she admits these limits:

> Men with the heads of eagles
> no longer interest me
> or pig-men. . . .
>
> All these I could create, manufacture,
> or find easily: they swoop and thunder
> around this island, common as flies. . . .

No different from all women, in fact, the Circe persona continues:

> I search instead for the others,
> the ones left over,
> the ones who have escaped from these
> mythologies with barely their lives;   (*SP*, 202)

Circe differs from Atwood's earlier protagonists in that she is
more aware of inhibiting mythologies. Her great understanding
— of individuals as well as of patterns and cultural expectations —
sharpens her perception but does not make her less vulnerable. She
can observe of Odysseus "Those who say they want nothing/want
everything," but she still loves him, and her loving is expressed
through her generosity:

> There are so many things I want
> you to have. This is mine, this
> tree, I give you its name,
>
> here is food, white like roots, red,
> growing in the marsh, on the shore,
> I pronounce these names for you also.
>
> This is mine, this island, you can have
> the rocks, the plants . . .   (*SP*, 209)

Tempering her love is one of the highly effective prose poems that
punctuate the "Circe/Mud" sequence, the story of the perfect mud
woman ("in the afternoon when the sun had warmed her [he
would] make love to her, sinking with ecstacy into her soft moist
belly, her brown wormy flesh where small weeds had already
rooted . . . His love for her was perfect, he could say anything to
her, into her he spilled his entire life"). The implicit question

Circe poses is, does every man dream of a perfect experience that is entirely physical, and entirely impersonal? Even after his lover has given him words, names, property, self, does her image pale beside his wormy fantasy?

As Odysseus' dissatisfaction grows (his basic greed is impossible to satisfy), he thinks often of Penelope, and Circe realizes the wife's power to draw him back. Besides, as she explains fatalistically, "It's the story that counts. No use telling me this isn't a story. . . . You leave in the story and the story is ruthless" (*SP*, 221). At the base of reality is the word. Despite omens and auguries, fire signs and bird flights, happenings return to the word, as Odysseus did:

> You move within range of my words
> you land on the dry shore
>
> You find what there is   (*SP*, 201)

Atwood changes the image of conquering male into the image of man lured by a subtler power. Verbal magic bests physical force; feminine wiles and words convince the male persona — no matter what the circumstance — that "you are happy." The ambivalence of the opening poem, "Newsreel: Man and Firing Squad" suggests the transitory and often indefinable quality of any happiness. One learns to say *No* to the most unpleasant of life's experiences; one counters fate and myth with strategy; one develops powers of his or her own kind and value, and for the poet, those powers are verbal. As Atwood says so well in the fifth poem of the "Eating Fire" sequence:

> To be the sun, moving through space
>
> distant and indifferent, giving
> light of a kind for those watching
>
> To learn how to
> live this way. or not. to choose
>
> to be also human, the body
> mortal and faded . . .   (*SP*, 229)

Atwood's poems suggest that the range of human promise is wide, that exploring that range — for woman, man, artist, or lover — should be a primary life experience: "To learn how to live," "to choose," "to be also human," and, as culmination, "to surface."

LORNA IRVINE

One Woman
Leads to Another

mothers like worn gloves
wrinkled to the shape of their lives,

passing the work from hand to hand
mother to daughter,

a long thread of red blood, not yet broken

— Margaret Atwood, "The Red Shirt,"
Two-Headed Poems

With the publication of *Two-Headed Poems*,[1] Margaret Atwood, for the first time in her writing, has created a dominantly female world. The male gods of earlier volumes of poetry fade into the background and the poetic dialogue no longer conjures up the ambiguous masculine other.[2] Here, the poet does not present herself as martyred; rather, she speaks with considerable assurance. Her representation of time has changed. Instead of trying to sever herself from the past, she reclaims it. Thus, although she knows that "history/breeds death," she also knows that "if you kill/it you kill yourself" (*THP*, p. 71). Furthermore, unlike, for example, *Power Politics*, where apocalypse controls the imagination, the poems of *Two-Headed Poems* illustrate continuance. Certainly, some of the imagery used is bizarre, even nightmarish. But the political violence that it illustrates neither dominates the world of these poems, threatening to end it, nor metaphorically images the disintegrating body.[3]

Spatially, the poet establishes herself in a rooted present. Instead of spiralling in towards the unconscious, as do such earlier poems as "A Descent Through the Carpet," "Journey Towards the Interior," or "Procedures for Underground," these more recent poems move outwards from this present. They are therefore more altruistic, avoiding the reflexive self and the mirrors that image it. As the poet suggests, the messages of these poems are "iron talismans, and ugly, but/more loyal than mirrors" (*THP*, p. 84). Specifically, they speak to a younger generation, a generation most persistently represented by the figure of the poet's young daughter.[4] For this child, and for herself, the poet needs to fill the lacunae of earlier poems with a female tradition. Thus, grandmothers, great-aunts, aunts, and mothers appear, like so many good fairies around a princess's christening, to protect the new generation by passing on the knowledge of the old.

The sense of female traditions also results in a new respect for the body, particularly the body that can reproduce. Atwood has certainly before now used images of creativity, but how ambivalent they have been. Think of Circe's disgust as she looks at the men she has manufactured, or, in *Power Politics*, the repeated creation of monstrosities. Now, represented in *Two-Headed Poems* by a healthy, living child, creativity becomes positive. Furthermore, this child alters the whole landscape. Translated into Christmas tree decorations, into stuffed animals, into puppets, the animals have been tamed. Although political tensions are present, particularly in the nine sections of "Two-Headed Poems," and the world does contain men with holes in their throat, hangmen, and torture chambers, the collection really celebrates the generative space of the home, the "land of hope/fulfilled" (*THP*, p. 20). In this space occur the rituals of Christmas and Hallowe'en, of gardening and preserving. Here, one can remember the ancestors and pass on that remembrance to one's children. This world is remarkably concrete; its central child seems real.

Children do not seem so in the first of Atwood's volumes of poetry, *The Circle Game*. In its title poem, the children playing on the lawn are obscurely frightening, not only trapping themselves in the circle of their game but also trapping the poet. Their voices are not human:

> (the children spin
> a round cage of glass
> from the warm air
> with their thread-thin
> insect voices)
>
> (*CG*, p. 44)

Solipsistic, the poem circles in on itself. The man and woman are cut off from their own childhoods. Locked in a deadly battle with each other, they inherit no tradition, only a bleak and empty space. The woman, "spineless," is caught in her "cage of bones" (*CG*, p. 43); the man, without a center, remains superficial, a "tracer of maps," a "memorizer/of names" (*CG*, p. 39). Regeneration does not occur. The circling children, the children who "aren't our children" (*CG*, p. 40), neither join with each other nor unite the watchers. Like the man and woman, they have no roots and thus must play the "orphan game," "the game of the waif who stands/ at every picture window" (*CG*, p. 41). Although the land passes through the vegetation cycle of spring, summer, autumn, winter, the cycle itself is dead, the game "closed" (*CG*, p. 43). Refuges are longed for, but those built by the children along the beach are eroded during the night and the museum, harborer of relics of the past, crumbles.

Other poems in this volume further illustrate emptiness and rootlessness. In "Evening Trainstation Before Departure," the poet, along with screaming children, a depressed woman, a threatening man, briefly inhabits a "pause in space" (*CG*, p. 15), a temporary and unsatisfactory asylum from her customary life on "all the edges there are" (*CG*, p. 16). Inner spaces are described negatively. Inside the body, tapeworms and other scavengers multiply:

> something is hiding
> somewhere
> in the scrubbed bare
> cupboard of my body
> flattening itself
> against a shelf
> and feeding
> on other people's leavings
>
> (*CG*, p. 33)

As in Yeats's "Second Coming," the imminent apocalypse does not imply a preparation for the building of a better world, but a more brutal one. The past is cut off; the poet can imagine no Eden, no sunken kingdoms. Her ancestors are "fossil bones and fangs" (*CG*, p. 23). Such a future and such a past imply a completely unstable present:

> These days we keep
> our weary distances:
> sparring in the vacant spaces
> of peeling rooms
> and rented minutes
> (*CG*, p. 31)

It is a present of capsized houses, of melting igloos, of people "each in his own private blizzard" (*CG*, p. 27). Except in the final poem, where children are imagined with "green smiles" (*CG*, p. 80), this volume concentrates on death. In it, the individual blots out the community and the circuitous, private journey into the unconscious denies outward-moving communication. Positive relationships among women are altogether absent.

A profound anxiety about the creation of offspring dominates *The Animals in That Country*. In "Speeches for Dr. Frankenstein," the monster emerges from an emptiness "barren as total freedom" (*AC*, p. 42), only to betray its creator. The nurturing that binds mother to child is here denied: "You have been starved/you are hungry. I have nothing to feed you" (*AC*, p. 45). Such foods as are mentioned in the poem are ironically presented: the pomegranate, symbol of fertility, of impregnation, becomes a red skeleton; yeast, living and expanding, turns instead suffocating; fruit is nothing more than core and rind; corn is a "kernel of pain," "my heart's husk is a stomach" (*AC*, p. 46). Thus, the winter myth of Demeter controls the world. Blood is not that of rebirth but of destruction. Certainly, the poem metaphorically illustrates the difficulties of poetic creativity. Yet so vivid are the images of physical birth that they betray a woman's fears of bearing deformed children, of suffering only to end up with the "chasm" (*AC*, p. 47) in the side.

Indeed, whereas the landscape of *The Circle Game* is frozen, usually eerily silent, that of *The Animals in That Country* is peopled, but the life it describes is frightening. The poet even fears her own body:

> I am the cause, I am a stockpile of chemical
> toys, my body
> is a deadly gadget,
> I reach out in love, my hands are guns,
> my good intentions are completely lethal.
> (*AC*, p. 30)

Children are foundlings or, like the poet herself, are destructive, playing in the trees with their guns. The "twisted" child, reflected in the window in "The Revenant" is "vindictive" (*AC*, p. 52), a mirror of the poet's sickness. Although, in one poem, children appear among strawberries, the squirrels eating out of their hands, and, in another, are pictured with their father and mother in a tourist brochure meant to lure Americans to Canada, these are fantasy children, remote from the poet. In this volume, as in the former one, the poet remains rootless. Houses do not become homes. Her real surroundings, the landlady "solid as bacon" (*AC*, p. 15), the rooming-house with its "ownerless letters," its "alien feet," its "unclaimed toothbrush" (*AC*, p. 28), are unstable. She continues to live on the edge. The "broken/line" (*AC*, p. 4) and the "separate/object" (*AC*, p. 6) dominate her imagination. Her barrenness is repeatedly evoked in "Chronology" and "After I Fell Apart": empty, she speaks of the uncovering of "incredible/blank innocence" (*AC*, p. 55); of the "hard, hollow" consciousness; of the skull, a "reversed/dry well, an absence" (*AC*, p. 56). In "Sundew," "silence and dead energy" (*AC*, p. 63) close in on the hot and decaying bay.

Other anxieties about bearing children are documented in *The Journals of Susanna Moodie,* that proud and lonely woman who becomes the poet's alter-ego. For Susanna Moodie, children mean loss. Thus, in "Death of a Young Son By Drowning," birth is obliterated by the child's long drowning. No longer real, he becomes a symbol of his mother's struggle with the harsh Canadian land; she plants him in "this country/like a flag" (*JSM*, p. 31). In "The Deaths of the Other Children," the mother's fragmented, disintegrating body dramatically illustrates the closeness between mother and child. To lose her children is to lose parts of herself:

> Did I spend all those years
> building up this edifice
> my composite
>   self, this crumbling hovel?
>
> My arms, my eyes, my grieving
> words, my disintegrated children
>   (*JSM*, p. 41)

Because of their association with death, children and therefore birth do not suggest regeneration: "I should have known/anything planted here/would come up blood" (*JSM*, p. 34); "unborn babies/fester like wounds in the body" (*JSM*, p. 42). And, because Susanna Moodie has been separated from her own country, she feels rootless, without a tradition. Alone, images of rape obsess her:

> they would be surrounded, stormed, broken
>
> in upon by branches, roots, tendrils, the dark
> side of light
> as I am.
>
> (*JSM*, p. 17)

These poems are fundamentally about a solitary struggle, not about a communal one. Thus, like those in earlier volumes, they are inward looking. In spite of the fact that Moodie's grand-children are mentioned towards the end, thereby establishing a tenuous genealogy, the landscape seems profoundly empty. Indeed, emptiness is evoked in the last line of the volume as Moodie's ghost imagines Toronto's disappearance: "Your place is empty" (*JSM*, p. 61).

Both *Procedures For Underground* and *Power Politics* are filled with apocalyptic imagery, a historical focus that extends itself to the disintegrating body. In "Stories in Kinsman's Park," damaged fathers and frightened children are forgotten in the sun and green leaves of the park; eternity is imaginable. But rejuvenation remains fantasy; the "bad dreams" (*PU*, p. 39) are the real world. These poems most commonly describe the ancestral past as a trap. Intruded upon, frequently split, the self is also represented as a gap or lacuna. Not reborn, the drowned body of "Delayed Message" rises to the surface, looking out at the world through the "empty holes" (*PU*, p. 19) of its eyes. In another poem, the poet imagines herself in water where she is "everywhere and nothing," where people walk through her without seeing her (*PU*, p. 30). Marriage does not join men and women together, is not "a house/ or even a tent" (*PU*, p. 60), does not nurture the human being. The human body of these poems is filled only when it is distended by water, as it is in the numerous images of drowning, or when it is malignant:

> our bodies
> are populated with billions
> of soft pink numbers
> multiplying and analyzing
> themselves
>
> (*PP*, p. 9)

The whole landscape reflects the body's illness and barren-

ness. Spring, like that in Eliot's *The Waste Land*, does not regener-
ate the world but is both ill and intrusive, raping its way into "the
earth, my head" (*PP*, p. 40). Rooms, houses, and buildings do not
shelter but are, like the body, either swollen or in the process of
disintegrating. Although, in one poem, children are imagined
into existence and the poet longs to be "reconciled to fur seeds and
burrows" (*PP*, p. 41), the Tarot cards deny her a future, pro-
phesying instead her death by water:

> the children, looking from
> the side of the boat, see their mother
>
> upside down, lifesize, hair streaming
> over the slashed throat
> and words fertilize each other
> in the cold and with bulging eyes
> (*PP*, p. 41)

Particularly in *Power Politics*, abortion seems preferable to birth:
"I should have used leaves/and silver to prevent you" (*PP*, p. 53).
Indeed, if the foetus is allowed to mature, in this world it will be
born crippled, "blind and one-handed" (*PP*, p. 53). Like that birth
imagined in "Speeches for Dr. Frankenstein," what will here be
born is catastrophe: it is brutal, aggressive, and male. In a world in
which the created attempts to annihilate the creator, reproduction
becomes a crime. Thus, the central question for the woman/poet
of this volume is a question superficially about art but fundamentally about reproduction: "Why did I create you?" (*PP*, p. 53).

With *Power Politics*, Atwood seems to have exhausted her
nihilism. The poems of the next volume, *You Are Happy*, are
considerably more positive. As we shall see, they seem transition
poems, moving towards what I consider to be a different philo-
sophical approach to creativity, an approach that alters even the
structure of the poems of *Two-Headed Poems*. Certainly, in *You
Are Happy*, the tension between destruction and creation
continues, as do the poet's obsessive concerns with intrusion and
rootlessness. However, more often now the focus is on generation,
and generation imagined somewhat positively. Although the poet
can still hear "death growing in me like a baby with no head"
(*YAH*, p. 14), she balances the anxieties of birth with its joys:

> we move still
> touching over the greening fields, the future
> wounds folded like seeds
> in our tender fingers
> (*YAH*, p. 23)

The landscape is healthier; water is more often an image of creation than it is of destruction. Women figures appear with increasing frequency and although they continue to seem projections of the poet herself, they are less victimized projections. They are able to imagine themselves nurturing and preserving another generation. Images of opening proliferate and the body, so diseased, malformed and frightening in earlier poems, gradually begins to mend:

> O body, descend
> from the wall where I have nailed you
> like a flayed skin or a war trophy

> Let me inhabit you, have compassion.on me
> once more
>
> (*YAH*, p. 73)

In the poems entitled "Eating Fire," "Four Auguries," and "Head Against White," metaphors of generation draw the reader's attention to the human flesh. Ripeness dominates "Late August." "Lush lobed bulbs" glow in the dusk; the plums

> dripping on the lawn outside
> our window, burst
> with a sound like thick syrup
> muffled and slow

> The air is still
> warm, flesh moves over
> flesh
>
> (*YAH*, p. 93)

Hopeful, *You Are Happy* describes towards the end of the volume the healing baptism that, following the self's burial, allows it, no longer empty, to "rise up living" (*YAH*, p. 91), to "offer life and remain/alive" (*YAH*, p. 96).

The reader has therefore been partially prepared for *Two-Headed Poems* in which temporal and spatial metaphors seem to me to emphasize a positive and healthy female tradition. In the poems of this volume, the poet emphasizes fresh beginnings (*THP*, p. 13) that make the present and, significantly, the future, meaningful. Similarly, she acknowledges the importance of time past. In "Five Poems for Grandmothers," the poet traces her own history through that of her ancestors — her great-aunts, her aunts, her mother — the offspring of the matriarch grandmother, the "old bone tunnel" (*THP*, p. 40) from which the poet has emerged. Clocks tick like the hearts of grandmothers (*THP*, p. 52); the black stone picked up at the lake's edge is a mother god. Filled with power, a survivor of the ravages of time, this mother god with her breast and buttock is the "knob of earth" (*THP*, p. 90) the poet worships. In "A Red Shirt," woman is, in a mythic flashback, witch and sorceress until, transformed by the poet, she becomes mother. The past cannot be discarded. Enclosed on a bus, the poet hears the whispering voices of the ancestors and accepts "the knowledge/of old lives continuing" (*THP*, p. 78). Her female ancestors reveal her to herself:

> Sons branch out, but
> one woman leads to another.
> Finally, I know you
> through your daughters,
> my mother, her sisters,
> and through myself
> (*THP*, p. 37)

But as well as dramatizing the past by describing her ancestors, the poet also confirms the future by presenting children. Even in poems in which the imagery is negative, they appear: the children of the man with the hole in his throat, the children of the man who cleans the floors of the torture chamber, the children in Beauharnois, Quebec, during the invasion of the British soldiers. Indeed, at the center of the volume, and the chief audience of its poems, is the poet's young daughter. This child dominates a remarkably concrete landscape. Outside the sleeping house of "Two Miles Away," the moonlight reflects the child's presence — the sandbox, the "green shovel," the "cracked white pail," the "red star" (*THP*, p. 21). Gone are the rented rooms and crumbling houses of earlier volumes; here, the central space is a home. The animals are tamed. The little girl seems to have made the natural world accessible to the poet:

> Downstairs, my daughter sleeps
> in her jungle of pastel animals
> with their milky noses and missing eyes;
> green leaves are rising around her cage,
> rubbery and huge, where she hunts and snuffles
> on all fours through the hours
> (*THP*, p. 29)

The legendary wolves of "The Animals in That Country" and of *The Journals of Susanna Moodie*, "the idea of an animal" that consumes the mind of the pioneer (*AC*, p. 37), the suffering animals of "Songs of the Transformed" (*YAH*) have, in *Two-Headed Poems*, become a child's toys. The Christmas tree of "Solstice Poem" shimmers with "tin angels, a knitted bear" (*THP*, p. 81) and, in "The Puppet of the Wolf," although the poet still fears the wolf's carnivorous mouth, the child "laughs at its comic/dance, at its roar" (*THP*, p. 100).

Most important, these are poems of instruction, a gathering up of the wisdom one generation wishes to pass on to the next. They do not circle inwards, are not maps of the unconscious, do not quarrel with the opposite sex. "Solstice Poem," addressed specifically to the poet's young daughter, establishes ancestral roots for the child. Spatially, it creates a home. Here imagined as an altar, temporarily out of range of the warring factions beyond the hills, this home protects the child in order to assure her a future. Like the solstice of the title, the temporary suspension that is the poem's space both acknowledges the sun's distance from the earth while it also celebrates its imminent return. This double awareness keeps the poet/mother's message from being naively optimistic. Although she longs to transmit only joy and peace to her child, she knows she must also warn her of the burden of sensitivity that makes ambivalent the struggle to be human. This poem, like many others in the volume, is, in this sense, two-headed. Nonetheless, the silver-festooned figure of the little girl seems the body that joins the two heads. Together, her father, "*onetime* soldier" (*THP*, p. 85, italics mine), and her mother, poet and prophetess, raise this "fragile golden/protest against murder" (*THP*, p. 85). Thus, they celebrate continuance.

In another poem, "Today," the poet relives her own fear of edges as she watches her fascinated child move toward the treacherous "bluegreen gold" (*THP*, p. 23) of the water. Here, the reader recalls not only all the images of drowning in Atwood's poetry (specifically the drowning of the self), but also those of splitting. Yet now, today, aware of the danger, the poet can also imagine a future clarity and singleness for the child. As well, the landscape of these poems seems more solid than that of previous poems. The "rocks will stay/where they are put" (*THP*, p. 28); the omphalos, symbol of the human joining with the earth, dominates:

> But there is one rift, one flaw:
> that vulnerable bud, knot,
> hole in the belly where you were nailed
> to the earth forever
>
> (*THP*, p. 96)

Even the seasonal cycle seems more dependable. Images of planting, growing, and ripening speak both for the ordered pattern of the seasons and for their constant regeneration. Then, too, sexual relationships have changed in these poems. The hidden gods, the messengers, the supermen and the heroes have disappeared, leaving in their place the husband/father. The poet no longer addresses the man as the other; through intercourse, they join:

> In this massive tide
> warm as liquid
> sun, all waves are one
> wave; there is no *other*
>
> (*THP*, p. 97)

Finally, menstrual blood and the blood of birth are symbols of union in this female world. In "Red Shirt," the poet and her sister, heads almost joined as they bend over their work, sew a red shirt for the poet's daughter. Taking from the color red its associations with anger, sacrifice, and death, the sisters purify it, offering it as a female birth-right to join all women to each other.

In none of her other writing does Atwood thus celebrate women. It is this celebration that she offers her child, stitching it into the red shirt in order to cancel all the negative myths about women. Nor has she elsewhere so captured the immediacy of being alive and the sensual satisfactions of simple objects. When the little girl, robed in the new red shirt, rushes through the air, the world does indeed "explode with banners" (*THP*, p. 106). Even "Night Poem," although somewhat muted, echoes the red shirt's message. The land protects this child:

> There is nothing to be afraid of,
> it is only the wind
> changing to the east, it is only
> your father   the thunder
> your mother   the rain
>
> (*THP*, p. 107)

Concrete and vivid, the volume paradoxically ends with "You Begin," a poem of teaching, a poem in which the shapes, sounds, and colors of the world begin and end with "hand," image, and object, both word and flesh. Indeed, *Two-Headed Poems* is a carefully stitched world, the work of women. In it, the poet joins the generations, mother to daughter, a "long thread of red blood" (*THP*, p. 103).

LEE BRISCOE THOMPSON

Minuets And Madness:

Margaret Atwood's *Dancing Girls*

Two-headed poems; polarities, mythic reversals: it may be from Margaret Atwood's own delight in oppositions and strong contradictions that critics often take their cue. One notices, at any rate, a tendency for commentators to deplore or dwell exclusively upon the clinical chill, the frightening detachment in Atwood's poetry, at the same time as they often criticize her fiction, particularly *The Edible Woman* and *Lady Oracle,* as shallow, flippant, frivolous, with silly protagonists, in a phrase, "not the essential Atwood."[1] The poetry is seen as cold, strange, mythical, ritualistic, while the prose is considered comparatively warm, full of common touches and ordinary bumblers; one intense and austere, the other almost frothy, rambling, diffused; one humourless, the other marked by considerable (to some tastes, too much) humour. This polarized view, while rarely pushed and almost always obliged to ignore *Surfacing* or term it a "poetic novel," implies a schizophrenia, a two-headedness of the poet, two separate and distinct psyches joined only at the body level for the mechanical purposes of writing and never overlapping territories.

For this interpretation there is reinforcement in Atwood's own analysis of her endeavours in verse and fiction. Interviewed for *The New York Times* (May 21, 1978) by novelist Joyce Carol Oates, Atwood was reminded that "You work with a number of different 'voices' in your poetry and prose" and asked, "Have you ever felt that the discipline of prose evokes a somewhat different 'personality' (or consciousness) than the discipline of poetry?"

Atwood replied, "Not just a 'somewhat different' personality, an almost totally different one. Though readers and critics, of course, make connections because the same name appears on these different forms, I'd make a bet that I could invent a pseudonym for a reviewer and that no one would guess it was me." She explained, further, that "Poetry is the most joyful form, and prose fiction — the personality I feel there is a curious, often bemused, sometimes disheartened observer of society." The appended remark, like a T.S. Eliot footnote, raises more questions than it answers. Poetry joyful? She must mean in its tight, rich creation, its soarings and plunges, its sophisticated levels of "naming." And the narrators of many of her fictions are indeed puzzled, uncertain, frequently demoralized. In this they stand contrasted to the assured tone of some of her poetic personae. But to argue that a reader is prompted to connect the fiction and poetry solely by the appearance of Atwood's name on both is to overlook or pay insufficient attention to importantly congruent elements which unify the genres. In so saying, Atwood underrates the organic quality of her writing.

A single case in point is the incidence of humour in Atwood. It is conceded by all but the grumpiest to be a significant force in her fiction. One thinks of the hilarious passage in *Edible Woman* when Marion sulkily retreats beneath the bed/chesterfield, realizes that her absence has gone unnoticed, but cannot then devise a graceful way to emerge from the dustballs. Or there's the memorable contemplation of how to smuggle Ainsley's lover out past the watchful landlady. *Lady Oracle* offers, among many other gems, the brilliant coup of "Bravo, Mothball," the passionate advances to obese Joan of the Italian restauranteur, the tender humour of her encounter with the Daffodil Man. It is admittedly more difficult to cite hilarities in the poetry, except of a sardonic turn. But the task becomes easier in the perspective of Atwood's article, "What's so funny? Notes on Canadian Humour."[2] She there distinguishes among British humour (based largely on class consciousness), U.S. humour (based on the tall tale, the confidence trick, and highly competitive and individualistic rather than "proper" British behaviour), and Canadian humour. Atwood unites the parody of *Sarah Binks*, the satire of *The Incomparable Atuk*, the genial humour of *Sunshine Sketches*, and Newfie jokes under the common heading of "concealed self-deprecation". Given the latitude of that definition, no side-splitters emerge, perhaps, but recognition is given to the comic talent of such funny passages as:

> I tightened my lips; knew that England
> was now unreachable; had sunk down into the sea
> without ever teaching me about washtubs
> ("First Neighbours," *JSM)*

or

> Come away with me, he said, we will live on a desert island.
> I said, I am a desert island. It was not what he had in mind.
> ("Circe/Mud Poems," *YAH)*

or the entire poem "They Eat Out," where

> the ceiling opens
> a voice sings Love Is A Many
>
> Splendoured Thing
> you hang suspended above the city
>
> in blue tights and a red cape,
> your eyes flashing in unison.
>
> The other diners regard you
> some with awe, some only with boredom:
>
> they cannot decide if you are a new weapon
> or only a new advertisement.
>
> As for me, I continue eating;
> I liked you better the way you were,
> but you were always ambitious.
> *(PP)*

Concession to the comic doesn't blunt the terrors and exorcisms of much of Atwood's poetry; it simply acknowledges a major aspect often buried in assessments of her as an ice princess with a gorgon touch.

What is perhaps even more useful is the way such a reevaluation of the "humourlessness" of the poetry stimulates a reviewing of the humour in the fiction. Almost at once one begins to detect the darker side, the alienation and essential isolation of Marian, the willful manipulation by Ainsley, the humiliation of Mothball through the perverted values of Miss Flegg, the pathetic loneliness of the Daffodil Man and the disastrous confusion of rescuer and villain in Joan's Gothicism-fuddled mind. Comedy slides into tragedy, minuets into madness, as they invariably do in the best of literature, and the categories of literary analysts fall into disarray.

Nevertheless Atwood's idea of two voices has a superficial validity, in that pulse readings of *Lady Oracle, Edible Woman,* and many of Atwood's short pieces undeniably detect a somewhat sunnier, more 'ordinary' approach to the universe than the bulk of Atwood's poetry. John Metcalf has pointed to the short story as the literary form closest to poetry by virtue of its intensity, brevity, and striving for a single effect. Assuming that is correct, one could then regard Atwood's short fiction, specifically her 1977 volume, *Dancing Girls,* as a visible bridge between the dominant 'voices' of her poetry and her long fiction. There are bemused fictive narrators, it is true, but there are also the characteristics of the poetry, especially the madness, the heightened consciousness, the mythic elements. Rather than speak in a voice utterly different from that of her verse, the short stories share the non-rational attributes of the poetry, and mingle the qualities of the mundane (minuets) and the poetic/mythic (madness) which have been misrepresented by some as exclusive to prose and poetry respectively.

The fourteen stories which appear in the Canadian version of *Dancing Girls* (an American version is apparently in the works) are resistant to glib systematization in that their original, individual publication spans fourteen years, from 1964 through 1977. Let us for convenience retain the loose terms "minuet" and "madness" to refer to the headsets which Atwood has suggested dominate her writing of prose and poetry. One is inclined to set in the "minuets" category: "The War in the Bathroom," "The Man from Mars," "Rape Fantasies," "The Grave of the Famous Poet," "Hair Jewellery," "Training," "Lives of the Poets," "The Resplendent Quetzal," "Dancing Girls," and perhaps "A Travel Piece" and "Giving Birth." Eleven out of fourteen: only "Polarities," "When It Happens," and "Under Glass" seem to commit themselves totally and immediately to the world of madness, in the dance metaphor a "danse macabre." Under examination, however, one finds that even these categories within categories, these voices within a genre, fluctuate and transform themselves. In the work of a lover of metamorphoses, surely this is to be expected.

"The War in the Bathroom" is a week in the life of a typical Atwood character — rootless, alienated, meticulous, relentlessly self-analytic, keeping madness at bay only by a series of rituals and inventories. Using the first person narration throughout, the story presents a deliberately ambiguous relationship between the narrator and the "she" whose slightest movements are described. Is it a mind-body split we are overhearing? A spontaneous, self-indulgent persona fused with a disciplined, self-denying persona?

The reader rummages for signals among the domestic details, the small joys and sorrows, coming up with only indirect evidence of time (modern, with supermarkets, fridges, apartments, and current products) and place (somewhere North American, far enough north to have snow) and no concrete bearings on the situation. But the narrator is not doing much better than the reader, carefully cataloguing everything to achieve the illusion of control. The minuet is reinforced by small standards ("I draw the line at margarine"), the madness by paranoia (suspicions of a check-out girl, of the German woman). The unsettling duality on the narrator's side of the apartment wall becomes echoed on Tuesday, the second day of the 'diary,' by the emergence of two voices in the next-door communal bathroom, one high and querulous, the other an urgent whisper, like daylight and nighttime selves. The narrator assumes that it is one person rather more swiftly than even the hearing of single footsteps would explain; this encourages the reader to notice that the puzzling and parallel "I-she" split is clarifying along lines of "she" doing all the physical action and "I" doing all the cerebral action and direction. "Perhaps she is a foreigner," the narrator guesses of the dual voices by Friday, forging yet another link between Atwood's poetry and fiction. On all fronts, one is a stranger confronted by foreigners, an alien subtly warring with aliens.

Actually the major war in this story focusses not on the enigmatic voices (whose secret is resolved before the week is up) but on a consumptive old man, a fellow tenant of the apartment block. The narrator takes an excessive and cruel dislike to him on account of his compulsively regular schedule in the bathroom, despite — possibly because of — her (?) own compulsiveness. (One is tempted to comparisons with such poems as "Roominghouse, Winter" and must fight the impulse to wander into a lengthy digression on bathrooms in Atwood's work.) The story concludes on the same terms as almost all of Atwood's poetry and fiction, the view of life as a series of small, uncertain battles on the fringe of madness: "For the time being I have won."

"The Man from Mars" presents a mother and daughter team much like the one in *Lady Oracle:* a fragile, dainty mom trying to manipulate a King Kong daughter. And like the fat Joan in *Lady Oracle,* Christine fits a dominant pattern of Atwoodian women: manless, acutely self-aware, inclined to animal imagery in her description of herself and others, making a wry, running commentary upon life in general and in particular. The narrator, while in the third person, concentrates on Christine's point of view. And the gothic combinations of pursuit, flight, and terror which play such large parts in *Lady Oracle, Surfacing*, and some of the poetry turn up here as the centre both hilarious and horrible of the story.

The title is a tip-off to the transitional quality of the tale: the foreigner again, here explicitly identified as about as alien as the common stock of metaphors permits: a Martian, a creature from other worlds. With that starting point, the movement of the story is rhythmic: the less-than-attractive Christine, whose life is so dull that she dreads the end of the school year; the slide into a magic, slightly mad phase, as she is mysteriously, hotly pursued by the "person from another culture"; the escalation of mystery into nightmare as she begins to brood over blood-drenched visions of assault and murder. The recession into mediocrity, the removal of the Martian/mystery/madness, finds Christine remembering her now romanticized pursuer and, when he is proclaimed "nuts," countering defensively that there is "more than one way of being sane." Graduation with mediocre grades is followed by a tolerable career and an adequate little life. Near the conclusion the Vietnamese conflict makes for a flickering revival of exoticism and Christine finds "the distant country becoming almost more familiar to her than her own" (a characteristic Atwood reversal). Predictably, however, the mood threatens again to become madness (shades of the poem "It is Dangerous to Read Newspapers"); the new nightmare visions provoke a deliberate retreat into the mundane, out of graphic modern television into genteel nineteenth-century novels and a carefully nondescript, domesticated final view. A certain control has been regained but only to the tenuous degree familiar throughout Atwood's writings.

The title story, "Dancing Girls", autobiographically set in the United States in the 1960s with a female grad student protagonist from Toronto, aligns itself with "The Wars in the Bathroom" in its boarding-house cheapness and with "The Man from Mars" in Ann's "encountering" another alien male, an Arab neighbour. Ann and her landlady, while staunchly defending the prosaic side of life, are acutely aware of and fascinated by the exotic and alien: Turkish Lelah with her gypsy earrings and gold tooth, the tattooed Arab with his noisy partying, dancing girls, and vacuumed-up dirt. Indeed, these polarities give Atwood a chance to voice the chagrin Canadians so often feel at the American view that "You're not, like, foreign." Parallel to the paradoxical approach-avoidance Atwood's characters experience regarding Gothic pursuers is the web of contradictory responses concerning aliens and alienation. One wants, simply, to be different — but not too different; the balance is rarely managed; hence the metaphor of the dance. And in a deft pirouette, Atwood casts the sober landlady and her sort as "cold, mad people" in the eyes of the amazed, terrified, and pursued alien. A wistful conclusion underscores the longing of so many of Atwood's creatures, from pioneer to highrise dweller, for escape, for gentle, green spaces, for a world where human contact is no longer measured out in razors in the bathroom or hair in the drain.

Four of the short stories in this collection concentrate on late stages of what Chaucer called the "olde daunce," the minuet between the sexes, and one finds again polarities of vulnerability and insensitivity, control and chaos, humour and rage. The war dance is cast, typically for this writer, as trivial guerilla warfare rather than overt bloodshed: surface minuet and subliminal massacre; it is this observance of the properties, this staying miserably within the rules of the dance floor, that gives the impact of a particularly Canadian truth.

"The Grave of the Famous Poet" and "Hair Jewellery" speak through the predominant Atwood voice, first person *very* singular female. "The Grave of the Famous Poet" involves the imminent split-up with an as-usual nameless "him." There is an emphasis on alienation, contrasted with the man and woman's joint purpose of a literary pilgrimage in England. The story ties itself closely to Atwood's poetry in its clinical tone, its emphasis on victimhood, emotional paralysis, traps and helplessness. "Hair Jewellery," dealing with similar circumstances, handles it somewhat differently. The diction is more formal, its self-consciousness the trademark of the literary academic (Atwood *and* her character), the analysis and delivery more amusing. Speaking of her preference for the safety of unrequited love, the narrator explains to her lover of long ago:

> If, as had happened several times, my love was requited, if it became a question of the future, of making a decision that would lead inevitably to the sound of one's beloved shaving with an electric razor while one scraped congealed egg from his breakfast plate, I was filled with panic. . . . What Psyche saw with the candle was not a god with wings but a pigeon-chested youth with pimples, and that's why it took her so long to win her way back to

true love. It is easier to love a daemon than a man, though less heroic.

You were, of course, the perfect object. No banal shadow of lawnmowers and bungalows lurked in your melancholy eyes, opaque as black marble, recondite as urns, you coughed like Roderick Usher, you were, in your own eyes and therefore in mine, doomed and restless as Dracula. Why is it that dolefulness and a sense of futility are so irresistible to young women?

She fluctuates, as we have seen elsewhere, between the mundane world of Filene's bargain basement and the Gothic horrors of such moments as the boyfriend's hand on her throat and announcement that he is the Boston Strangler. But in this story, the sequel to terror is regularly ironic humour and then wistful, romantic melancholy, a posture with implicit self-mockery. One realizes at the last the appropriateness of the title "Hair Jewellery — memorial jewellery made from the hair of the dear departed — for the story presents just such dusty, obsolete, romantic kitsch, with all the right macabre undertones.

"The Resplendent Quetzal" carries on the basically humane tone of "Hair Jewellery," but offers this time a bit of insight into both dance partners' steps. The story makes use of dramatic, mythic, poetic effects from the very first line: "Sarah was sitting near the edge of the sacrificial well." However, Atwoodian *reductio* operates throughout; here, "Sarah thought there might be some point to being a sacrificial victim if the well were nicer, but you would never get her to jump into a muddy hole like that." Her husband, Edward, exhibits the same vacillation between fantasies of the mythic past and glum realization of modern mediocrity; his vision of himself, "in the feathered costume of the high priest, sprinkl[ing] her with blood drawn with thorns from his own tongue and penis," becomes debased to a Grade Six special project with scale models of the temples, slides, canned tortillas and tamales. Atwood tells of an abrupt reversal of roles near the end. Yet, even in the intense scene of ritual sacrifice of the doll baby, practical Sarah has noted wrinkles in her skirt and the likelihood of more flea bites. A moment of potential reconciliation or at least the introduction of strangers arises:

Sarah took her hands away from her face, and as she did so Edward felt cold fear. Surely what he would see would be the face of someone else, someone entirely different, a woman he had never seen before in his life. Or there would be no face at all. But (and this was almost worse) it was only Sarah, looking much as she always did.

The still point at the centre of the dance between the mundane and the mad has been reached again.

The fourth of the stories about deteriorated romance is "The Lives of the Poets," which opens with Julia speaking but, as she realizes her lack of control, shifts quickly into third person. Starting with the indignities of an actual, boring nosebleed, the tale alternates complexly through relationships not only between lovers but also between a person and his environment, a writer and his audience, words and the mind, reality and metaphor, before coming to a closing drenched in symbolic blood. In the midst of increasing emotional pain, Julia humorously anatomizes the small idiocies of the visiting poet's lot. Once more Atwood's conclusion combines the self-deprecating wit of an edible woman with the raging, apocalyptic visions of many of her poetic personae:

> They park the virtuous car and she is led by the two young men into the auditorium, grey cinderblock, where a gathering of polite faces waits to hear the word. Hands will clap, things will be said about her, nothing astonishing, she is supposed to be good for them, they must open their mouths and take her in, like vitamins, like bland medicine. No. No sweet identity, she will clench herself against it. She will step across the stage, words coiled, she will open her mouth and the room will explode in blood.

The story which best fits the critical stereotype of Atwood's "bubbleheaded/ladies' magazine fiction" (vs. her "serious poetry") is probably "Rape Fantasies." Agreed, its lower-middle-class diction, full of babbling asides and slang, is far removed from the fine intuitions of the *Power Politics* voices. And the subject matter, the dynamics of a female office/lunch room and the "girls' " revelations of their extremely unimaginative rape fantasies, hardly seems in the same league as the mythic patterns of *You Are Happy* or the multiple metaphors of *The Journals of Susanna Moodie*. Nevertheless, when the intellectual snobberies are put aside (and appropriately so, since that is one of Atwood's satiric targets here), the narrator does demonstrate an admirable sense of humour, appreciation of the ridiculous, and considerable compassion. For once in Atwood the cutting edge seems thoroughly dulled by the sheer zaniness of the monologue.

One imaginary rapist is "absolutely covered in pimples. So he gets me pinned against the wall, he's short but he's heavy, and he starts to undo himself and the zipper gets stuck. I mean, one of the most significant moments in a girl's life, it's almost like getting married or having a baby or something, and he sticks the zipper." She ends up drawing him out and referring him to a dermatologist. In another incarnation, she and the rapist are both slowed down by ferocious headcolds, which make the would-be assault "like raping a bottle of LePage's mucilage the way my nose is running." The cheerful remedy here is conversation, Neo-Citran and Scotch, plus the Late Show on the tube. "I mean, they aren't all sex maniacs, the rest of the time they must lead a normal life. I figure they enjoy watching the Late Show just like anybody else." As the reader is introduced to these and other alternatives, it becomes apparent that the naïve narrator's innocent premise is the power of the word. "Like, how could a fellow do that to a person he's just had a long conversation with, once you let them know you're human, you have a life too, I don't see how they could go ahead with it, right?" That we see so easily the flaws in this simplistic and determined optimism serves to underscore a subtle counterpoint Atwood strikes throughout her writing — the actually severe limitations of language, and the doubtfulness of real communication. The sunny normalcy of this lady's world view glosses over a chaotic realm even she must tentatively acknowledge: "I mean, I know [rape] happens but I just don't understand it, that's the part I really don't understand."

What is also noteworthy is that this story explicitly draws men into the circle of victimhood that Atwood tends to populate with women. Rapists, yes, but failed rapists; they are betrayed by their jammed flies, their sinuses, their gullibility, their pimples, their inadequacies. And one sees that the filing clerk's rape fantasies are actually scenarios of kinship, friendship with and support of other mediocre, in fact worse-off, human beings.

"A Travel Piece" also operates in a chatty, colloquial (here third-person) voice, with a heavy measure (even for Atwood) of run-on sentences and comma splices presumably bespeaking a slightly mindless protagonist skimming on the surface of life. The story is less successful than "Rape Fantasies" in that we, like Annette, never quite penetrate to the reality of her being. But the juxtaposition of her everlasting calm/numbness with the increasingly dramatic events has a definitely surreal power, and demonstrates ably Atwood's skill at combining minuets and madness, the mundane and the bizarre. Drifting in a life raft after a plane crash, surrounded by masks and bloody markings which it is

increasingly hard to remember are merely plastic sandwich trays
and lipstick donned for protection against the sun,

> Annette feels she is about to witness something mundane and
> horrible, doubly so because it will be bathed not in sinister blood-
> red lighting but in the ordinary sunlight she has walked in all her
> life. . . . she is . . . stuck in the present, with four Martians and one
> madman, waiting for her to say something.

Annette's predicament, in Atwood's work, is not all that unusual.

"Training" too concerns itself with emotional paralysis and
human inadequacies, but here the reader becomes far more
involved. The story centres on the unorthodox relationship of a
healthy teenaged boy and a nine-year-old cerebral palsy victim
confined to a wheelchair. Jordan's cages are explicit: the uncon-
trolled body, the "metal net" of machinery upon which she must
depend; "that mind trapped and strangling." Rob's are subtler: his
overachieving medical family and their and everyone else's expectations for him; feeling the "bumbling third son in a fairy tale,
with no princess and no good luck." Superficial antitheses are set
up — the "crips" or the "spazzes" vs. the "norms." Then the distinctions are gradually demolished. Rob feels abnormal regarding
his sexuality; the possibility of the healthy person failing to cope
with reality introduces madness ("Real life would be too much for
him, he would not be able to take it. . . . He would go crazy. He
would run out into the snow with no galoshes, he would vanish,
he would be lost forever.") And steady-eyed Jordan, meanwhile,
comes to represent the honest, psychologically whole person. In
the grotesqueries of the compelling conclusion, the polarized
worlds are poignantly united in the "danse macabre": the wheelchair square dancers "danced like comic robots. They danced like
him."

"Giving Birth," which with "Training" and "Dancing
Girls" comprise the only previously unpublished material in the
collection, has been taken by some critics as autobiographical
evidence of a mellowing of the formidable Atwood as a result of
motherhood. In fact, one reviewer has summarized the story as
"good reading for many parents, past or prospective;"[3] another,
less pleased, considers it "a mass magazine approach to a lesson in
childbirth, tinged, of course, with female chauvinist irony."[4]
Sniffs a third, it will have appeal only for those who have "been
there."[5]

Certainly the story *is* a detailed account of one birthing experience, told with Atwood's remarkable clarity and precision and having some fun with prenatal classes and maternity fads. It is also correct to say that most readers will notice a warmth and positivity, a wholeness, that is very scarce in Atwood's writings. Nor is the male figure here a nebbish; both the narrator's mate and the pregnant woman's companion, "A.," are supportive, helpful, reasonable, in no way threatening. But Atwood's concerns in the collection have not been abandoned in this, the last story. Split and multiple personalities have appeared elsewhere, and in "Giving Birth" one has not only the complications of the narrator differentiating herself from but obviously in some respects coinciding with Jeannie, but also the fluctuating presence of Jeannie's mysterious brown alter ego. There is "pain and terror" as well, an undercurrent of fear, a consideration of death, the need for talismans against the Evil Eye, cages of conventional thought, descent into a "dark place," the "tubular strange apparatus like a science fiction movie," the screams. " 'You see, there was nothing to be afraid of,' A. says before he leaves [after the birth], but he was wrong."

Most important, "Giving Birth" tackles yet again Atwood's intense interest in the relationship between language and the body. The story opens with contemplation upon the title phrase and its true meaning. Numerous explanations are discarded; "Thus language muttering in its archaic tongues of something, yet one more thing, that needs to be re-named." The narrator abandons that struggle for the moment, but almost at once resumes it in the form of naming the universe with her child — dog, cat, bluejays, goldfinches, winter. The young daughter "puts her fingers on my lips as I pronounce these words; she hasn't yet learned the secret of making them, I am waiting for her first word; surely it will be miraculous, something that has never yet been said. But if so, perhaps she's already said it and I, in my entrapment, my addiction to the usual, have not heard it." This compares remarkably closely with the considerations of several selections in the recent *Two-Headed Poems*, but also traces its lineage to pieces from *The Journals of Susanna Moodie, Power Politics, The Animals in That Country,* and *Circle Game.* The struggle of birth gives the relationship between flesh and the word a focus, but offers no answers: "indescribable, events of the body . . .; why should the mind distress itself trying to find a language for them?" When, in the middle of a contraction, a nurse speaks of pain, *"What pain?* Jeannie thinks. When there is no pain she feels nothing, when there is pain, she feels nothing because there is no *she*. This, finally, is the disappearance of language." In a surreal postpartum illusion Jeannie sees the watery fragility of a solid building and is overwhelmed by the enormity of her maternal perception that "the entire earth, the rocks, people, trees, everything needs to be protected, cared for, tended." But that technically mad anxiety is counterbalanced by the normalcy of her baby, "solid, substantial, packed together like an apple. Jeannie examines her, she is complete, and in the days that follow Jeannie herself becomes drifted over with new words, her hair slowly darkens, she ceases to be what she was and is replaced, gradually, by someone else." As with Rob in "Training," too much "reality" might have driven Jeannie permanently insane; protective metamorphosis is a necessity.

The justice of this view is demonstrated by a look at the three short stories one may clearly designate as tales of madness rather than mundane minuets: "Polarities," "Under Glass," and "When It Happens." Least successfully realized of the three (and arguably of the entire collection), "When It Happens" anticipates the apocalypse with an unruffled certainty and overlay of domestic chores which serves to heighten the atmosphere of insanity. Agreed, the characters, Mrs. Burridge and her husband Frank, are too cardboard and plodding to infuse the contrast of the mundane and the mad (personal and global) with real terror. But the closing intimation of bloody destruction, restrainedly expressed as "the burst of red," juxtaposed with Mrs. Burridge's final housewifely gesture of adding cheese to the shopping list, does play its part in the cumulative effect of *Dancing Girls*.

From the first semi-insane paragraph of "Under Glass," it is clear that this female narrator is holding herself and her universe together with only the flimsiest of threads. She notes with satisfaction that, on this good day, "the trees come solidly up through the earth as though they belong there, nothing wavers. I have confidence in the grass and the distant buildings, they can take care of themselves. . . ." Her identification with the plant world is intimate, speaking as she does from the start of "all of us [greenhouse plants and the narrator] keeping quite still." "Today, however . . . I walk on two legs, I wear clothes," she explains, making a distinction between the human and the natural very near to that of the *Surfacing* narrator. Similarly, it is abundantly clear where her real allegiances lie, how strained her human "affiliation."

As in "When It Happens," the narrator of "Under Glass" maintains an impeccably "normal" surface and a deranged interior. The story moves quickly from her vegetarian fantasies into her relationship with a man, the description of which dazzles with its authenticity and all the fancy footwork of the sexual dance. A favourite: "I'm annoyed with him for some reason, though I can't recall which. I thumb through my card-file of nasty remarks, choose one: You make love like a cowboy raping a sheep." And closer to the bone: "I steer my course so he will have to go through all the puddles. If I can't win, I tell him, neither can you. I was saner then, I had defences."

From contemplation of self as "something altogether different, an artichoke" through her abrupt self-admonition, "None of that," to moving a moment later "about the room in a parody of domesticity," the narrator dances among animal, vegetable, and human incarnations. References abound to animals in zoos, "under glass," hunted, huddled, hiding. Her death fantasy is crazily followed by visions of ducks and a line of cartoon dancing mice. Angered, she uses animal and plant images, serene and "doing nothing," to get a grip on her rage. Estranged from her lover, she feels "bloodless as a mushroom," finds "he's too human." Turning her metaphoric tables when she wants a reconciliation with him, she sees her lover's face as "a paper flower dropped in water," spreading tendrils, becoming "inscrutable as an eggplant." The couple appear to have made up their differences by the conclusion of the story but Atwood inexorably slows the action from the normal, mundane pace of the purposefully departing narrator ("I ponder again his need for more glasses and consider buying him a large bath towel") to the motionless, insane world under glass, the dream of no more dancing, the longing for annihilation or zerodom:

> I find myself being moved, gradually, station by station, back towards the 7-B greenhouse. Soon I will be there: inside are the plants that have taught themselves to look like stones. I think of them; they grow silently, hiding in dry soil, minor events, little zeros, containing nothing but themselves; no food value, to the eye soothing and round, then suddenly nowhere. I wonder how long it takes, how they do it.

"Polarities" is the story whose titular metaphor competes most strongly with dance for control of the entire collection. It begins with an excerpt from a Margaret Avison poem which complements the other Margaret's survival ethic of "beyond truth, tenacity":

> Gentle and just pleasure
> It is, being human, to have won from space
> This unchill, habitable interior. . . .
> ("New Year's Poem")

The obvious introductory contrast is between no-nonsense, brisk Louise and shambling, slothful Morrison, a false effect the omniscient narrator begins reversing almost immediately. Louise's progression into complete madness is handled in slyly paradoxical fashion, for her vision of Blakean wholeness looks remarkably reasonable, a sort of metropolitan yin and yang, in comparison with those "sane" friends who eagerly tuck her away in the loony bin and violate her privacy. Like the aphorisms and short poems in her notebooks, "which were thoroughly sane in themselves but which taken together were not," Louise's understanding is frequently perfect, as in her fine assessment of Morrison, even when her total picture is askew. "Morrison is not a complete person. He needs to be completed, he refuses to admit his body is part of his mind. He can be in the circle possibly, but only if he will surrender his role as a fragment and show himself willing to merge with the greater whole." Morrison, rather impressive in his awareness and swift comprehension, interprets Louise correctly in turn: "she's taken as real what the rest of us pretend is only metaphorical."

All these polarities, then: of wholeness and partiality, exposure and retreat, the mind-body split, interchangeable madness and sanity, energy and the inert, decorating apartments and facing the void, zoos and asylums, living colour and glacial whiteness, chosen and involuntary isolation, inclusion and exclusion, the dream of the "unchill, habitable interior" and the reality of Morrison's "chill interior, embryonic and blighted." Morrison, the American, the actual and metaphoric outsider, can understand but not change; the reader's position, Atwood suggests by the act of writing, is less bleak.

Travels through these tales make quite unworkable the Atwoodian notion that her poetry and fiction are expressed in two entirely different, stylistically unrelated, philosophically dissimilar voices. Two voices there are, and more, but they are found throughout her work and come from a remarkably unified consciousness. It may be that Atwood's theory is subtly related to her own two public faces: mythic Margaret, the fox-woman, laconic even at readings, reserved, cool, detached, distant, vs. earth-mother Maggie on the farm, folksily recommending Aussie french fries and chatting about Jess's cute tricks. Behind the promotional masks, however, Atwood seems to have no confusion about who she is, and reading her stories and poems, her audience has no doubt about the quality of her dance. Proceeding from a single, powerful sensibility, *Dancing Girls* is a virtuoso performance.

CATHERINE McLAY

The Dark Voyage:

The Edible Woman as Romance

On a first reading, Margaret Atwood's novel *The Edible Woman* seems to differ greatly in both theme and tone from her poetry, her early short stories, and the two later novels, *Surfacing* and *Lady Oracle*. In these later novels, while the protagonists are, like good Canadian heroines, in search of their identity, the novels are an exploration of inner space, the exterior landscape becoming a projection of the inner mental journey. Both novels are set in the present but proceed through an exploration of the narrator's past. The tone of *Surfacing* suggests clearly the dark underside of experience, the voyage to the centre of self, and while *Lady Oracle* seems less sombre and nightmarish, Joan's preoccupation with Gothic romance indicates her fascination with fear and terror which gradually move out to possess her waking reality. *The Edible Woman*, in contrast, seems to be a comedy. The prevailing tone is light, even effervescent. The novel occurs almost completely in the narrative present; the protagonist Marian seems to have little contact with her past and her family exists only as a shadowy projection of her own mind and attitudes. The settings which, in *Surfacing* and *Lady Oracle*, are clearly symbolic, even surrealistic, are here realistic, everyday modern urban scenes. While in *Surfacing* and *Lady Oracle* the protagonists change and die, to be reborn into newer and more complex selves, Marian seems to alter very little from beginning to end. She is the modern young woman, sensible and clear-headed. Indeed she represents one side of Peggy Atwood who described herself in an interview with Linda Sandler: "[In high school] I was supposed to be practical and sensible; that was my 'image.' "[1]

If, however, we examine *The Edible Woman* from the perspective of the later novels, we may discover beneath the surface dissimilarities a common pattern. For the novel is a disguised romance. While it is clearly not a typical romance as described by Northrop Frye in his study *The Secular Scripture*, it does employ many features of romance, albeit in a rather unusual manner.[2] In an interview with Graeme Gibson, Atwood refers to Northrop Frye's theory of comedy in defining *The Edible Woman* as anti-comedy. In the *Anatomy of Criticism*, Frye described the basic comic action: a young man desires a young woman but is thwarted in his pursuit of her by a blocking character, usually a father or father substitute. The comedy is resolved when this father and his generation are defeated, the hero wins the bride, and the new society forms around the young couple.[3] Atwood's discussion implies her knowledge of Frye's theory; indeed Frye was her professor at Victoria College, Toronto. As she explains:

> [The term] sort of determines not only what happens in the book but the style. . . . I think in your standard eighteenth-century comedy you have a young couple who is faced with difficulty in the form of somebody who embodies the restrictive forces of society and they trick or overcome this difficulty and end up getting married. The same thing happens in *The Edible Woman* except the wrong person gets married. And the person who embodies the restrictive forces of society is in fact the person Marian gets engaged to. In a standard comedy, he would be the defiant hero. As it is, he and the restrictive society are blended into one, and the comedy solution would be a tragic solution for Marian.[4]

But the change from comedy to anti-comedy has more serious implications than a mere inversion of plot. Atwood has remarked to Linda Sandler: "the book does make a negative statement about society. . . . The complications are resolved, but not in a way that affirms the social order." The ending too is more complex. As Atwood remarks in the same interview:

> The tone of *The Edible Woman* is light-hearted, but in the end it's more pessimistic than *Surfacing*. The difference between them is that *Edible Woman* is a circle and *Surfacing* is a spiral. . . . the heroine of *Surfacing* does not end where she began.[5]

Considered as a romance, however, the novel reveals a number of interesting features. The romance necessarily involves a love relationship and a series of adventures which provide the complications of the courtship. According to Frye, a central theme is the loss and regaining of identity and a common form is that of the quest. Progressively the worlds of dream or wish-fulfillment and of nightmare become polarized. The action involves a descent, a movement downward from the ideal, the "once-upon-a-time" world, into nightmare. This latter world is marked by a break in consciousness, increasing restriction of action, isolation, imprisonment and even death, real or symbolic. The escape from this world involves a reversal of the spell: a revolt of the mind, a growing detachment and even comic irony, a freedom from restraint and ultimately a rebirth and a reaffirmation of society through ritual, as represented by marriage and/or the feast.[6] That Atwood is familiar with this pattern is indicated both in her choice of Rider Haggard's romance fantasies for a never-completed doctoral thesis and in her remarks to Sandler on *Lady Oracle:*

> The maze I use is a descent into the underworld. There's a passage in Virgil's *Aeneid* which I found very useful, where Aeneas goes to the underworld to learn about his future. He's guided by the Sibyl and he learns what he has to from his dead father, and then he returns home.

And in the same interview, she refers to her poem "Procedures for Underground" as "a descent to the underworld."[7]

Certainly Marian is not the traditional virgin heroine, threatened with rape and violence, a pattern parodied in *Lady Oracle* in Louisa K. Delacourt's Costume Gothics. Yet in some sense, the ending fits the pattern. There is a clear implication that it is indeed the virgin who wins the hero and becomes the accepted bride of society. And Ainsley, the self-proclaimed feminist and liberated woman, comes to accept the traditional role of wife and mother that Marian rejects; her capitulation is even symbolized by a honeymoon in Niagara Falls, that cliché of honeymoon cities.

Yet Marian is, in a sense, the romantic hero/heroine who searches for her identity through a quest which takes her on a dark voyage into the underworld and back. The structure of the novel supports this interpretation. At the beginning of Part I Marian's life, if hardly idyllic, is at least quite satisfactory. She has a not-too-permanent job related to her university training, a secure home with a not-too-obtrusive roommate, and a satisfactory relationship with a lover who does not place many demands on her. She is moving towards the conventional ending of happy-ever-after which she, like her family, equates with marriage. And she begins Part I complacently: "I knew I was all right on Friday when I got up; if anything I was feeling more stolid than usual" (p. 11).[8]

In the next two days, however, her security is disturbed. Her job with Seymour Surveys takes on an ominous significance when she must sign the pension plan, her signature being locked away in a filing cabinet until that day when she turns sixty-five and must live in "a bleak room with a plug-in electric heater" (p. 21). The same day her sense of permanence is threatened when Ainsley announces her determination to produce a baby without benefit of clergy and to conceive it in Marian's apartment (even her bedroom as it turns out). And Peter, the young bachelor who has carefully cultivated his *Playboy* image and seems to be averse to legal commitments, suddenly becomes domestic and proposes. In the light of this, Clara, Marian's old university friend, now married and ever-pregnant, assumes significance as a possible model of Marian's future self. Finally Duncan, the eccentric graduate student, begins to play a central role in her life and thus to threaten her whole relationship with Peter.

In Part I, as Marian moves toward captivity and imprisonment, the episodes become more bizarre and the nightmare intensifies. In Chapters 8 and 9, Marian recognizes the impulse of this nightmare and the need for escape from a world of which she has lost control. But she ignores the demands of her subconscious mind and accepts her bondage to Peter and to the conventions of society. As a consequence, in Part II she must undergo another ordeal which reaches a climax in Chapters 24 to 27, and only a rejection of her marriage to Peter will lead to liberation from the prison of society and a return to freedom and new life. Although Atwood has described the ending as pessimistic, Part III is not simply the completion of a circle, the return to the beginning, but a spiral like *Surfacing* and *Lady Oracle;* the point to which Marian returns is on a higher level of reality. While she is faced with the same decisions as before and must search for a new job, new accommodations, and a new lover, she has gained a sense of identity and a new knowledge of self. And she has discovered, in a world seen as alien and threatening, the need for integration not only of mind and body but of multiple aspects of the self, a discovery which anticipates the discoveries to be made by "I" in *Surfacing* and Joan in *Lady Oracle.*

Atwood's treatment of point of view in the novel indicates, at least in part, this cycle. *Surfacing* and *Lady Oracle*, like many of the stories of *Dancing Girls*, employ a first person narrator, all events and characters being transmitted to us through this central vision. *The Edible Woman*, however, employs a novel and striking technique. Parts I and III are narrated in first person while Part II is narrated in third person. Atwood suggests the significance of this in Marian's tongue-in-cheek remark in Part III: "Now . . . I was thinking of myself in the first person singular again" (p. 278). Atwood uses a somewhat similar device in an early story "War in the Bathroom," where the protagonist is split into two distinct and co-existing entities, "I" and "she," I narrating and she acting. The change of viewpoint in *The Edible Woman* suggests not only a loss of identity but also an entry into enchantment. Her body is now seen as external and can be observed from the outside by her mind; the two are no longer parts of a unified self.[9]

The settings of the novel seem at first highly realistic, even super-real. We recall them with the vividness of cinema images; the shabby-genteel third floor apartment presided over by Atwood's omnipresent landlady; the unfinished shell of Peter's apartment building with its brittle surfaces and modern emptiness; the darkened lounge on the top floor of the Park Plaza; the sweeping marble staircase and the many corridors and rooms of the Royal Ontario Museum; the supermarket with its shelves and shelves of enticingly-packaged commodities; and the seedy streets and cheap hotels of the inner city where Marian and Duncan seek a room. All these settings exist in actuality more obviously than the island of *Surfacing* with its maze of waterways and its symbolically tangled undergrowth, or the castles and prisons of Joan's fiction, or even her refuge in Italy. Yet these settings, like the paintings of the New Realists, suggest something beyond the surface, a quality described by one critic of the paintings as "a purity which is both super-real and unreal at once."[10]

And on closer examination, many of these settings approach more closely to Surrealism. Like the fantasies of Henri Rousseau, they are simplified, abstracted, belonging to the world of dream or nightmare rather than to the everyday world of taste, touch, sight, and smell. This abstraction is most apparent in the climactic episode of the novel, Peter's engagement party. Here Marian, who has just congratulated herself prematurely on coping, on having evoked from Peter the image of the domesticated male, moves directly from the real scene in Peter's bedroom to dream:

> It had been a long search. She retraced through time the corridors and rooms, long corridors, large rooms. Everything seemed to be slowing down. . . . She opened a door to the right and went in. There was Peter, forty-five and balding but still recognizable as Peter, standing in bright sunlight beside a barbecue with a long fork in his hand. . . . She looked carefully for herself in the garden, but she wasn't there and the discovery chilled her.
>
> No, she thought, this has to be the wrong room. It can't be the last one. And now she could see there was another door, in the hedge at the other side of the garden. She walked across the lawn, passing behind the unmoving figure, which she could now see held a large cleaver in the other hand, pushed open the door and went through.
>
> She was back in Peter's living-room with the people and the noise, leaning against the doorframe holding her drink. Except that the people seemed even clearer now, more sharply focussed, further away, and they were moving faster and faster, they were all going home. . . . She ran for the next door, yanked it open.
>
> Peter was there, dressed in his opulent winter suit. He had a camera in his hand; but now she saw what it really was. There were no more doors and when she felt behind her for the door-knob, afraid to take her eyes off him, he raised the camera and aimed it at her; his mouth opened in a snarl of teeth. There was a blinding flash of light.
>
> "No!" she screamed.   (pp. 243-4)

In this passage, the nightmare qualities are accentuated: the terror, the slow-motion of time, the sense of captivity and isolation, even paralysis, and the fear of death. In contrast with Joan's Costume Gothics where the fear and terror are cultivated by reader and writer alike for their erotic thrill, the terror here absorbs us, re-creating our own dark journeys into nightmare. The tone indicates the real mood of the novel underlying the light frothy surface. It is not dispelled until Chapter 30 where the return to comedy marks the end of nightmare and the recovery of detachment and control.

The first suggestion of a nightmare world underlying the everyday reality occurs in Chapters 8 and 9. The image patterns here make clear what is really happening in the action. As elsewhere in Atwood, the relationship between male and female is presented as a battle, symbolized by the image of the hunt. Frye notes that in the descent pattern, the dream world becomes "a world of increased erotic intensity": "the hunt is normally an image of the masculine erotic, a movement of pursuit and linear thrust, in which there are sexual overtones to the object being hunted."[11] The image is introduced early in the Moose Beer Survey which Marian conducts; the advertisement here is calculated to create in the male viewers "a mystical identity with the plaid-jacketed sportsman . . . with his foot on a deer or scooping a trout into his net." (p. 26) The scene is totally clean, deodorized, and bloodless. The hunt scene described by Peter is, however, not so unreal. The meeting of Peter with Len in the Roof Lounge of the Park Plaza precipitates the crisis. In this scene, there is a Hemingway bond between the two men, a masculine mystique which unites the two men and explicitly identifies their prey as feminine. It is Len who introduces the image: "you've got to watch these women when they start pursuing you. They're always after you to *marry* them. You've got to hit and run. Get them before they get you and then get out" (p. 66). However, it is Peter who makes the key comparison; in his description of an old hunting scene, he relates metaphorically the gun and the camera. He first describes shooting a rabbit "right through the heart" and disembowelling her:

> [I] took her by the hind legs and gave her one hell of a crack, like a whip you see, and the next thing you know there was blood and guts all over the place. All over me, what a mess, rabbit guts dangling from the trees, god, the trees were red for yards. (p. 69)

In the sentence immediately following, he connects the two sports: "Lucky thing Trigger and me had the old cameras along, we got some good shots of the whole mess." While the attention of the men shifts to camera lenses, Marian's mind imagines the scene in the forest with intense and magnified clarity, as if projected onto a screen:

> [I saw] the colours luminous, green, brown, blue for the sky, red. Peter stood with his back to me in a plaid shirt, his rifle slung on his shoulder. A group of friends, those friends whom I had never met, were gathered around him, their faces clearly visible in the sunlight that fell in shafts down through the anonymous trees, splashed with blood, the mouths wrenched with laughter. I couldn't see the rabbit. (p. 69)

She equates the violation and destruction of life in the hunt with the violation of the camera. And her response to the primitive colours is also primitive; from this point on she subconsciously plays the role of the hunted creature, the rabbit. We may note that in the hunt imagery, the predator is not always male, the prey, female. Lucy, one of the "office virgins," is described as "trailing herself like a many-plumed fish lure with glass beads and three spinners and seventeen hooks" (pp. 111-2). And Ainsley, whose choice of Len as an appropriate begetter for her illegitimate child forms the "sub-plot," is condemned by Marian as unethical: "it's like bird-liming, or spearing fish by lantern" (p. 70), and later as menacing, with the "inert patience of a pitcher-plant in a swamp . . . its hollow bulbous leaves half-filled with water, waiting for some insect to be attracted, drowned and digested" (p. 75).

But the predominant image is of Peter as hunter, Marian as prey. Reacting to the implied threat, Marian retreats to the washroom where she sees the cubicle as a "cell" and the roll of toilet paper as the rabbit: "It crouched in there with me, helpless and white and furry, waiting passively for the end." On returning to the lounge, she feels an overwhelming sense of claustrophobia; the looped curtains are "concealing things" and the air is "filled with a soft menace" (pp. 70-1). At first in running from the hotel, with the others in pursuit, Marian sees the comic perspective, but suddenly the game of tag reveals its sinister side; for her, as for the rabbit, it is a matter of life and death.

At first Peter's capture of her is reassuring; his reality disperses the nightmare. But it recurs in Len's apartment and she seeks a retreat in the "dark cool space" under the bed. While even to Marian this scene is comic, it is also absurd and the comedy is undercut by hysteria. The imagery indicates the real meaning: like the rabbit, Marian is in a "private burrow" and "underground"; she is in a coffin-like space, six feet long and "two or three feet lower than the rest of them," where the outside world is muffled and obscure (p. 76). Although she scrambles out of the space, she does not escape the situation and her engagement to Peter is in defiance of her own mood. It is a capitulation to the flesh. The chapter ends with a striking image. Marian's remark: "I could see myself, small and oval, mirrored in his eyes" points up the spell or enchantment which prepares for her entry into the underworld.

In the next two chapters Marian surrenders her freedom, even her identity. The two men, Peter and Duncan, represent the two poles of experience. Rationally she submits to Peter, the symbol of society, as decision-maker: "I'd rather leave the big decisions up to you" (p. 90). Emotionally, however, she inclines towards Duncan who symbolizes total withdrawal into the self. Duncan's appeal for Marian is similar to that of the protagonist's boyfriend in Atwood's story "Hair Jewellery":

> No banal shadow of lawnmowers and bungalows lurked in your melancholy eyes, opaque as black marble, recondite as urns, you coughed like Roderick Usher, you were, in your own eyes and therefore in mine, doomed and restless as Dracula.[12]

From the beginning, Duncan is dehumanized, even grotesque, related to the grotto or underground caves. Both playful and animal, he is the guide who accompanies Marian on her downward journey, her descent into the dark side of self. As guide he permits her to free herself from Peter and society. But then his function is complete: Marian must reject him and return alone to the daylight world of freedom and true selfhood.

Increasingly in Part II of the novel, Marian moves away from the "normal," the practical sensible young woman, and towards the world of madness. The change from "I" as teller to "she" as character marks her altered perception of herself and others. Her vision is distorted. In the Park Plaza, she has observed her companions as dehumanized, reflected in the mirror of the table surface: Peter and Len "all chin and no eyes" and Ainsley with downward eyes magnified (pp. 70-1). Now she sees others as animal-like. The women at the office, in continual turmoil, are "like a herd of armadilloes at the zoo" (p. 108). Clara in the last stages of pregnancy is "a swollen mass of flesh with a tiny pin-head" or "a queen-ant, bulging with the burden of an entire society" (p. 115). Ainsley's capture of Len reminds Marian of primitive Biblical sacrifices, though she admits to some confusion as to which is human and which animal: "she didn't know exactly whether an early Christian was being thrown to the lions, or an early lion to the Christians" (pp. 122-3).

Marian also comes to see human beings as divided into multiple selves, with no constant core. The pregnant Clara she imagines as "a semi-person" or "several people, a cluster of hidden personalities that she didn't know at all" (p. 115). Peter too is changeable; behind the façade of the urbane young lawyer she imagines the Underwear Man who phones women to inquire about their personal linen:

> Perhaps this was his true self, the core of his personality. . . .
> Perhaps this was what lay hidden under the surface, under the
> other surfaces, that secret identity which in spite of her many
> guesses and attempts and half-successes she was aware she had still
> not uncovered. (p. 118)

Duncan's comment when he sees her in his dressing-gown,
"Hey. . . . you look sort of like me in that" (p. 144), suggests that, as
she withdraws more and more, she becomes like him. And his
action of breaking the mirror — "I've got my own private mirror.
One I can trust, I know what's in it" (p. 140) — suggests Marian's
rejection of the outside world, her retreat within to her own private
reality.

    Even language becomes suspect. She begins to question her
whole role at Seymour Surveys as a "manipulator of words" (p.
110). Part of Duncan's appeal is his form of communication. He
too is drowned in words. He remarked earlier "Words . . . are
beginning to lose their meanings" (p. 96), and Marian comments
concerning his monologues: "all this talking, this rather liquid
confessing . . . seemed foolhardy to me, like an uncooked egg
deciding to come out of its shell: there would be a risk of spreading
out too far" (p. 99). Duncan's true communication is through
symbols, the messages he leaves behind him in the movie house
through the little pile of pumpkin seed shells "like some primitive
signal, a heap of rocks or a sign made with sticks or notches cut in
trees" (p. 126). Despite his role as a graduate student in English, he
is controlled not by reason, the logic of words, but by emotion,
primitive non-verbal images similar to the rock paintings which
fascinate the father in *Surfacing*. In Part II, Marian finds words
become more threatening. They are a "labyrinth" (p. 140) or
"prehensile . . . like snakes, they had a way of coiling back on you
and getting all wrapped up" (p. 134).

    At this point, Marian undergoes her transformation. In
romance, as Frye notes, the descent involves a metamorphosis, a
change into a lower order of nature, either animal or vegetable.[13]
Like the narrator of *Surfacing*, who moves through successive
changes from animal to tree to place, Marian too regresses through
previous stages of human development. Identifying with lower
forms of life, she refuses to eat, and therefore prey upon, first steak
and all meats, then eggs, then carrots; nor can she destroy the
lowest form of life, mould. Her identification with the hunted is
precipitated by her growing realization that she is powerless to

control her own life. Her horror at the act of consuming flesh occurs, then, at the point where she becomes detached from society, even alienated from it. She is an observer, no longer an actor, and she sees with shocking clarity, like E.M. Forster who reputedly described eating as "people sitting around a board shoving things into a hole in their heads." Eating she comes to see as a "violent action," concealed behind the social façade of dining, just as the sacrifice of the victim in the Moose Beer Ads is concealed as sport. The cookbook description of preparing turtle soup, the directions to feed and nurture the victim before plunging it into water brought to the boil, suggests to Marian "the deaths of early Christian martyrs" (p. 155). Finally Marian's revulsion spreads outward from the thing eaten and the act of eating to the body which lives by ingesting and regurgitating. She sees with detachment and even alienation the women of Seymour Surveys as they celebrate her engagement:

> What peculiar creatures they were; and the continual flux between the outside and the inside, taking things in, giving them out, chewing, words, potato-chips, burps, grease, hair, babies, milk, excrement, cookies, vomit, coffee, tomato-juice, blood, tea, sweat, liquor, tears and garbage . . .   (p. 167)

And, like the narrator of *Surfacing*, Marian discovers that she too is "one of them." The scene in the supermarket where she dreams of being trapped in at closing time and found in the morning in a coma, surrounded by overflowing carts, expresses, then, both her sense of claustrophobia within, and her identification with, a consumer society where life preys upon life.

In Chapter 21, set in the Royal Ontario Museum, Marian moves into the world of death and negation. The heavy doors, domed roof, marble staircase, and "church-like atmosphere" all deny the validity of the flesh. Here, in the maze of entries and "labyrinthine corridors," Marian loses her sense of direction. The imagery points up the significance of the chapter. Marian's symbolic journey leads to the mummy room and to ancient Egypt, linked to the descent as the "land of death and burial."[14] Here Duncan is the appropriate guide with his narcissism, his fascination with death, and his similarity to the mummies, entombed in their coffins. He is attracted particularly to two mummies, one stylized in figure and make-up and decorated with a painted bird, orange suns, and gilded figures, and the other the size of a child. His remark: "When I really get fed up with this place [the univer-

sity] I'm going to go and dig myself in" (p. 188) suggests his desire
to retreat from life into the silent world of the dead, and his kiss
seals Marian's captivity in the world of death.

More and more Marian loses her sense of choice and free will
and more and more she is controlled by fate. While she rejects the
role of Clara, symbolized at one point by the "cave" or "culvert"
and at another by the bars of the child's playpen through which
she peers, Marian also envies her for knowing her role:

> She only wanted to know what she was becoming, what direction
> she was taking, so that she could be prepared. It was waking up in
> the morning one day and finding that she had already changed
> without being aware of it that she dreaded. (p. 206)

In Chapter 24 Marian is, like the heifers of pagan religious rites,
prepared for the sacrifice. In the beauty parlour she becomes an
object; her hair is decorated "like a cake, something to be carefully
iced and ornamented" (p. 208). Her dress "short, red and sequin-
ned," is chosen not by her but by the saleslady who remarks: "It's
you, dear" (p. 208). When Ainsley adds to her costume gold earrings, painted nails and lashes, she gazes into the mirror and sees
not herself but the beautiful Egyptian mummy whose open eyes
reveal a "serene vacancy": "[She] stared into the egyptian-lidded
and outlined and thickly fringed eyes of a person she had never
seen before " (p. 222).

Nor is she able to act. Her destiny is controlled by the decisions of both Ainsley and Len who are arguing over Ainsley's right
to produce a child without the permission of the father, but her
remarks are unheeded and she describes herself as "a child's
wheeled wooden toy being pulled along by a string" (p. 213). Her
comment on the argument and indeed on her own situation at this
point summarizes her current view of her life: "Thinking would
be of no use anyway. Whatever course it took, there would be
nothing she herself could do to prevent it " (p. 215). And her
acceptance of her role as victim or sacrifice is indicated by her
refusal to move the dirty dishes out of the sink, thereby displacing
the scum, for "perhaps the mould had as much right to life as she
had" (p. 217).

To this point, Marian has seen herself increasingly as divided
into two: I and she, mind and body, essence and object, like I in
Surfacing. In her preparations for the engagement party, however,
she comes to see herself further divided into three distinct and
equal selves, like Joan in *Lady Oracle*. Looking into the mirror of

the bathtub taps she sees her three-fold self, only a reflection of reality and caught there by a spell. She even fears annihilation: she is "dissolving, coming apart layer by layer like a piece of cardboard in a gutter puddle" or "spreading out, not being able to contain herself any longer" (pp. 218-9). And the engagement ring which she sees as a "protective talisman, that would help to keep her to-gether" (p. 218) is in fact the centre of the spell which holds her there, imprisoned. She is unable either to integrate these identities within one self or to accept the existence of multiple selves. In the bedroom mirror she sees reflected herself as centre between the two dolls of her childhood past. The blonde doll represents the outer shell which she has taken on, the social façade, and the dark doll, with its frizzy hair and worn painted face, represents her asocial self:

> She saw herself in the mirror between them for an instant as though she was . . . inside both of them at once, looking out; her-self, a vague damp form in a rumpled dressing-gown, not quite focussed, the blonde eyes noting the arrangement of her hair, her bitten fingernails, the dark one looking deeper, at something she could not quite see, the two overlapping images drawing further and further away from each other; the centre, whatever it was in the glass, the thing that held them together, would soon be quite empty. By the strength of their separate visions they were trying to tear her apart. (p. 219)

The party at Peter's apartment focuses all these conflicts and tensions. As Alan Dawe comments, in this chapter "all her alter-natives are brought together . . . and the moment finally arrives when she must choose."[15] First Marian's society prefers the shell to the reality. Each of her friends and associates, beginning with Peter, comments on the beauty of the artificial self and suggests that she should always dress in this manner. Only Duncan dissents, observing the incongruity between surface and reality: "You didn't tell me it was a masquerade. . . . Who the hell are you supposed to be?" (p. 239).

As Marian feels more and more the victim, identified in her red dress as "the perfect target," the images of the hunt become predominant. Marian sees her overshoes, sitting with Peter's outside the apartment door, as "black leathery bait in a large empty newspaper trap," and her coat on his bed becomes "a decoy" (pp. 227-8). Peter's remark, "It's almost zero hour," and his request for "a couple of shots of you alone," with the ominous addition: "that red ought to show up well on a slide," evokes in

Marian a reaction immediate and paralyzing: "She couldn't move, couldn't even move the muscles of her face as she stood and stared into the round glass lens pointing towards her" (pp. 231-2). As in the poem "Camera," the protagonist sees the very act of photographing as an act of violation, an indication of a desire to stop the clock and to capture the other in time: "once he pulled the trigger she would be stopped, fixed indissolubly in that gesture, that single stance, unable to move or change " (p. 245). And as in the poem, the only solution is escape. In her dream of the future corridors and rooms, Peter is transformed from a domesticated family man beside the barbecue to a primitive hunter with a large cleaver. And as she runs through the snowy streets, fearing Peter to be "tracing, following, stalking her," she finally sees what she interprets as the real Peter under the veneer of civilization: "That dark intent marksman with his aiming eye had been there all the time, hidden by the other layers, waiting for her at the dead centre: a homicidal maniac with a lethal weapon in his hands" (p. 246).

But the escape to Duncan, Peter's antithesis, is not a solution either. As they search for a hotel which will ask no questions, Marian conspicuous in her red dress and dangling earrings, the scene suggests the outskirts of Hell with its cheap hotels patronized by prostitutes and their clients. And the attempt to make love with Duncan becomes an attempt to unite with death itself, a union which annihilates meaning and reveals the absurdity not only of death but also of life:

> At this moment to evoke something, some response, even though she could not predict the thing that might emerge from beneath that seemingly-passive surface, the blank white formless thing lying insubstantial in the darkness before her, shifting as her eyes shifted trying to see, that appeared to have no temperature, no odour, no thickness and no sound, was the most important thing she could ever have done, could ever do, and she couldn't do it. The knowledge was an icy desolation worse than fear. No effort of will could be worth anything here.   (p. 254)

With this act, her body cuts itself off completely: "the food circle had dwindled to a point, a black dot, closing everything outside" (p. 257).

Yet Duncan's acceptance of her, his moving away from the foetal crouch, marks for Marian the end of the descent. The change in setting marks the change in mood. As they leave the tawdry district to make their way towards the ravine, the winter imagery turns to that of spring: melting snow, growing bulbs and damp earth (although the romanticism is countered by the realism of rotting leaves and the "Winter's accumulations of the cats"). Death gives way to rebirth: "old people [are] coming out of the grey doors with shovels, creaking over the lawns, burying things. Spring cleaning: a sense of purpose" (p. 259). The setting of the ravine, narrow and deep, symbolizes Marian's situation at this point. Below them a roadway spirals down to a circular pit and, at its centre, the brickworks and a concealed prison. The hills above them are "closed in by trees" but far above, near the rim, children are playing. Marian moves progressively upwards towards the city, to which she is now connected by the bridge spanning the ravine, with its clinging subway trains. Behind her she leaves Duncan, still part of the underworld: "a dark shape against the snow, crouched on the edge and gazing into the empty pit" (p. 265).

The ending of *The Edible Woman* is both surprising and comic. In the final section of Part II, Marian rejects passivity. She prepares the cakewoman as a test of the hero, a test "simple and direct as litmus paper" (p. 267). Atwood has remarked to Gibson that she cannot explain in critical terms what happens here, that she chose the ending by intuition rather than reason:

> When writing the filmscript we had long conversations on just exactly what that means. Obviously she's acting, she's doing an action. Up until that point she has been evading, avoiding, running away, retreating, withdrawing. . . . She commits an action, a preposterous one in a way, as all the pieces of symbolism in a realistic context are, but what she is obviously making is a substitute of herself.[16]

If Peter passes the test, unscrambles the riddle, he will become the bridegroom. The end of the descent is often marked by riddles or ciphers and by a trial. But while Marian has been on trial throughout, a false trial, it is Peter who is on trial here. For the cakewoman is a parody of human sacrifice, of the "cannibal feast, the serving up of a child or lover as food" which, Frye notes, marks the bottom of the night world.[17] As Marian looks at Peter's back, she comments: "The face on the other side of that head could have belonged to anyone"; he could be the Underwear Man or, more frightening, one of the future killers: "those in the newspapers, those still unknown, waiting for their chance to aim from the upstairs window." She explains her motive in creating the cakewoman: "the price of testing this version of reality [the daylight side] was testing the other one" (p. 271). If Peter can accept

Marian's claim, "You've been trying to destroy me, haven't you?" and her offer of the cake-woman as substitute, he will have recognized his own dark side, his need to exploit. When he flees however, Marian believes that the dark self has remained concealed and is thus potentially dangerous. Her final image of Peter combines his roles as suave business man and primitive hunter; she imagines him featured on a poster, elegantly costumed, his foot posed on a stuffed lion's head and with a revolver strapped under his arm.

Marian's release is immediate. In Part III she returns once more to her own voice, fusing the "she" and the "I" once more into a unity. In washing the floor, the sink and the windows, and in cleaning out the refrigerator, she rejects kinship with lower forms of life which had been "sprouting hair, fur or feathers, each as its nature dictated" (p. 277). The narcissism of Duncan now no longer attracts her: "I found my own situation much more interesting than his" (p. 278). In this active mood she is prepared to take an active role in her life, to find a new home, a new job, and, presumably, a new boyfriend.

Like the traditional romance, the novel does end with a marriage, perhaps two marriages. Ainsley captures Fischer, a student of womb symbolism, and Marian is pleased to have her faith in Ainsley's ingenuity confirmed. Lucy presumably lands Peter in her net (his last description of her is "it's nice to know there are *some* considerate women left around . . ." [p. 266]) and in any event Peter's bride will be the traditional wife expected by his society. Even Clara, although she is unsure of how to cope with Len's regression to the age of her own four-year-old, sounds "more competent than usual" (p. 280).

The comic perspective is restored with the feast, the celebration of Marian's new freedom and even rebirth. While Ainsley has protested: "You're rejecting your femininity!", Marian's reply, "Nonsense . . . it's only a cake" signifies her release from the spell, from her identification of herself with the victim. No longer isolated and alien, Marian has rejoined society; as Duncan observes "you're back to so-called reality, you're a consumer" (p. 281). No longer divided, in danger of disintegration, she can detach herself from her cake-creation, and she joyfully attacks the carcass with a fork, "neatly severing the body from the head" (p. 273). A cake is a cake, an edible; a woman's a woman, not edible. The dark voyage, downwards and inwards, is over. She has returned to life and to consuming.

ANNIS PRATT

Surfacing
and the Rebirth Journey

Margaret Atwood's *Surfacing* has been generally accepted as an archetypal narrative dealing with a quest for rebirth and trans-formation. Thus, in a *New York Times Book Review* column, Francine du Plessix Gray suggested that Atwood has taken a "primeval, matriarchal direction" in her "quest for religious symbols," and that the "stages of the heroine's quest are starkly archetypal: Heroine of the thousand faces, she descends, like Perse-phone, into the world of the dead; she tests, like Perseus, the extreme limits of human endurance; she finds her ultimate vision in the self-enforced solitude."[1] Theologian Carol Christ points out that the hero's spiritual discoveries by no means alienate her from her own or nature's body: Atwood, she writes, creates a quest in which "spiritual insight surfaces through attention to the body," leading to an "achievement of authentic selfhood and power which depends on understanding one's grounding in nature and natural energies." Contrasting the spiritual quest, defined as the "self's journey . . . in relation to cosmic power or powers," to the social quest for integration into a collective, Christ nonetheless recognizes that the interiority of such quests as that which structures *Surfacing* does not necessarily preclude "acommunal dimensions."[2]

The journey into the solitary world of the psyche is a process which feminist theoreticians are beginning to recognize as trans-formational in both the individual and the collective sense. Arche-typal narratives, as well as theological formulations and the rituals by which women enact them, are being examined as repositories of power; sources of energy which can enable women to break through social norms dictating gender rigidity into a "new cosmosis," as Mary Daly puts it, beyond patriarchal space. My intent as a feminist archetypal critic has been threefold: first, to describe the archetypal patterns informing women's literature; second, to study the way in which such patterns effect literary structures; and third, to speculate about the process by which such texts act upon their audience. In this essay I will be concerned with defining the archetype of the rebirth journey as it applies to the feminine experience in a set of analogous texts. My approach to *Surfacing* will thus be archetypal and contextual, a process which Black English more aptly defines as "diggin' out the meaning by shakin' out the context." Having placed *Surfacing* in the context of archetypal and fictional analogues, finally, I will look into the way that such an archetypally informed literary text might effect social change.

The Rebirth Journey

Feminist archetypalists find it helpful to engage in a process which French feminists call *volant,* punning on the dual connotations of *voler* as meaning both to steal and to fly away. Descriptions of the process of transformation or "individuation" provided by Jung and his followers are highly informative in elucidating literature. It is important to note, in this context, that Jung deplored the term "Jungian" and disliked his theories to be too rigidly applied, urging each scholar to come to terms with his or her own interpretation of unconscious materials.[3] Insofar as it applies to the individual life span (in contrast to the rebirth process of reincarnation or metempsychosis) Jung defines *Wiedergeburt* as involving either renovation or transformation of an individual so that all of his or her faculties are brought into conscious play. This may involve a "renewal without any change of being, inasmuch as the personality which is renewed is not changed in its essential nature, but only its functions, or parts of the personality, are subjected to healing, strengthening, or improvement." It may, moreover, take the form of transformation of personality in that the individual undergoes an "essential transformation" or "total rebirth" by taking on the characteristics of a superhuman figure to whom he or she is "initiated in mystery, rite, or dream."[4]

The process by which such a crystallization of the personality comes about is one by which the self, which Jung differentiates from the ego, leaves the narrow bounds of its persona or social mask and plunges into the unconscious. The ego, as Jung defines it, "extends only as far as the conscious mind," whereas the self comprises the *"whole* of the personality, which includes the unconscious as well as the conscious component. The Ego is thus related to the self as part of the whole."[5] The inner or rebirth journey is at one and the same time personal and communal, in that the world of the unconscious is one shared with the entire human race. The problem which Jung acknowledged, however, is that there is less likely to be a correlation between the world of the unconscious and that of the conscious mind in the feminine as in the masculine experience, since a man can easily discern "definite recognizable patterns" in his inner world bearing analogues to mytho-religious structures provided by his society or mesocosm. A woman's unconscious, however, is less likely to reflect the received myths of society as known, having its analogues in the pre- or acivilizational worlds of a lost culture. I am suggesting that the various stages of the masculine rebirth journey are likely to be symbolic vehicles for learned experience, whereas the stages of woman's rebirth quests conform to codes and hieroglyphs alien to western culture. As a result, the male quester will have far less difficulty as a transformed personality in reintegrating into his culture than the woman hero, whose adventures increase her chances for death, madness, self-sacrifice, and accusations of "deviance" at the level of culture.

After reading widely in the field of British and American women's fiction, I found it possible to develop a description of the woman hero's quest as to some degree different from that of the male. Woman's ego or persona can be understood as having its day to day life in the world of cultural experience, by definition a world of gender and social norms. This same layer of being, in my formulation, finds its reflection in the layer of unconscious materials, which for convenience I term the subconscious, immediately "below" that of conscious experience. It is from these two "upper" realms of culture and of subconscious reflections of personal and familial roles that the normative values of much of women's fiction derive, and these realms play an important role in determining the accommodationist denouements of many novels of manners, family life, and even of social protest. When a woman author wants her character to enact possibilities unsuitable to these realms, she cannot choose material from them but must delve into unconscious materials necessarily alien to her mesocosm or social matrix. In taking her hero down into the unconscious and in returning her from it, however, the author almost never lets her bypass these "upper" worlds but depicts her absorbing them and transcending them in a process of working through inauthentic role behaviours. The world of the unconscious in such fiction is quite likely, moreover, to be a timeless one, precisely because it has no correlation to historical time; and, correspondingly, spaceless or obscure in landscape, patriarchal space being alien to it. In such a world the identity of the self seems in flux, undergoing shifts and leaps in harmony with the interior vision and with the universe as a whole but "deviant" in the sense of being strange to the normative perspective. Because the images, symbols, and archetypal narratives of such a world are puzzling, bizarre, even "crazy," they are extremely difficult to absorb into the day to day life of consciousness, and hence comes the tearing apart of narrative structure, tacked-on denouements, and sense of irresolution characterizing so much of women's fiction.

The creation of any schema carries with it the danger of being too absolute, of becoming a model so rigid that texts have to be distorted to fit its dictates. In setting forth the following series of stages in fictional rebirth journeys I intend to indicate only the broadest outlines and to call attention to the fact that not every novel proceeds in this particular sequence of phases. There is, nonetheless, significant enough recurrence of most of the phases in such fiction to make the outline helpful in elucidating the texts.

Phase I: Splitting Off from the World of the Ego

This first aspect of the interior journey takes the form of an acute consciousness of dissatisfaction with the roles and norms typically assumed by the persona and of a consequent turning away from society. Marge Piercy, in *Small Changes*, shows her hero Beth setting out on a social quest after a particularly awful evening with her husband; Nin's Lillian in *Seduction of the Minotaur*, like Lessing's Martha in *The Four-Gated City*, crosses an ocean to a new world of endeavour; in Woolf's *To the Lighthouse* Mrs. Ramsay's plunge into interior space is precipitated after a trying day with her husband, and Atwood's hero in *Surfacing* is introduced to the reader driving away from the city where she has had a traumatic experience.

Phase II: The Green World Guide or Token
Helps the Hero Cross the Threshold

As in the epiphanic visions of childhood and adolescence, naturistic moments which help fictional heroes aspire to a different realm of being from the ordinary, the rebirth journey hero is helped to cross the threshold into the unconscious world by some ordinary phenomenon which takes on extraordinary portent. Rhoda, in Woolf's *The Waves,* enters a trance through the simple device of a puddle; Kate, in Lessing's *The Summer Before the Dark,* dreams of a seal which she is to carry on her journey; Mrs. Ramsay's lighthouse and Beth's turtle in *Small Changes* perform similar functions. As for Atwood's hero, "the lake was the entrance for me."

Phase III: Confrontation with Parental Figures

In women's rebirth fiction this confrontation most often takes place with memory figures rather than with actual persons, and constitutes an experience which belongs both to the realm of subconscious or societal experience and to the powerful mother- and father-imagos haunting the deepest reaches of the unconscious. It is thus a key phase if the hero is to complete the full plunge to the nadir of her unconscious, and frequently becomes an *agon* or terminal struggle if unsuccessful. As we shall see below, the heroes in *The Four-Gated City* and *Seduction of the Minotaur,* like Atwood's hero, experience this struggle as a difficult passage crucial to their final developments.

Phase IV: The Green World Lover

Whether as an actual or a reverie figure, an ideal and distinctly non-patriarchal lover often aids in the final journey of the self into the fountainhead of Eros or Libido which contains the drive and energy of the transformed personality. In Willa Cather's *O Pioneers!* a tall corn god of fertility and death bears Alexandra through despair to survival; Heathcliff provides such a quasi-naturistic figure leading Brontë's Catherine on to a consummation after death or *liebestod* in *Wuthering Heights;* the lovemaking of a character called "Three" in June Arnold's *The Cook and the Carpenter* becomes a catalyst in the integration of the Carpenter's personality, and in Atwood's *Surfacing* Joe, a figure from the world of the Ego and of the City, is transformed in the hero's mind into a primevally naturistic lover, a furry buffalo. Sometimes the Green world lover actually *is* an animal, as may be the case with the unicorn archetype which appears so often in women's poetry and needlework.[6] It appears as a heron in Sarah Orne Jewett's "A White Heron," a fox in Mary Webb's *Gone to Earth*, a donkey in May Sarton's *Joanna and Ulysses*, a stag in witchcraft rituals, and a bull in the Cretan mysteries of Minos. The hero may love it, pretend to be it (as in Jo March's identification with a horse in *Little Women*), or follow it. In the modern novel of rebirth such figures seem to represent the incorporation into the personality of one's sexual and natural energies, one's Pan, as it were, one's own internal Adonis.

Phase V: The Shadow

Although the figure of one's "shadow" or worst personality, one's anti-self, does not necessarily appear as such in all rebirth novels, at some phase in the inner journey there tends to be a coming to terms with all that is negative or destructive prior to tapping one's deepest streams of creativity. Martha, in Lessing's *The Four-Gated City*, overtly struggles with a figure she calls her "self-hater" as she is guided by the "devil" through a series of self-recognitions which she calls the "stations of the cross." Nin's Lillian finds herself denying help to her animus-figure or potential guide in *Seduction of the Minotaur*, and, indirectly, taking responsibility for his death; the shadowy or life-denying side of Mrs. Ramsay's lighthouse seems to claim her for death a third of the way through the novel, and Atwood's hero is constantly aware of her brother as the technologically violent, murderer-side of her own personality.

Phase VI: The Final Descent to the Nadir

Psychoanalytically, the plunge to the nadir of the unconscious is a fulcrum of danger, taking one to the self beneath self, and as likely to lead to madness as to transformation. Fictional heroes often experience a chaos of surreal images and symbols at this phase, disassociated fantasies and chaotic noises that mimic clinical madness. This experience, which I would term "literary insanity" in contrast to the objective horrors of true madness, can either disintegrate the hero entirely or provide the turning point in her quest. The problem is that "insanity," as Phyllis Chesler and others have documented, tends whether literary or clinical to mimic the accepted role of women in society, that of a victim trapped and suffocating within an enclosure. Even if she is able to take the leap through this layer of being, the transformed hero is going to have difficulties at the ascent phase in re-integrating herself into "normal" society.

Phase VII: Ascent and Re-Entry into Society as Known

Although there is no doubt that the masculine hero who has assimilated his "anima" or "feminine other" as well as his "shadow" into a fully integrated personality may have some difficulty in a gender role oriented society, such heroes are depicted returning to the level of the ego and contributing the elixir they have won to their civilizations. For the fully transformed woman hero, however, re-entry is far more problematical, since her assumed role in society is by necessity secondary or auxiliary and thus her elixir is not only devalued but a threat to civilization. She is met upon her ascent, thus, with a forceful backlash, an attempt to dwarf her personality and re-accommodate her to secondary status. It is for this reason that so many women's rebirth novels are, at best, open-ended, the hero's precise place in society being left to guesswork on the part of the reader. Sometimes, however, a non-civilizational "new space" is actually provided for her, as in the case of the post-nuclear-holocaust island where Lessing's Martha finds her collective. Although the returning woman hero is unlikely to be able to affect a broad sector of her society, however, she is quite often depicted as passing on her boon or elixir to one apprentice, a younger woman who may in turn pass the tradition of transcendence to her own initiate. Lily Briscoe is such an apprentice to Mrs. Ramsay, Rita to Martha in *The Four-Gated City*, the young woman interviewer to Mrs. Stevens in Sarton's *Mrs. Stevens Hears the Mermaids Singing*, etc. In many cases the hero seems to initiate *herself*, looking back to her own mother or to an idealized mother-figure as model. This seems to me to be the case with Atwood's hero in *Surfacing* and with Nin's Lillian in *Seduction of the Minotaur*. Sometimes, finally, the transformed woman hero seems to be transferring her boon of power not to any figure within the text but to the woman reader herself.

Although a full scale textual analysis of a series of rebirth novels would be too cumbersome for my purpose here, it seems helpful to approach *Surfacing* obliquely, by comparison to several texts structured in conformity to the same archetypal narrative. Since I have written elsewhere about Mrs. Ramsay's rebirth journey in Woolf's *To the Lighthouse*,[7] I will summarize here those broad features which are of help on providing a context for *Surfacing*, and then develop an analysis of *Seduction of the Minotaur* for the purposes of comparison and contrast.

Mrs. Ramsay and the Androgynous Elixir

With a markedly erotic set of kinesthetic images, Woolf describes Mr. Ramsay in *To the Lighthouse* as barren and sterile, having to be completed by Mrs. Ramsay's pouring of a "delicious fecundity," a "fountain and spray of life" into his empty being. This experience of plunging down into her own "fountainhead" of energy and giving life to the world through it is linked consistently with the figure of the lighthouse through imagery of rising, illumination, circling, and stroking. The actual lighthouse, contemplated by the weary Mrs. Ramsay, thus becomes an inner imago or archetypal symbol around which she rallies her self by repeated journeys into the depths of her unconscious. The rays of the lighthouse become, thus, emanations of an inner or green world lover, "as if it were stroking with its silver fingers some sealed vessel in her brain whose bursting would flood her with delight." Wholly an inward and nonsocial force, the lighthouse provides her with escape from her world, "something real, something private, which she shared neither with her children nor with her husband." Ultimately, then, Mrs. Ramsay turns away from those she has attempted to fructify with her inner elixir, and dies of "a stroke."[8]

Although empowered by an unusual androgynous fusion of forces normatively considered "male" and "female" in sexual import, Mrs. Ramsay is not able to survive with the totality of self she has achieved, the process having, apparently, been too one-sided. "When the libido leaves the bright upper world," writes Jung, "whether from choice, or from inertia, or from fate, it sinks back into its own depths, into the source from which it originally flowed." Once back at the sources of being, however, a fulcrum is reached which is a "dangerous moment when the issue hangs between annihilation and new life."[9] It is at this point, I would conclude, that Mrs. Ramsay becomes unable to return to the level of the ego, and perishes. In the structure of the novel, "Time Passes" in turn constitutes a fulcrum of the tripartite plot division, in which Mrs. Ramsay becomes embodied in the "ebb and flow" of objects which take over the abandoned house at their will, arranging themselves not according to human dictates but according to a timeless and spaceless essence. The process by which the house and its contents settle into a personless flux of "things as they are" and are rescued only at the last moment by the return of the family constitutes a rebirth experience within the wider rebirth structure of the total text. As a *tour de force* of lyric prose, "Time Passes" provides a variation on the tranquil, personless state of mind which is at one and the same time Mrs. Ramsay's elixir and her nemesis.

The third section of *To the Lighthouse* reverses the archetypal Demeter/Kore narrative (although Jane Ellen Harrison notes that mother/young woman or mother/daughter are always interchangeable in import) in that Lily Briscoe is apprenticed to the spirit of the mother figure who is depicted as having descended into the world of the dead. Brooding over the painting and adding in brush strokes in a kinesthetic pattern reminiscent of Mrs. Ramsay's lighthouse trances, Lily seems to perceive the older woman leaving the world behind for the realm of the dead. She sees that she has let her "flowers fall from her basket, scattered and tumbled them on to the grass and, reluctantly and hesitatingly, but without question or complaint," is journeying away "Down fields, across valleys, white, flower-strewn."[10] The field of flowers suggests the Rharian plain at Thria which Demeter fructified after the restoration of Persephone, and the spilled basket the basket of flowers which Persephone dropped when she was abducted from a field by Pluto. The basket may also represent Demeter's *Cista Mystica* of the Eleusinian mysteries, the basket in which she keeps the sacred (and purportedly androgynous) symbols sought by the initiate. Lily is able to put the final stroke to her painting when Mr. Carmichael, whom she perceives as Neptune, stands erect and looks out to sea: she has perhaps been empowered by an appearance of Poseidon, lover of Demeter and father of Persephone. Where in the Demeter/Kore narrative and in the rites based upon it the mother grieves after the abduction and rape of her daughter and quests through heaven and earth to bring her back to life, in *To the Lighthouse* Lily as daughter or younger woman apprentice seeks the meaning of Mrs. Ramsay's life after her death. Her role is one of enquiry into the source and nature of Mrs. Ramsay's unique elixir, of absorption of it into her own art, corresponding perhaps to the quest of the Eleusinian initiate for an understanding and assimilation of the power of the goddess. As a rhetorical structure,

To the Lighthouse constitutes a ritual of passage in which a younger woman learns, on the one hand, to preserve herself from such tyrannical (and gender-rigid) demands as Mr. Ramsay's; and, on the other hand, to absorb sufficient inner and asocial powers to pursue her own creativity.

Seduction of the Minotaur and the Hieroglyphic Elixir

Anais Nin's *Seduction of the Minotaur* is the last novel in the five volume *Cities of the Interior*, a multivolumed work which differs from such novel sequences as Lessing's *The Children of Violence* and Dorothy Richardson's *Pilgrimage* in being less sequential than cyclical, dealing not with the development of one hero but with the interaction of three — Lillian, Sabina, and Djuana. The first and last volumes nonetheless are chiefly concerned with Lillian's quest for selfhood, and the final volume is structured as a rebirth journey which she undertakes upon a "solar barque" to the land of "Golconda," which is also the land of her own unconsciousness. Lillian's descent into the underworld parallels Mrs. Ramsay's in some ways, but the denouements form an interesting contrast: where Mrs. Ramsay's power is explicit in nature and absorbed by Lily, Lillian is left without a full understanding of what she has experienced, her elixir or goal of her quest being hieroglyphic.

Before she is able to proceed into the depths of the unconscious, Lillian must come to terms with personal material having to do with memories of her mother and father and of how they perceived her. "Already," she muses, "she regretted having come. This was not a journey in her solar barque. It was a night journey into the past, and the thread that had pulled her was one of accidental resemblances, familiarity, the past. She had been unable to live for three months a new life, in a new city, without being caught by an umbilical cord and brought back to the figure of her father." Lillian's problem is that she cannot perceive herself adequately behind the mirrors of her parents' eyes: "Lillian had never seen herself with her own eyes . . . You retained as upon a delicate retina, your mother's image of you, as the first and the only authentic one, her judgement of your acts." What Lillian needs to grow is the ability to possess her own self-vision, in spite of or in contrast to the way husband/lover/mother/father have previously defined her personality. She is beset and confused not only by these familial distortions of her authenticity but also by gender expectations to which she does not conform. As an adolescent, Nin remarks in the first volume of the sequence (*Ladders to Fire*), she has been both "aggressive" and "womanly," and although Nin associates the one with masculinity and the other with femininity she sees her hero as one human unity: "She had two voices, one which felt deep like the voice of a man, and another light and innocent. Two women disputing inside of her."[11]

As an inner and empowering imago paralleling Mrs. Ramsay's lighthouse, Lillian carries inside of her mind an "inner chamber" containing a figure which is neither herself nor her own mother but an idealized archetype of maternity:

> The mother madonna holding the child and nourishing it. The haunting mother image forever holding a small child.
>
> Then there was the child itself, the child inhabiting a world of peaceful, laughing animals, rich trees, in valleys of festive color. The child in her eyes appeared with its eyes closed. It was dreaming the fertile valleys, the small warm house, the Byzantine flowers, the tender animals and the abundance. It was dreaming and afraid to awaken. It was dreaming the lightness of the sky, the warmth of the earth, the fecundity of the colors.
>
> It was afraid to awaken.[12]

As in the Demeter/Kore archetype, in which mother and daughter mingle in being and take on each other's powers, Lillian, in this passage, is at one and the same time mother and child. The inner world of the child is the paradisiacal vision of the green world filled with friendly animals which occurs so often in women's embroidery and tapestry work as the tree of life or the island of animals dominated by a beneficent goddess and her maidens. The madonna figure represents a positive imago in contrast to Lillian's maternal experiences both with her own mother and as a mother to her children, whom she has left behind with her husband because they were imposed upon her by social norms and not sprung from the inner authenticity of her own choices:

> Who had desired the children? She could not remember the first impetus, the first choice, the first desire for these, nor how they came to be. It was as if it had happened in her sleep. Lillian, guided by her background, her mother, her sisters, her habits, her home as a child, her blindness in regard to her own desires, had made all of this and then lived in it, but it had not been made out of the deeper elements of her nature, and she was a stranger in it.[13]

The world to which she turns for renewal of self in *Seduction of the Minotaur* is the green and tropical land of Golconda, and she attempts through it to undo the alienation from nature that has made her bear children in this absent-minded fashion. During her re-immersion into the plant and animal world of Golconda the memories of mother and father are dealt with, and Lillian is enabled to undertake the plunge into the unconscious through the guide or *animus* figure of Dr. Hernandez. He dies before he is able to help her to complete her quest, however, and she realizes that having failed him, she has failed herself: "If only they had gone down together, down the caverns of the soul with picks, lanterns, cords, oxygen, x-ray, food, following the blueprints of all the messages from the geological depths where lay hidden the imprisoned self." He cannot go with her, however, and she must undertake a journey without the help of all the tools that he might have provided. As a result:

> She was now like those French speleologists who had descended thousands of feet into the earth and found ancient caves covered with paintings and carvings. But Lillian carried no searchlight and no nourishment. Nothing but the wafer granted to those who believe in symbolism, a wafer in place of bread. And all she had to follow were the inscriptions of her dreams, half-effaced hieroglyphs on half-broken statues. And no guide in the darkness but a scream through the eyes of a statue.[14]

This chaotic world of jumbled signals is that timeless realm of surreal imagery and confused voices which Lessing's Martha as well as Woolf's Mrs. Ramsay and Atwood's hero experience. She has no true nourishment with her, only a "wafer" which is at one remove from bread, a merely sacramental food which is useless to Lillian since she does not have any "blueprint" to the mythological or theological system informing it. Like the hieroglyphs in the caves and the inscriptions in her dreams, the bread is at a level removed from helpful substance, a symbolic and ritual vehicle which has lost its referent. In this way it corresponds to the empty forms and puzzling masks surviving from prepatriarchal times, coded ciphers which are confusing, at best, and more often horrifying to the visitor from the world of "normal" society.

The incomplete nature of Lillian's inner quest is recapitulated in a vision that she has of her own reflection in the window of the airplane in which she is flying home. She sees not herself but a "minotaur," which "was not a monster. It was a reflection upon a

Mirror, a masked woman, Lillian herself, the hidden masked part of herself unknown to her, who had ruled her acts." In the pre-Hellenic Cretan religion the minotaur was the animal lover of the queens, the "bull of Minos" corresponding to the horned god of the witches. He thus represented the animus and the green world lover for the queen, who participated in a *Hieros Gamos* or love-making ritual with him in order to establish her erotic, political, and religious hegemony. Queen and Minotaur, like Lady and Unicorn, Indian Maiden and Buffalo, are powerful figures of feminine autonomy and erotic power. For Lillian, however, the minotaur is merely at the level of "mask" worn as cover to the self, the indication being that the archetype is not wholly assimilated or integrated with her self and that she is not fully transformed. Her persona or ego is thus at the denouement in disjunction with its own unconscious materials, the hieroglyphs containing her elixir remaining encoded.

Margaret Atwood's *Surfacing* and the Elixir of Maternity

Where the outcome of Lillian's quest is problematical, that of the hero of Atwood's *Surfacing* is as precise as Mrs. Ramsay's. As in *To the Lighthouse,* a quest is described in which the hero plunges down through subconscious to unconscious materials and is empowered by absorbing the archetypal symbols available to her at the fountainhead of her personality and being. This achievement, moreover, is at one and the same time a spiritual and a markedly naturistic one, the green world and a green world lover or erotic figure making the outcome an integration of body and soul. As in Woolf and in Nin, moreover, the text is structured according to a penetration of a world of unconscious materials which are at one and the same time so wholly new as to seem bizarre and, through analogy with such archetypes as the Demeter/Kore narrative, wholly and radically "old."

The island in the Canadian lake constitutes a green world of childhood remembered and a locus of transformation or rebirth, thus conflating Lillian's child's dream and the land of Golconda as well as unifying the consciousness Woolf divided between Mrs. Ramsay and her disciple, Lily. The hero brings her own patriarchal space or subconscious gender world with her in the form of David and Anna, a couple hideously involved in normative "male and female" behaviour.

The hero's mother and father provide her with figures both

from the subconscious or familial and from the unconscious realms. On the one hand, they represent her memories of her actual parents, but on the other hand they bring gifts, like Mrs. Ramsay's, which transcend the personal. These gifts, moreover, constitute hieroglyphs which, unlike Lillian's, are translatable into agents of transformation. The hero comes to the island because of reports that her father, who has been living alone following her mother's death, is missing. Looking at his scribbled notes, she is at first fearful that he has gone mad but soon realizes that they are sketches of ancient Indian cave drawings and symbols. Whether her father is dead, mad, or returned from the dead becomes all one to the hero, who finds herself drawn by the power latent within these archetypal figures into a world which she seeks for her own sake. Having found the site of the drawings, and having dived down to it from her canoe, she comes upon a "dark oval, trailing limbs. It was blurred but it had eyes, they were open, it was something I knew about, a dead thing, it was dead." It is, in actuality, her drowned father, but it also suggests the memory of the foetus whose abortion had traumatized her and of the frogs and snakes that her brother had put to death in closed jars, "evil grails." She realizes that her father had achieved a new and powerful world, whose elixir she in turn desires to absorb.

> He had discovered new places, new oracles, they were things he was seeking the way I had seen, true vision; at the end, after the failure of logic. When it happened the first time he must have been terrified, it would be like stepping through a usual door and finding yourself in a different galaxy, purple trees and red moons and a green sun.[15]

The "new places" which she will seek are repositories of power finding their expression in an old/new language of hieroglyphs, alinguistic, prespeech, and implicitly acivilizational like so much of the content of women's unconscious realms. Where the father has translated them for scholarly interpretation, the hero will have to find some far less culturally acceptable use if she is to become an effective woman self.

"It would be right for my mother to have left something for me also, a legacy," she realizes. "His was complicated, tangled, but hers would be simple as a hand, it would be final." To a certain extent the mother's legacy is the image of herself as a strong figure close to nature, able to scare away bears, rescue her son from drowning, and tame the wild birds. More personally, the hero finds her mother's boon in a scrapbook of her own childish drawings, specifically one of "a woman with a round moon stomach: the baby was sitting up inside her and gazing out. Opposite her was a man with horns on his head and a barbed tail." The gift of her own drawing is a gift from her own unconscious, and although at first glance Atwood seems to be sexually stereo-typing these figures, they represent, when taken together, the same type of androgynous projection as Mrs. Ramsay's "masculine" and "feminine" qualities and the mixture of two voices, "male" and "female," in the unitary woman, Lillian. The dual symbol is analogous to the powerful queen and her horned consort, and in turn to the figure of a witch with her stag lover. The hero has deplored the split in herself between "head," which she associates with "the gods of the head," "antlers rooted in the brain," and the round moon body. The goal of her quest is to integrate body and head, nature and mind, in one personality. Her transformation consists, thus, in taking over one by one the faculties which she has projected upon others rather than bring them to consciousness as parts of an integrated selfhood. Thus her decision to get pregnant by Joe, whom she associates, archetypally, with a buffalo, seems at first glance to be one which will force her back into a social role but is actually a self-actualizing choice, in that it is derived not from the subconscious realm of personal or gender role expecta-tions but from an unconscious world where maternity is a form of power. Her act of conception, self-initiated and self-contained, is one in which she is wholly central and authentic:

> He trembles and I can feel my lost child surfacing within me, forgiving me, rising from the lake where it has been prisoned for so long, its eyes and teeth phosporescent; the two halves clasp, interlocking like fingers, it buds, it sends out fronds. This time I will do it by myself, squatting on old newspapers in a corner alone; or on leaves, dry leaves, a heap of them, that's cleaner. The baby will slip out easily as an egg, a kitten, and I'll lick it off and bite the cord, the blood returning to the ground where it belongs; the moon will be full, pulling. In the morning I will be able to see it: it will be covered with shining fur, a god, I will never teach it any words.[16]

The lost child is in one dimension the aborted foetus, the imagery of leaves and fronds contrasting to the metallic imagery sur-rounding an operation which the hero regrets. It is also, however, her own lost child or childhood, surfacing to empower her, an inner self that she is delivering into personal transformation that is the rebirth experience. By uniting herself with nature, literally floating naked in the water and wandering at one with the island in a prelinguistic, "mad" state, she conceives new life in an affirmation of a woman's unique powers of birth. All of this is done wholly in rejection of her culture, which, in the guise of David, considers her a deviant, a man hater. In Mary Daly's terminology, she goes "crazy" deliberately in order to empower herself through "the role of witch and madwoman . . . tantamount to a declaration of identity beyond the good and evil of patriarchy's world, and beyond sanity and insanity."[17] Where Mrs. Ramsay dies, leaving Lily a heritage which she can personally assimilate but which has little import for her role in society; and where Lillian returns to her family without having fully absorbed her elixir; Atwood creates a hero shockingly deviant precisely because, having fused in her personal transformation both spiritual and natural powers, she fully intends to complete her rebirth journey by returning to the mesocosm.

The Rhetorical Effect of Rebirth Fiction

Feminist critics have sometimes worried that writers like Woolf, Nin, and Atwood focus too narrowly upon inward, "personalistic" visions, to the point of suggesting a retreat from social life rather than engagement with it. "For Mrs. Ramsay," writes Elaine Showalter, "death is a mode of self-assertion. Refined to its essences, abstracted from its physicality and anger, denied any action, Woolf's vision of womanhood is as deadly as it is disembodied. The ultimate room of one's own is the grave."[18] My hypothesis, in contrast, is that the retreat into sanctuaries and rooms constitutes a *reculant pour mieux sauter*, a drawing back in order to leap further; and that fantasies are indeed prevalent in women's fiction but to a positive effect, constituting projections of worlds of being desired by author, hero, and reader alike, treasure houses of energies locked into symbols whose import has been forgotten. As Mary Daly puts it, the contents of our inner selves constitute "those flames of spiritual imagination and cerebral fantasy which can be a new dawn." It becomes the task of the feminist archetypalist to decipher these symbols through comparison to a broad range of analogues not only in literature but in the preliterary materials of folklore, craft, and mythology.

As I have indicated throughout this essay, one variety of archetypal rebirth narrative seems particularly helpful in elucidating *Surfacing* and analogous texts — the Demeter/Kore story, dealing with the *Anabasis* of the daughter from the world of the dead and leading to mysteries or rituals in which initiates reenact Demeter's quest and rescue. Scholars have long recognized that the Demeter/Kore archetype and its embodiment in the Eleusinian rituals constitutes a uniquely feminine experience, in the sense that its appeal and ultimately its empowering effects are felt far more strongly by women than by men. Jane Ellen Harrison was perhaps the first to point out that the material is "almost uncontaminated by Olympian [Aryan/Patriarchal] usage" and that it derives from pre-Hellenic Thrace and Crete.[19] Jung recognizes that, although a male initiate might experience the Demeter/Kore figures as animas, they are of far greater importance as imagos representing the superordinate or fully integrated feminine personality of the woman: "The Demeter-Kore myth," he asserts, "is far too feminine to have been merely the result of an anima-projection. Although the Anima can, as we have said, experience herself in Demeter-Kore, she is yet of a wholly different nature. She is in the highest sense *femme à homme*, a man's woman, whereas Demeter-Kore exists on the plane of mother-daughter experience, which is alien to the man and shuts him out. In fact, the psychology of the Demeter cult has all the features of a matriarchal order of society, where the man is an indispensable but on the whole disturbing factor."[20] The effect of participation in the Demeter/Kore mystery, and of absorbing its underlying archetype, Jung feels, is one in which by a mutual empowering, an intermingling of the elixirs of mother and daughter, an individual achieves "a place and a meaning in the life of the generations" and, at the same time, "is rescued from her isolation and restored to wholeness. All ritual preoccupation with archetypes ultimately has this aim and this result."[21]

Women's rebirth fiction represents, it seems to me, one form of "ritual preoccupation with archetypes" having as its effect the transformation not only of the hero but of the reader. The archetypal narratives and symbols that one finds in such fiction (and which may indeed be remnants of a far more coherent tapestry than has been imagined) make of each novel a ritual experience for the reader analogous to participation in such mysteries as that enacting the Demeter/Kore narrative. The novel, and indeed all of our literature, might be defined as a literate or written-down variation on pre-literary and folk practices which are available to the reader as to the author in the realm of the unconscious, even when they have long been absent from day to day life. A woman knitter once wanted to learn to spin wool for herself, and found the directions in the handbook to spinning difficult to follow. When she actually picked up her spindle and began to wind the threads through it and to twirl it in rhythm she found that her fingers knew already what was arcane to her intellect. She coined the term "unventing" for such a rediscovery of a lost skill, through intuition, a bringing of latent knowledge out of oneself, in contrast to "invention" or creation from scratch. Following this model, I would suggest that the woman's novel is a form of "unvention," depending upon a repository of knowledge lost from the mesocosm but still available to the author and recognizable to her reader as deriving from a world with which, at some level of her inner mind, she is already familiar.

In very few instances in women's fiction do we find a hero who has been able to return to the "upper world" of the ego wholly in control of the "unvented" archetypal materials experienced in the rebirth journey. What makes *Surfacing* so unique in this genre is that the hero seems wholly transformed and wholly determined to "surface" in her full powers back into the world of culture. What has happened to her is that she has been so empowered by her fusion of spiritual or psychic and natural energies that she has brought about an implosion of her own world, a shifting of her selfhood from its stance on the margins of male society to a state of being in which her own feminine personality is central and patriarchy has itself moved to her margins. She thus transforms herself from victim to hero, turning patriarchal space inside out so that it can no longer limit her being. Although the reader does not experience the hero's return to society, her impression is that she can never be returned to a peripheral or secondary status.

In what way, then, does the novel as experienced ritual affect the reader and lead, in turn, to social change? The restorative power of women's fiction upon both the individual and her collective, it seems to me, consists in the dialectical nature of its rhetorical process. Most novels, indeed, seem to be strung upon a deadlock between contrary forces — societal and gender norms, on the one hand, and the desire of the heroes for human development, on the other — and rarely is this polarity resolved into synthesis within a given text. Even, as in the case of *Surfacing*, when the process which dialecticians describe as *aufheben* — to negate, absorb, and transcend — seems most fully carried out, the social future of the hero remains uncertain. Such texts seem to provide a description of blue and yellow and of the process by which they will become green, only to launch their messages into a color blind society. Insofar as it negates patriarchal behaviour patterns, absorbs (via the hero's coming to terms with the materials of the subconscious) social roles, and points towards a consciousness that transcends gender, the novel is a symbolic vehicle indicating a state of being which it does not in and of itself contain. It asks a question, poses a riddle, cries out for action, but remains essentially rhetorical, an artifact or ideal equation but not a mode of action. Life does not, however, consist in hypotheses or in ideas but in the affecting of society by individuals. In my hypothesis, the final element in the fictional dialectic, the synthesis, does not occur within the text but in the mind of the reader, the text being social only insofar as he or she is prepared to put the symbolic message into action. Such a relationship between fiction and its audience, or between any work of imagination and the perceiver, is comparable to the relationship between dream and dreamer. In our waking life we derive benefits from those long hours of the night spent in the world of the unconscious, where we flex our psychic muscles in the face of nightmare and vision alike. Fiction is recreational in the same sense as the dream, "made up" for essentially ethical ends, for *praxis,* and its effect is to bring us face to face with both negative experiences and visions of the good so that we may negate the one, absorb the other, and thus prepare ourselves for transcendence.

Women novelists (to put it another way) have been gathering us around campfires where they have "spooked" us with horrific lore and provided us with adventures for emulation. They have given us maps of the patriarchal battlefield and of the landscape covering our ruined subculture, and they have brought out of those ruins the lost symbols of our power. Most importantly, they have puffed up the worst aspects of the enemy so that he/she becomes laughable, a paper monster. They have strengthened us with moments of epiphany when we feel a quality rising from our depths which altogether transcends gender polarities so destructive to human life. They have dug the goddess out of our ruins and cleansed the debris from her face, casting aside the gynophobic masks hiding her power and her beneficence. In so doing, they have made of women's fiction a pathway to the authentic self, the roots of our selves before consciousness of self, and shown us the way to the healing waters of our innermost being.

CLARA THOMAS
Lady Oracle:
The Narrative
of a Fool-Heroine

Ellen Moers' study of Heroinism in *Literary Women* (1976) just preceded the publication of *Lady Oracle* and provides a splendid context for the adventures of Joan Foster. When she parted from Chuck Brewer it was not because she didn't love him. "I did, in a peculiar way, but I knew I couldn't live with him. For him, reality and fantasy were the same thing, which meant that for him there was no reality. But for me it would mean there was no fantasy, and therefore no escape."[1] Up to its very end, *Lady Oracle* is Joan Foster's own account of her unremitting exercises in heroinism — when the story is finished she is just beginning to relinquish what she calls her compulsive escape-artistry. Throughout her story what has become increasingly evident to the reader — and in flashes to Joan herself — is the self-destructive buffoonery of a Fool-Heroine.

Ellen Moers talks about Traveling Heroinism, Educating Heroinism, and Loving Heroinism, but she does not use the term Fool-Heroine, though Jane Austen's Catherine Morland, whom no one "would have supposed born to be a heroine," verges dangerously on being one. Like Austen, Margaret Atwood is gifted with a comic vision; when she wrote *Lady Oracle* she found, I believe, her true fictional métier. Her story of Joan Foster is a true comedy for our time with the Fool-Heroine at its centre and her education into individual and social responsibility its central theme. *Lady Oracle* demonstrates the idea that Suzanne Langer worked out in *Feeling and Form* (1953), of comedy as the expression of the irrepressible vitality of life, the "rhythm of fortune," and of the figure of the fool or buffoon as its central symbol.

Joan Delacourt-Foster always has longed to love and be loved, to be accepted and supported within a group, whether it be her family, the Brownie pack, her high-school class, or Arthur's anarchist friends. Her essential kindness, warmth, and decency are discernible throughout her story as the rock-solid foundations of a personality that has veered off in mad tangents from them. The pattern of the outsider and that of the buffoon were at first forced on her and then became both her defence and her revenge. When she was six years old her mother stopped taking pictures of her — "She had decided I would not do." When she was seven, both heavier and taller than other children, her mother and Miss Flegg, the dancing teacher, would not let her dance as the butterfly, but put her in a white teddy-bear suit and made her be a moth-ball instead:

> Then I danced. There were no steps to my dance, as I hadn't been taught any, so I made it up as I went along. I swung my arms, I bumped into the butterflies, I spun in circles and stamped my feet as hard as I could on the boards of the flimsy stage, until it shook. I threw myself into the part, it was a dance of rage and destruction, tears rolled down my cheeks behind the fur, the butterflies would die; my feet hurt for days afterwards (p. 47).

What Joan found out, however, was that her dance won more applause than had the butterflies'. That puzzled her and she refused to go back to dancing-school, but the experience was the first of many compensations for being forced to — and then choosing to — play the fool.

In Joan's eyes this episode is a landmark in her constant victimization by others. What is not clear to her as she writes her story, but what becomes abundantly clear to the reader, is that Joan Delacourt-Foster, child and woman, has a will of iron, as inflexible as that of any of the pale, pure Gothic heroines she later writes about, and as inflexible as that of her mother. In her relentless war with her mother, she wins all the battles: she will eat grossly, she will not diet, she will not go to boarding school, she will not go to university, she will take jobs, she will buy clothes that emphasize her grotesque size, she will leave home. "The war between myself and my mother was on in earnest; the disputed territory was my body." That such sweet revenge against her

mother could also be her own terrible loss she never realized at all
as a child and very rarely later:

> "What have I done to make you behave like this?" my mother
> cried. . . . I stomped past her up to my room, feeling quite satisfied
> with myself. But when I thought about it I had doubts. She was
> taking all the credit for herself, I was not her puppet; surely I was
> behaving like this not because of anything she had done but
> because I wanted to (p. 86).

The recital of causes that Joan weaves into her narrative does
not nearly cover their effects and this, too, is abundantly evident to
the reader. The unwanted daughter of an aggressive, insecure,
unhappy woman and a passive, guilty man does not command our
sympathy and is not meant to command our sympathy to the
extent of obscuring the freak of will and fortune that makes Joan
turn herself into a fool. It is one of the conventions of classic
comedy that the combination of character and circumstance
setting off Don Quixote on his quest or Darcy and Elizabeth
Bennet towards an eventual reconciliation of their "Pride and
Prejudice" does not and cannot adequately explain the case. As
Joan tells her story she thinks she is giving us all the data needed to
explain her past and her present; actually she is engaged in a
highly selective, self-rationalizing, and self-excusing process. A
comedy is a process towards proportion and balance, and
Atwood's purpose in the telling of Joan Foster's story is to have us
see her as irrepressibly in process, not as an irreversibly fated
product either of heredity or of environment.

The timing of Joan's telling of her story is important to its
meaning and effect. It seems to move along in incidents and
memory contemporaneously to her arrival and stay in Terremoto
after her fake suicide. Actually, however, as the first paragraph
indicates, it is all remembered after the arrival of the letter from
Sam's lawyer when she finds out that Sam and Marlene have been
arrested for murder:

> I planned my death carefully; unlike my life, which meandered
> along from one thing to another, despite my feeble efforts to
> control it. . . . The trick was to disappear without a trace, leaving
> behind me the shadow of a corpse, a shadow everyone would
> mistake for solid reality. *At first I thought I'd managed it* (p. 3).

The subsequent story that we read must be substantially the same
as the one that Joan told to the reporter who found her after she

made her final, panic-stricken bid for freedom and an indulgence that would relieve her from living with her past's reality: "I talked too much, of course, but I was feeling nervous. I guess it will make a pretty weird story, once he has written it; and the odd thing is that I didn't tell any lies. Well, not very many. Some of the names and a few other things, but nothing major."

Joan's narrative is set down in a five-part structure with the first and last parts, each of about thirty pages, framing the interior three (91, 65, and 116 pages). Part I establishes Joan and all her mysteries. All the questions are raised and left unanswered; a reader's curiosity, already aroused by the first words, "I planned my death carefully," is teased on by a further and complicating series of questions. To the "why" of the faked death is speedily added the "who" of a galaxy of characters headed by Arthur:

> There in front of me, across an immense stretch of blue which I recognized as the Atlantic Ocean, was everyone I had left on the other side. . . . Arthur was the nearest; behind him was the Royal Porcupine, otherwise known as Chuck Brewer, in his long, pretentious cape; then Sam and Marlene and the others. Leda Sprott fluttered like a bedsheet off to one side, and I could see Fraser Buchanan's leather-patched elbow sticking out from where he lurked behind a seaside bush. Further back, my mother, wearing a navy-blue suit and a white hat, my father indistinct by her side; and my aunt Lou . . . (p. 5).

Arthur is the nearest; earlier in the paragraph Joan has called him both "lanky, uncertain, stoney-faced, rescue-minded . . . not knowing whether I would be there or not." Chuck Brewer, aside from the preposterous title, "the Royal Porcupine," is linked to the adjective pretentious. Leda Sprott flutters and Fraser Buchanan lurks. Her father is indistinct and her mother is a female cipher, symbolized by the utter conventionality of her clothing, a navy-blue suit and a white hat. This is Joan's cast and among them only Aunt Lou seems to be refusing to play in Joan's drama, not looking at her, "marching along the beach, taking deep breaths and admiring the waves and stopping every now and then to empty the sand out of her shoes." Then, to her dismay, Joan realizes that these imagined people are waving at each other and not at her; they are not centering their attention on the proper heroine of her drama — herself.

Joan Foster, "celebrated author of *Lady Oracle*, looking like a lush Rossetti portrait, radiating intensity, hypnotized the

audience with her unearthly . . . (The Toronto Star)," is added to
the accumulation of mysteries, as is, finally, her other persona,
Louisa K. Delacourt, the secret author of Costume Gothics. Like
Joan herself, Charlotte, the heroine of *Stalked by Love,* her current
opus, is presented *in medias res,* alone in an alien and probably
hostile environment. Joan finds that the first eight pages of her
manuscript are missing — "It wouldn't be too difficult to recon-
struct the opening pages." Joan's subsequent story of her life is the
reconstruction of her own opening pages, a major, lengthy, and
intermittently painful exercise, far different from her easy plan for
the filling in of Charlotte's first pages. In fact as Joan progresses
with her own narrative and it becomes more painful to her, the
parallel story of Charlotte becomes more and more intractable as
well, until finally the two stories merge in a nightmarish fantasy,
just before the reporter knocks on Joan's door: "the flesh fell away
from his face, revealing the skull behind it; he stepped towards her,
reaching for her throat. . . ."

Joan's opening scenario in Part 1 also establishes her as a
vulnerable, lonely, insecure, disaster-prone, and self-berating
young woman. Anything will trigger her imagination into fantasies, but they very quickly turn back on herself. The balcony of
her apartment suggests a dark stranger climbing towards her, but
that stranger is replaced by Arthur, who "would rather crunch
than climb," and then by a great crying fit made more painful
because of Joan's self-mockery: "I snorted, my eyes turned the
colour and shape of cooked tomatoes, my nose ran . . . the grief was
always real but it came out as a burlesque of grief" (p. 6).

Her faked suicide plan has seemed to work perfectly thus far,
but now she is beset by doubts and regrets. She is lonely for Arthur,
who was in Terremoto with her the year before; she will be recognized and found out:

> "It was my own stupidity, my own fault. I should have gone to
> Tunisia or the Canary Islands or even Miami Beach, on the Grey-
> hound Bus, hotel included, but I didn't have the will power; I
> needed something more familiar. A place with no handholds, no
> land marks, no past at all: that would have been too much like
> dying" (p. 7).

Joan has played a game of dying, but the thought of a touch of
reality impinging on the game terrifies her.

When she brings herself to act, she advances the "game" by
moves which put her into situations of absolute farce, which are

very funny, and situations of absolute self-delusion, which are not funny at all. The idiocy of the hair-cutting and burning episode, interrupted by Mr. Vitrioni and his "neon Coliseum" painting is one of the funniest vignettes in Canadian literature, matched only in its hair-category by the classic "scrape" of Anne of Green Gables, when she dyes her red hair with black shoe-polish and it turns green (a further exploration of Anne, the child, and Joan, the stubbornly childish, suggests a number of other correspondences).[2] Both the hair-cutting and burning episode and the clothes-burying one which follows are sharply and ridiculously visual, an impelling invitation to identify oneself with such nonsensical strategies, to laugh hard both with Joan and at her. Such laughter is then undercut by the uneasy recognition of Joan's self-delusion:

> I climbed back up to the balcony, feeling relieved. Once I'd dyed my hair, all the obvious evidence would be taken care of and I could start being another person, a different person entirely (p. 16).

Joan is obsessed with thoughts of Arthur. She would like to change the past: "That was the one thing I really wanted to do. Nostalgia convulsed me." But she has absolutely no confidence in herself. She also does not notice the contradiction between wanting to change the past and wanting to treasure it in nostalgia. She wants to let Arthur know how clever she has been in carrying out her plan: "I always wanted to do something he would admire." Arthur has never known about her Costume Gothics: "Why did I never tell him? It was fear mostly . . . he talked a lot about wanting a woman whose mind he could respect." As she finishes the preamble to her story she has turned her back once again on all temptations to tell Arthur the truth. Furthermore, she has successfully rationalized her constant duping of him:

> I should have trusted him more. I should have been honest from the beginning, expressed my feelings, told him everything (but if he'd known what I was really like, would he still have loved me?). . . . But it wasn't more honesty that would have saved me, I thought; it was more dishonesty. In my experience, honesty and expressing your feelings could lead to only one thing. Disaster (p. 33).

At this point Joan has recommitted herself to her old game where she is the pawn between chance and her own bizarre inventions. Parts II, III, and IV are her account of how she got to the place where she is and the way that she is.

The crying fit that followed her fantasy of Arthur and the beach-group had been triggered by her memory of Disney's film, *The Whale Who Wanted To Sing At The Met*, the story of the whale who approached the ship and sang arias, but was harpooned by the sailors. This is the clue to the central mystery set up in Part I, the one that Joan herself considers the *raison d'être* of everything else in her life. It is the story of Fat Joan and her stubborn refusal to be exorcised that Joan Foster now proceeds to tell us.

In Part II she tells the story of her life up to the time of her leaving home. For the most part this is written as a straight flashback. There are no switches in setting between her present in Terremoto and her past childhood and girlhood in Toronto. The narrative is continuous, but with references to Arthur that not only tie it to Part I, but also point beyond it to the central place of Arthur among Joan's many mysteries: "That was one reason I never told Arthur much about my mother," or, "As Arthur pointed out more than once, my politics were sloppy," or, "I knew how Arthur would analyse this fantasy." Essentially, however, Part II is a self-contained story, a drama told by Joan herself, the story of and her explanation of the appearance and disappearance of Fat Joan. It rises to a climax with Aunt Lou's death and its dénouement is Joan's weight-losing exercise, culminating in her final scene with her mother and her leaving home.

Throughout this narrative Joan swings back and forth between self-pity and self-mockery. She thinks of herself as a victim and the "pity the unwanted child" tone is very strong, but she also sees and shows herself to be ridiculous as well as pathetic. Fat Joan made herself into a clown-fool with her size, the garish clothes she bought to emphasize her size, and her various adventures in the process of trying to make friends and gain affection. Then everyone began to see her as a clown (except her mother, who saw her as a tragic grotesque). The Fat Lady role became expected of her, then the only one that was acceptable to others, and, finally, the only one that was possible for her to play:

> As for the Fat Lady, I knew perfectly well that after her death-defying feat she had to return to the freak show, to sit in her oversized chair with her knitting and be gaped at by the ticket-buyers. That was her real life (p. 102).

Joan's pain had been real and her understanding of others' pain had grown as a compensating impulse in her. She had been and still is a basically kind human being. But the misery of Fat Joan's early life and her resentment of that misery had made her see her mother first and then life itself as her adversary and had carried over into her actions and attitudes long after Fat Joan had vanished. One of the interpolations about Arthur made in the narrative of Part II makes clear the legacy of pain and resentment that she still bears and that still holds her back to Fat Joan's past:

> As Arthur pointed out more than once, my politics were sloppy.... What he didn't know was that behind my compassionate smile was a set of tightly clenched teeth, and behind that a legion of voices, crying, *What about me? What about my own pain? When is it my turn?* But I've learnt to stifle these voices, to be calm and receptive (p. 90).

One effect of her past that begins to come strongly to the fore in Joan's telling of Part II is that of the designating of all the people whom she has known as fools together. When she says, "Sometimes I was afraid I wasn't really there, I was an accident; I'd heard her call me an accident," the roots of Joan's devaluation of herself are clarified for us; so, however, is the effect of that self-devaluation, her inability to see anyone at all outside the context of her own lopsided scenario. Psychologically, the basis of her problem is completely understandable: her mother's attitudes to her deprived her of any sense of her own worth. Therefore, with her worthless self at the centre of her universe, she is quite unable to believe in anyone else's individual worth and dignity.

Only two people in Joan's early story took her with complete seriousness — her mother, who was her first and constant adversary, and Aunt Lou, who was her ally. Her mother is painted into her story not as a woman, but as a fetish or witch-doll, as grotesque with her frustrated ambitions, restlessness, dissatisfaction with Joan and her father, and obsessive, sterile neatness as the terrifying three-headed mask she became whenever Joan remembered her at her make-up mirror. Aunt Lou, by contrast, is given her full human dimensions, but while their total presents a woman who is warm and affectionate, they also show that Aunt Lou is as much an outsider in her way as is Fat Joan. Though her affection was the one constant, undemanding element in Joan's life, her effect on Joan was as ambiguous as her remembered words, which always might be taken to mean several different things. She provided a warmth that Joan desperately needed, but she also encouraged her escape into movie or opera fantasies so that Joan was led further away from, not towards, the actualities of her self-willed outsiderdom.

In death, however, Aunt Lou had an enormous and a positive effect on Joan: the loss of the one person on whom she could depend for easy acceptance, together with the promised inheritance of two thousand dollars as soon as she had lost a hundred pounds, propelled her into a reformulation of herself that made her abandon the battle with her mother as the lodestone of her life and substituted for it the goal of transformation into Thin Joan and then escape:

> "Where do you find them?" she sobbed. "You're doing it on purpose. If I looked like you I'd hide in the cellar." I'd waited a long time for that. She who cries first is lost. "You've been drinking," I said, which was true. For the first time in my life I experienced, consciously, the joy of self-righteous recrimination   (p. 86).

At the end of Part II, Joan has moved from her defensive, passive, adversary role into temporary aggressive action with regard to her own life. Part III describes her early days of action; then her relapse into her old familiar role of victim; then the central complication of the story she is telling us, her falling in love with Arthur and the various deceptions she practiced on him, partly through her absolute lack of confidence in herself and partly because of her defensive dependence on fantasy. One hundred pounds lighter and two thousand dollars richer, Joan moved to England, but though Fat Joan had physically disappeared, her attitudes and her insecurities were still all Joan Foster knew. The battle with her mother was over, she thought, but it was the only way of life she knew and since she had always thought of herself as a victim, she moved into a kind of play-victim, imprisoned-heroine role with the Polish Count. She also discovered her talent for the easy writing of Costume Gothics and these became an extension, rationalization, and romanticizing of her own situation. Just as the play threatened to become serious, when Joan was becoming a little frightened of Paul's jealousy and his gun, she met Arthur. As with Paul, chance arranged their meeting, but a combination of Joan's need and her pre-conditioning determined her reactions and the outcome of their meeting. One day she simply moved in with Arthur and his friends, telling her version of an orphan-in-the-storm tale to ensure her welcome: "I've been evicted. . . . Because of my political sympathies." . . . "Oh," said Arthur, "Well, in that case." . . . "I was a political refugee."

The narrative technique of Part III is crucial to the success of *Lady Oracle*. On the one hand Atwood is involving us more and more closely with a narrator we must care about, whose adventures, misbegotten or hilarious, must be read with some acceptance of Joan's own logic about them. On the other hand it is also essential for the reader to retain the detachment required by comedy. To be fully appreciated Joan must be recognized as both self-deluded and distinctly unreliable as the narrator of her own dealings with others. Unlike Part II, a continuous flash-back with a few intermittent references to Arthur, Part III begins with a continuation of *Stalked By Love*, the unfinished story of Charlotte, Felicia, and Redmond, which Joan had brought with her to Terremoto. Initially, then, we find ourselves back in Terremoto with the present, post-suicide Joan. Her account of her life after leaving home is touched off by loneliness when she goes to Rome for a typewriter and some hair-dye and remembers Arthur and herself together there the year before. As in Part I, the sense of Arthur's physical distance from her sets off her tears, so in Part III the same sense of separation sets off her account of their story. In both cases self-dramatizing and sentimental nostalgia for the past are activating forces. Joan copes in a random way with the present, but she yearns for the past, even a bad past. Her sense of a possible future, beyond day to day extemporizing, is non-existent:

> Arthur had been with me, he wasn't with me now, we had been walking along a street like this once and then the future swept over us and we were separated. He was in the distance now, across the ocean on a beach, the wind ruffling his hair, I could hardly see his features. He was moving at an ever-increasing speed away from me, into the land of the dead, the dead past, irretrievable (pp. 133-34).

As Joan tells her story of Arthur she also comments on the story and thus leads on to other essential episodes in her narrative: "I never told Arthur about Paul, which was perhaps a mistake;" or "If Arthur had known about my little dramatisation of Lord Russell, he would've been appalled." Sometimes she wonders about her own crucial mistakes, and certainly the reader comes more and more to consider Arthur as the central pivot in her present, just as her mother was in her past, and to recognize the irreversible train of events that were set in motion by their meeting and Joan's self-protecting deceptions. Furthermore, we also see that Joan was still tied to her old adversary-role with her mother;

her mother's spectral visit to Arthur's apartment terrified her, but still, when she heard of her death she left Arthur to go back home to Toronto.

Joan's story in Part III is framed by her trip to Rome. It ends with two converging lines of action in apparently irreconcilable tension. On the one hand the faked suicide seemed to have worked. Joan had received Sam's coded message indicating success: "Relief flooded through me, I was really free now." On the other hand her heroine, Charlotte, is in desperate peril, "drawn towards the maze, irresistibly, against her will, yet she knew if she went in, something terrible would happen to her." Joan, hearing footsteps outside her balcony, is likewise terrified: "I am not afraid of you. I don't trust you. . . . Our love is impossible. I will be yours forever. I am afraid." To go on with her story, Joan too has to enter a maze, the bewildering complex that her own choices have created. Understandably, she is terrified. When she gets to its centre all the part-Joans, the Fool Joans, are going to be stripped away and only the unknown, essential Joan Foster will be left to take on the responsibilities of her own life and actions.

Part IV begins with the immediate continuation of Charlotte, Felicia, and Redmond's crisis-situation in *Stalked by Love* and by the confirmation of Charlotte's (and Joan's) terror. It breaks away into the book's third nostalgic, tear-laden recalling of Arthur, his finding her in Toronto, their marriage, and all the bizarre escapades that led up to her faked suicide and her arrival in Terremoto. This is the section of *Lady Oracle* that is most superficially memorable and that, because of its kaleidoscopic colour and event, has obscured for some reviewers and critics what is going on in the story as a whole. In it Joan's choices, past and present, erupt into a surreal circus of people and events, with Arthur and herself supposedly at the centre, but dimming and dulling by contrast to the Royal Porcupine and Lady Oracle. The affect of this section of the book is enhanced by Atwood's skill with Toronto's settings and, especially, with the sleazy trapping of the *avant-garde* world she portrays: the muddled-headed reforming zeal of Arthur, Sam, and Marlene; the flaunting exhibitionism and the idiotic but endearing childishness of Chuck Brewer, the Royal Porcupine; the malicious journalistic blackmail of Fraser Buchanan; the publicity and market-crazy media world; and the total disproportion of response between the *Lady Oracle* poems and the adulation of their author and Joan's ostensibly random, unconscious composition of these poems.

As she tells her story in Part IV, Joan still sees herself as a largely passive victim. Increasingly, however, the web of her self-rationalizing argument breaks down; increasingly the fabric of her narrative fragments into contradicting pieces; and increasingly as her fear grows, so does her realization that she has made a vast muddle of her life and that she must take the responsibility of restoring it to some kind of order. It was Arthur's decision to get married, but it was Joan's decision to keep her identity as Joan Delacourt a secret from him. The *Lady Oracle* poems were supposed to be the chance outcome of an automatic writing experiment and this, in turn, the outcome of a writing-block in one of her Costume Gothics. However, as she reveals, she did work on the poems and she did send them to, not only one publisher, but two: "I would stare at the words, trying to make sense of them; I would look them up in Roget's Thesaurus, and most of the time, other words would fill in around them."

She has not confronted crises, she has extemporized responses to them. When Sam and Marlene embarked on their crazy dynamiting scheme because of a thoughtless remark of hers, she did not openly refuse to help, but secretly she foiled them. She said that she did not mean to go home with the Royal Porcupine, but she could not refuse to help him carry home a dead dog and so, once at his apartment, they made love. She hated and still hates her ensuing further deceit of Arthur, but she could not bear to give up the acted-out fantasies of her adventures with the Royal Porcupine. She says that she did not mean to tell the truth about her *Lady Oracle* poems to her interviewer, but she did tell him about their genesis in automatic writing and so created a sensation. She shows herself to be still locked into her Fool-Heroine role, craving attention as avidly as did the mothball among the butterflies. Even Fraser Buchanan's blackmail was better than no attention at all. She pretended to come to terms with his demands, but she also foiled him by stealing his black notebook. In certain moments of crisis, however, she was incapacitated and her weird tricks and deceptions were excused, rationalized to herself by the fantasized return of Fat Joan:

> Wads of fat sprouted on my thighs and shoulders, my belly bulged out like a Hubbard squash, a brown wool beret popped through my scalp, bloomers coated my panic-stricken loins. Tears swelled behind my eyes. Like a virus meeting an exhausted throat, my dormant past burst into rank life   (p. 231).

The remembering Joan, in Terremoto, is still mocking herself
with all this descriptive grotesquerie, but she is also still indulging
herself in her old refuge from all responsibility, the lost but still
hovering figure of Fat Joan.

Twice in Part IV through the words of others Joan reveals
herself being pushed towards her own responsibilities. Leda
Sprott (Eunice Revele) lectured her about her gift, her "great
powers," and climaxed her lecture with both criticism and
warning:

> "People have faith in you," Leda said. "They trust you. That can
> be dangerous, especially if you take advantage of it. Everything
> catches up to you sooner or later. You should stop feeling so sorry
> for yourself. . . . Don't say what you don't mean," she said irritably.
> "You do enough of that already" (p. 207).

Chuck Brewer's speech, when he dropped the Royal Porcupine
role and wanted her to marry him, got through to her as well:
"That's the trouble with you, you have no motives. You're like an
out-of-control school bus."

Part IV ends with the inextricable tangling of all Joan's roles
and responsibilities propelling her into her final ruse to escape
both her past and her present in the faked suicide. "I was safe," the
final words of this section, bring us round again to the first part of
her narrative, her arrival in Terremoto and the speedy dispelling
of that illusion of safety. The narrative of Part V carries on with
Joan's growing sense of imminent danger, but also with a series of
self-revelations which began to free her from fear.

She has a final spectral vision of her mother whom she now
recognizes as the tragic lady of the *Lady Oracle* poems:

> She'd never really let go of me because I have never let her go. . . .
> My mother was a vortex, a dark vacuum, I would never be able to
> make her happy. Or anyone else. Maybe it was time for me to stop
> trying (p. 331).

She also recognizes that she has always made traps for herself and
then exercised her ingenuity in getting out of them. She has,
however, begun to stop immobilizing herself through guilt. She
has begun to find and accept herself, not as a shadowy fantasy-
being who both detests her past and yearns for it, but as a clearly-
regarded "I" who is moving into a future:

> I might as well face it, I thought, I was an artist, an escape artist.
> I'd sometimes talked about love and commitment, but the real

> romance of my life was that between Houdini and his ropes and locked trunk; entering the embrace of bondage, slithering out again. . . . this thought did not depress me. . . . I washed my hair, humming, as if I were getting ready for a big evening. A lot of the brown came out, but I no longer cared. . . . From now on, I thought, I would dance for no one but myself   (p. 335).

From now on she is really playing with her fears. Though she has determined to make one more final and successful escape, when she gets the letter from Sam's lawyer she knows that she must go back home. As she hides, waiting for the expected intruder to arrive, she is more bored than fearful: "I began to be restless. It struck me that I'd spent too much of my life crouching behind closed doors, listening to the voices on the other side." Finally, in the last sequence of *Stalked By Love*, Felicia and all the Joans, including Fat Joan, converge, caught in the centre of the maze together and menaced by Redmond, who becomes a death's head. Joan's past, and her past selves, still beckon and threaten her, but now that she recognizes them as her own self-devised "embraces of bondage" she can also recognize and act in her own area of choice. When the intruder's knock does come on her door, she chooses the future, now knowing and accepting that it will contain her past and her present as well:

> I still had options. I could pretend I wasn't there. I could wait and do nothing. I could disguise my voice and say I was someone else. But if I turned the handle the door would unlock and swing outward, and I would have to face the man who stood waiting for me, for my life. I opened the door   (p. 343).

Joan did not rid herself of her past by her faked suicide, but she did engage in the process of bringing herself to real life, as it were, through telling her story. As the story ends she is having a last brief respite from the process of responsibility that she now knows she must engage in: "The first thing is to get Sam and Marlene out of jail, I owe it to them;" and "I'll have to see Arthur, though I am not looking forward to it;" and then, "I'll feel like an idiot with all the publicity, but that's nothing new;" "I won't write any more Costume Gothics, though; I think they were bad for me." The reporter, her discoverer, has promised not to give her away for a week; meanwhile she walks to the hospital everyday to visit him: "I've begun to feel that he is the only person who knows anything about me. Maybe because I've never hit anyone else with a bottle, so they never got to see that part of me. Neither did I, come to think of it." And finally, "It did make a mess; but then, I don't think I'll ever be a very tidy person." At the end Joan is triumphantly herself, still irrepressibly adventuring and in process. When she says, "I keep feeling I should have learnt some lesson out of all this, as my mother would have said," the reader already knows that she has — she has chosen to accept her responsibilities, preeminently the responsibility of her own life. In Joan's mother's world, however, to learn a lesson was indistinguishable from accepting a punishment. This conception of guilt Joan has finally and successfully resisted. In her mother's world to be tidy was to be good — Joan is not tidy, nor will she ever be; nor, most important, will she allow herself to be inundated by guilt and fear because she is not.

To write thus about the meaning or, heaven forbid, the "message" of *Lady Oracle* is very like the moth-ball stamping out a clumsy dance in the midst of the butterflies. For *Lady Oracle*, like all true comedies, is written with a light touch and to analyze it in other and academic language is inevitably to desecrate it. This is a funny book and we are carried along on the crests of its fun with all the buoyancy of swimming in salt water. Joan is not going to be entirely swamped by a wave and therefore we, her readers, are allowed to ride the waves with her. The most we are asked to do is to share the salt-spray — and the odd inundation in bitter brine — with her. In my experience of teaching the book, it is also one with which all women identify and which repels many men, or at best leaves them ever-so-slightly defensive, as before some mystery that they neither can nor desire to penetrate. Women students recognize themselves in Joan with the comprehension that to "escape," to leave home, is a basic impulse for women, mirrored in countless heroines' stories, just as for men the complementary impulse is signified in literature by Odysseus' dogged voyage *towards* home. When in *The Diviners* Morag Gunn tells Val Tonnerre that Wolfe's *You Can't Go Home Again* is a mistaken title, for, try as we will, our Manawakas never leave us, she is illustrating as clearly as possible these contrasting urges in men and women and the contrasting literary patterns for heroines and heroes that express them. Like Morag, Joan Foster has to learn that, while the past will always be a part of her, it need not and must not be either prison or refuge.

Women students also recognize and share in the misadventures of Joan in a kind of joyful release as in a laughing sisterhood of buffoons. Men students seem often to believe that certain of

Joan's adventures are overdrawn beyond credibility — the cutting off of her hair, for instance, and being caught in the act of trying to burn it; the burying of her jeans and T-shirt and the landlord's ceremonial presentation of them to her, all carefully washed and ironed, a hilarious, stubborn Nemesis. All women have had ridiculous experiences comparable to these; we seem to have been educated from childhood in what Carlyle called "the horrible animosity of inanimate objects" and the sense of recognition and expectation that events will from time to time make fools out of us makes us easy and eager sharers of Joan Foster's dilemmas. Men, at least many male students, seem to live with the expectation of an intact personal dignity and they feel embarrassed and obscurely offended by Joan's constant pratfalls. Women students laugh with, not at, her; her misadventures are too close for condescension, too recognisable as our own writ large, and they bond us to her with laughter.

There is another important factor beyond the male-female differentiation which somewhat obscured the impact of *Lady Oracle* when it was published. It was not what readers and critics expected from Margaret Atwood and, even more important, it was not what they expected of a major Canadian novel at this time. In her earlier prose works, Atwood was fulfilling Flannery O'Connor's dictum — "For the blind you draw large pictures; for the hard-of-hearing you shout." *The Edible Woman* was unmistakeably satire and *Surfacing* was melodrama, the *angst* of its heroine and its message of personal and environmental waste and pollution both arousing and alleviating the matching guilts and anxieties of its readers. *Survival* is essentially a self-help manual, its exhortations pounded in by means of a fast-paced and often very funny theme-study of Canadian literature. But the balance of comedy, at the same time quieter, deeper, and more comprehensive in its implications than any specific Canadian here and now, is more subtle, unexpected, and, therefore, more easily missed or dismissed. Like Hugh Hood's *The Swing In The Garden*, another comedy which has been inadequately treated by critics, *Lady Oracle* has not been compatible to our contemporary mood of urgent and self-conscious literary nationalism. In an article "Theatre, Self, and Society: Some Analogues," Robert Heilman has recently written:

> Comedy does not so much hope for better things as it assumes
> the presence of some good things; it does not so much castigate

faulty actuality as it assumes imperfection to be insuperable but endurable. It does not endeavour to destroy evil and render good omnipotent; it has a healthy respect for the survival value of original sin, but likewise for the human talent to make adequate, if only partial and temporary, escapes from total sinfulness. In the comic way of life, "the moral sense" often manifests itself as good sense, and good sense has, at least in the long run, a slightly better than even chance against nonsense, dimwittedness, irrationality, and the perversities of calculation and studiously thoughtless self-gratification.[3]

Like Susanna Moodie, whose characterized Susanna is at many points in her story the great progenitor of Fool-Heroines in our literature, Margaret Atwood shows Joan Foster moving stage by stage through a slow, hilarious, painful, and ultimately reassuring process towards a personhood which will incorporate its necessary component of good sense.

ROBERT LECKER

Janus through the Looking Glass:

Atwood's First Three Novels

I enter with you
and become a mirror.[1]

At one point in *Lady Oracle* Joan Foster pauses to reflect that her
affair with the Royal Porcupine marked "the beginning of my
double life."[2] Then she wonders: "But hadn't my life always been
double? There was always that shadowy twin, thin when I was fat,
fat when I was thin . . ." (*LO*, p. 246). Finally, she admits that "I
was more than double, I was triple, multiple, and now I could see
that there was more than one life to come, there were many" (*LO*,
p. 246). Joan's words direct us to the duplicitous nature of the
novel as a whole. *Lady Oracle* is not only full of the mirrors,
masks, and masquerades which dress up Joan's Janus-like perceptions, but of reduplicating interior narratives which enclose us in
their shared distortions as well. Joan does not find identity, nor
does she surface to survive. Rather, the end of *Lady Oracle* returns
us to its beginning, and to yet another version of Joan's celebrated
ability to be many people, and to speak in many tongues, all at
once. The circular structure of the narrative also implies that the
concept of self-identity, traditionally associated with narrative
resolution, has become a sham; the multi-vocal heroine gives us
her fragmented visions of modern life.

    If it is true that the final "message" of this novel which
parodies the motifs and conventions associated with the search for
self is ironic, that irony may also constitute an implicit comment

on Atwood's previous fiction, and provide further confirmation of Eli Mandel's notion that Atwood tends to create self-reflexive works which comment on each other.[3] The duplicity of *Lady Oracle* and Lady Oracle suggests that all of Atwood's fiction may be read as an expression of the need to see truth as a shifting construct, or as a series of — to use the title of one of Atwood's poems — tricks with mirrors. After all, does *The Edible Woman* really end with an affirmation of Marian MacAlpin's singular identity, or does the resolution remain ambiguous, indicating that, like Joan in *Lady Oracle*, Marian is a composite of confused personae? Does the unnamed narrator of *Surfacing* really transcend the past to find new meaning in the present, or is she, again like Joan, caught in a costume-room realm between roles and tenses, on a stage where "façades were at least as truthful" as "passionate revelation scenes" (*LO*, p. 197) and where "Every myth is a version of the truth" (*LO*, p. 92)? The strength of Atwood's novels may well be the result of the permeating sense of irony and ambivalence which they evoke, both in terms of structure and characterization. This ambivalence is often overlooked because of the theories advanced in *Survival* — theories which to many have suggested that Atwood's heroines can only survive by becoming something other than what they were (victor rather than victim, hunter rather than prey).

I

> If the head extended directly into the shoulders like a worm's or a frog's without that constriction, that lie, they wouldn't be able to look down at their bodies and move them around as if they were robots or puppets; they would have to realize that if the head is detached from the body both of them will die. (*S*, p. 76).

In his introduction to *The Edible Woman* Alan Dawe comes close to identifying the novel's two-sidedness when he writes that the ending is "ambiguous but somehow triumphant."[4] It might be more accurate to say that Marian MacAlpin's story is triumphant *because* it is ambiguous, not only in its ending, but from the start. Yet the book has usually been seen in terms of contrasts which are manifested as the choices with which Marian is confronted: she must be either a victor or a victim, either consumer or consumed; she must speak either in the self-affirming voice of the first person, or in the disembodied voice of the third.

At first, the three-part structure of the book seems to confirm the presence of these choices and distinctions. We meet Marian as an "I" in Part I. In Part II the "I" is replaced by "she" as Marian ostensibly becomes the packaged product of a male-dominated corporate society which thrives on clichés and stereotypes. In Part III, the first person voice returns as Marian rejects her role as prey, transcends her role as product, and consumes her disembodied self as she confirms her new identity. Or so we have been told. From this perspective, the cake which Marian finally bakes and eats is seen as symbolic evidence of her development, and of her ultimate refusal to be a victim. As Frank Davey has observed, however, a reader is likely to accept this viewpoint "not because of the clarity of the symbolism but only because such an interpretation *seems* consistent with the rest of the novel. . . . "[5]

But that interpretation is not consistent at all. Marian seems to stop eating for two reasons: a) because her job with an advertising research agency has led her to reject the artificial forms of sustenance provided by an artificial society, and b) because she equates the consumption of food with her feeling that she has been assimilated and exploited as a female object. Yet the end of the novel depicts her as partaking in the very metaphor of eating which was originally seen as taboo. Moreover, by symbolically offering the cake to Duncan and Peter (and by eating it herself) Marian re-enacts her female as food role. Ainsley is therefore quite correct to argue that "You're rejecting your femininity!" (*EW*, p. 272) while Duncan pinpoints the irony of Marian's fate when he says that "you're back to so-called reality, you're a consumer" (*EW*, p. 281). Duncan's words suggest that Marian's plight is not resolved, and that the plot of *The Edible Woman* is metaphorically circular. Duncan also implies that Marian's story is like a series of plays in which each actor eventually gets to experience every part: "One of us has to be the sympathetic listener and the other one gets to be tortured and confused. You were tortured and confused last time" (*EW*, p. 278). Sometimes, Duncan notes, the role-playing itself becomes deceptive: "Peter wasn't trying to destroy you. That's just something you made up. Actually you were trying to destroy him" (*EW*, p. 280). At this point, Marian begins to wonder, "Is that true?" and her question allows Duncan to provide an answer which explains a good deal about the story: "Maybe Peter was trying to destroy me, or maybe I was trying to destroy him, or we were both trying to destroy each other . . ." (*EW*, p. 281). Maybe, or, maybe, or. The equivocations emphasize the ambivalent aspects of the novel's characters. Marian lives in a world where distinctions tend to be obliterated and the reflector and the reflected become one.

When distinctions between characters' motives become confused, it is time to examine the extent to which this confusion echoes throughout the story. And when we look at the ostensible dichotomies which make up *The Edible Woman*, we do discover that they tend to cancel each other out. In refusing to eat, for example, Marian seemingly refuses to be labelled as the victim of a system which treats people as if they were popovers (it is quite clear that Marian sees her life in terms of the synthetic, mass-market foods and commercial jingles by which she is surrounded). Fine. But as Marian's anorexia intensifies, she finds herself withdrawing from meat, eggs, and vegetables as well, and finally, she is forced to rely on vitamin pills in order to maintain her strength. The boundary between natural and synthetic begins to disintegrate, for the vitamin pills represent the ultimate replacement for real foods. Or, as T.D. MacLulich puts it, "Marian is using the products of the consumer society to sustain a rebellion which is ostensibly directed against that very society."[6] Paradoxically again, Marian's rejection of food is predicated on the assumption that in order to survive one must starve, and that by starving one can survive. Marian's non-eating turns into a metaphor of sustenance, and the non-eating/eating conjunction becomes an oxymoron. Marian is thriving on death as life.

If we look at what the food metaphor says about the role of women the result is much the same. Marian's rejection of food is synonymous with her rejection of a culture which tends to exploit women and treat them as edible objects. Logically, Marian's refusal to eat should lead her to discover the "natural," "real," and untainted female self which is buried somewhere in the gooey centre of a slogan sandwich. But what happens when the food is gone? Marian becomes more artificial than ever as the disembodied and calorie-reduced "she" of Part II. Only when she resumes eating does she once again become the "I" of Part III. Thus to deny the entrapments of consumer culture in favour of a more natural, non-consumer-oriented lifestyle is to discover that the natural and the culturized are identical. No wonder then that the "real world" to which Duncan refers in the book's closing pages is the same as the synthetic universe that Marian has seemingly left behind. The putative resolution of the novel begins to confirm the suspicion that, like the triple mirrors in *Lady Oracle*, the three parts of *The Edible Woman* are only reflections of each other. Marian is no more or less herself in Part III than she is in Parts I and II, and the fact that she eats a cake which symbolizes herself makes her into a mixture of consumer and consumed. So Marian dreams of dissolving or of becoming transparent (*EW*, p. 43), and in keeping with her bifocal vision, her perceptions begin to blur (*EW*, p. 44). It is also fitting that her disorienting ride in Peter's car should shake her up enough to admit that "I must have been thinking of myself as plural" (*EW*, p. 81).

This is the plurality that draws Marian into her third person existence as the ultimate female commodity, and as Peter's so-called prey. Her role as victim is first evoked through the symbolism of the "festive red dress" (*EW*, p. 219) which she wears to her engagement party in Peter's apartment. Predictably, however, the initial symbolism of the dress becomes multi-faceted. Well before Peter stalks her outside the building, Marian realizes that "She should never have worn red. It made her a perfect target" (*EW*, p. 244). Yet as she leaves the apartment, she purposefully takes off her coat to *reveal* this "perfect target," now picturing it as camouflage:

> She had to hurry. Now there was the living room to negotiate. She would have to become less visible. She took her coat back off and bundled it under her left arm, counting on her dress to act as a protective camouflage that would blend her with the scenery.
>
> (*EW*, p. 245).

The irony here is inescapable: Marian is best camouflaged at her gaudiest moment because the women at the party provide a background scene which is uniformly gaudy. When she is outside, however, the camouflage doesn't reassure. Marian begins to think of how "even now Peter might be tracing, following, stalking her through the crisp empty streets as he had stalked his guests in the living room" (*EW*, pp. 245-46), and she is reminded that "Once he pulled the trigger she would be stopped, fixed indissolubly in that gesture, that single stance, unable to move or change" (*EW*, p. 245). The red dress therefore comes to be associated not only with Marian's vision of Peter's camera as gun, but with her fear of the trigger-happy hunter who will zero in on his red-dressed victim as well.

However, the symbolism attached to the dress also transforms

Marian — two-headedly again — into a seductress, the female equivalent of the male hunter figure. Duncan sees the dress as a sign that Marian is "The Scarlet Woman herself" (*EW*, p. 247), and no sooner has he identified this role than Marian begins to play the part. Although she tells Duncan that "I had to come and find you," because "you need me" (*EW*, p. 247), it is clear that Marian has sought out Duncan with the intention of seducing him. It doesn't take him long to realize that "tonight's the night, it's now or never" (*EW*, p. 247), nor does it take Marian long to suggest that "we will have to find some sort of hotel" (*EW*, p. 248). Marian is forced to admit that "if I'm dressed like one and acting like one, why on earth shouldn't he think I really am one?" (*EW*, p. 251). Thus she appears as a cheap · prostitute — the female commodity *par excellence*. By the next morning, however, Marian and her costume seem to fall apart once more. As she heads towards the ravine with Duncan "She had a vision of the red dress disintegrating in mid-air, falling in little scraps behind her in the snow, like feathers" (*EW*, p. 260).

Are we to interpret this vision as evidence of Marian's final ability to shed her status as an exploited female object, or is it simply another sign of Marian's disintegrated identity? Marian's experience at the ravine seems to confirm her notion that "Now she knew where she was" (*EW*, p. 265) and we tend to make the assumption that now she knew *who* she was as well, and that she achieves some form of new insight which prompts her to bake the edible woman and emerge as a self-assured "I." The penultimate chapter in Part II, however, suggests that this assumption is incorrect. Although Marian would like to believe that she can shed her various disguises and become her "real" self, she must admit that her quest has failed, and that she remains as confused about the nature of her identity as she was in the beginning. Thus when Duncan observes that "I thought you were the capable type" (*EW*, p. 263), Marian can only respond equivocally: "I am,".... "I was. I don't know" (*EW*, p. 263). She also confesses that in all these last months "she hadn't been getting anywhere. And she hadn't accomplished anything" (*EW*, p. 263).

It is the frustration which this discovery engenders that drives Marian to reject Duncan and Peter in the hope that without anyone on whom to rely she will be forced to become productive by relying on herself. And so she is led back to the supermarket for food, and back into her kitchen to create the cake which symbolizes the artificiality of her existence. Marian believes that when Peter consumes the cake, his need for edible women will be satisfied and she will have effected the exorcism that will leave her uneaten and free. But Peter refuses to devour the cake, and Marian is left to consume most of it herself. She is forced to acknowledge that "As a symbol it had definitely failed" (*EW*, p. 271). By eating the symbol of her own artificiality, then, Marian only reaffirms the fact that she still thrives on artifice. In other words, she continues to be sustained by the symbol of all that she once was. That Marian's present is part of a prior state of awareness (or unawareness) is also implied by the fact that the cake-doll is a smaller version of Marian — hence a child — as well as a reminder of the two dolls with which Marian associates her own childhood. The dolls from the past seem to reflect Marian's own shifting identity. They "were staring blankly back at her from the top of the dresser. As she looked at them their faces blurred, then re-formed, faintly malevolent" (*EW*, p. 219). Marian can be the calculating, cold-blooded woman out to conquer her male foe, at the very moment that she possesses "a swift vision of her own monumental silliness, of how infantile and undignified she would seem in the eyes of any rational observer" (*EW*, p. 270). She is even willing to accommodate the thought that "if Peter found her silly she would believe it, she would accept his version of herself" (*EW*, p. 270). Later, she contemplates the dual perspective from which she has viewed Peter, and realizes that "The price of this version of reality was testing the other one" (*EW*, p. 271).

Throughout the novel, this dual perspective leads Marian to see those around her as two-sided as well. In one moment she can claim that "Peter was not the enemy after all, he was just a normal human being like most other people" (*EW*, p. 271). Within the space of half a page, however, Marian turns to this non-enemy and says "You've been trying to destroy me, haven't you" (*EW*, p. 271). In an interesting series of images, Duncan comes to embody the union of life and death, infancy and old age. Marian and Duncan are sitting in the laundromat, and, as she looks at him, Marian begins to feel "serene as a stone moon, in control of the whole white space of the laundromat" (*EW*, p. 99). With the moon in mind, Marian begins to feel like Duncan's mother: "I could have reached out effortlessly and put my arms around that huddled awkward body and consoled it, rocked it gently" (*EW*, p. 99). This picture of Duncan as babe, however, is immediately countered by the next sentence. "Still," Marian thinks, "there was something most unchildlike about him, something that suggested rather an unnaturally old man, old far beyond consolation" (*EW*, p. 99). Not surprisingly, the doubleness Marian sees in Duncan leads her to consider "his duplicity about the beer-interview," and to conclude, in a tellingly equivocal manner, that Duncan's response, "may have been real enough; but then again, it may have been calculated to evoke just such a mothering reaction . . ." (*EW*, p. 99). Here, Marian equates motherhood with her ability to control — a strange connection considering the extent to which she has previously seen Peter's control over her as an undesirable masculine trait to be avoided. Does this represent an ironic comment on the dehumanizing aspects of a contemporary culture in which the distinctions between male and female have become obsolete and unisex reigns triumphant? If we look ahead to the next important "mummy" scene involving Marian and Duncan (one which is capped by Duncan's statement that a withered mummy represents his personal "womb symbol" [*EW*, p. 187]) the confusion between male and female, death and life, becomes apparent. They are at the museum. Duncan leads Marian to the Ancient Egyptian section and shows her "my favourite mummy-case." Marian looks, and says, "She's beautiful." Duncan responds, "I think it's supposed to be a man" (*EW*, pp. 186-87).

When it becomes possible to confuse the sexes in this way some inversion of the natural order is obviously at hand. Duncan proceeds to show Marian another mummy that was shrivelled enough to resemble a child: "it was a skeleton, still covered in places with skin, lying on its side with its knees drawn up" (*EW*, p. 188). Soon, Marian is seeing the shrunken mummy "with its jutting ribs and frail legs and starved shoulder-blades" as a rendition of Duncan, who is, we recall, "cadaverously thin" (*EW*, p. 48), and he feels the need to assure her that "I'm not going to return from the tomb" (*EW*, p. 188). The childlike Duncan of the laundromat turns into an old man, but, as the museum scene suggests, he is also one of the "living dead" figures which appear in so many horror films about beings with double identities. The ramifications of the various mummy incidents in *The Edible Woman* do not stop here, for when Marian looks at the shrivelled mummy as child, she is also looking at the emaciated, shrunken body of her starved-to-death self. Equally, the shrunken mummy represents a foetus with "its knees drawn up," and so foreshadows the "foetal position" (*EW*, p. 254) which Marian later assumes in the hotel with Duncan. Finally, the relationship between the large mummy (which appears to be androgynous) and the small mummy (which is mother, child, and foetus) corresponds to the relationship between Marian (who confuses sex roles) and the cake-doll (which represents Marian as mummy, child, and self-impregnated woman). In Marian's world, the fact that people can be simultaneously old and young, mother and child, dead and alive, reaffirms the notion that there is no final sense of definition and that Marian's existence can only be defined in terms of duplicity.

Duncan's observations on the final page of the novel serve as a pointed reminder of this role-blending, as do Marian's thoughts and actions. In the end, she derives "a peculiar sense of satisfaction" (*EW*, p. 281) from watching Duncan eat the cake. The satisfaction is peculiar because in offering Duncan the cake, Marian does more than offer up a symbol of her artificial self; she simultaneously affirms her role as the great little woman of the Swanson T.V. Dinner advertisements who is defined by her ability to provide her great big man with food. "I like to cook when I have the time" (*EW*, p. 281), Marian says as she confirms the stereotype and Duncan swallows the cake's remaining "one eye." When we realize that the "eye" is the symbolic equivalent of Marian's one "I," the puzzling nature of her final act of self-observation becomes consistent with the double-edged nature of the narrative. "I smiled comfortably at him," we are told as Marian watches Duncan devouring the "I" who has turned into an other.

Now it is one thing to say that the novel's ending is consistent only in so far as it confirms the larger inconsistencies of the novel, but the question remains: why the sustained ambivalence and confusion? On one level, Atwood seems intent on suggesting that people aren't what they think they are, and that (to echo Flannery O'Connor once again) everything that rises must eventually converge. *The Edible Woman* is often seen as a contemporary comedy of manners — as a satire on modern society. But comedies of manners in general are by no means as straightforward as they might at first appear to be. The genre, it should be remembered, reached its peak in Restoration comedy which purposefully incorporated motifs of disguise, duplicity, mistaken identity, and mistaken sexual identity. Moreover, comedies of manners offer, in the final analysis, a depressing vision of life which depicts men as the propagators and victims of corruption, vice, avarice, lust, and greed. It is in the debased, alienated lifestyle of the secular world that the comedy of manners character remains caught, and all that he can do is to delude himself into believing that his own debasement is a form of freedom. Marian MacAlpin is not debased; she is not even immoral. But she does participate in a comedy of manners which comments tragically on a contemporary world in which even the semblance of identity has disappeared and men (and women) are seen only as faceless non-entities in a zombified crowd. In such a world, the hope that one can find one's "true identity" can only lead to the "sinking feeling" which plagues Marian at the end of *The Edible Woman.*

II

> It was my subconscious getting ahead of my conscious self, and the subconscious has its own logic. The way I went about doing things may have been a little inconsistent with my true personality, but are the results that inconsistent? (*EW*, p. 101)

Like Marian, the unnamed narrator of Atwood's second novel lives in an ambivalent world in which apparent distinctions tend to cancel each other out. Although the final pages of *Surfacing* bring the narrator full circle back to an uncertain beginning, and although the ending is shot through with irony, many critics have argued that the heroine emerges transformed from a descent into primeval, preconscious awareness as a reborn woman who has discovered identity, meaning, and purpose. Only Eli Mandel and Rosemary Sullivan have observed that *Surfacing* may actually work toward negating plot and character development. Sullivan argues that "Atwood leaves her character in the ironic world and even though her intent seems to have been to expose the perfect circle of the mind as demonic, we end in the tautology of self."[7] Mandel puts it more bluntly: "At the end, nothing is resolved."[8] While Sullivan sees this unresolved ending as "one of the most evasive postures of our contemporary culture,"[9] Mandel suggests that the ambiguity inherent in the novel provides the material with its haunting power. I agree. Atwood could easily have allowed the narrator to return illuminated and transformed as the new woman; she could easily have given her a name and permitted her to reject the artificial, culture-bound aspects of her previous existence. Such epiphanies are *de rigueur* in literature which traces the development of alienated consciousness. But life, as the saying goes, is not always like that. Atwood chooses to send her character down the much more perilous and authentic path between nature and culture, an ambiguous path which she follows from the beginning of the novel.

To begin with the closing pages, we find the narrator asserting that she must "refuse to be a victim" (S, p. 191). The statement appears to constitute a final realization. But does the refusal really arise from any new sense of clarity? Just before the narrator contemplates her refusal to be victimized she admits that "from now on I'll have to live in the *usual* way" (S, p. 189 — emphasis added), and the "usual way" for her is to be confused about who she is. "I turn the mirror around," she tells us, and "in it there's a creature neither animal nor human" (S, p. 190). Neither/nor. She no longer wants to be the animal woman whose "lips move by themselves. This," she senses, "was the stereotype . . . talking nonsense or not talking at all" (S, p. 190). She knows that the "natural woman" in modern life is inseparable from culture's torso, the "tanned body on a beach with washed hair waving like scarves" (S, p. 190). The woman with "skin grimed and scabby" will be seen as nothing but a new social commodity, "A new kind of centrefold" (S, p. 190).

Centrefold. Pinned in the middle. By surfacing, the narrator only returns to the beach to take her place among the sunbathers; if she remains submerged, she will be defined in terms of the back-to-nature cliché provided by the very world from which she is ostensibly trying to escape. You have them both at once. And so when the narrator emerges in the last chapter of the book, her action announces that she has simultaneously become submerged. No wonder then that her perceptions tend to embody this duality as they mediate between extremes. She sees Joe as a kind of tightrope walker, "balancing on the dock which is neither land nor water" (S, p. 192), and she understands that "he is only half-formed, and for that reason I can trust him" (S, p. 192). But then again, she thinks, "he may have been sent as a trick," or he is "a mediator, an ambassador" who offers "captivity in any of its forms" — the same captivity which may be, paradoxically, "a new freedom" (S, p. 192). The ambiguity which the narrator finds in Joe at the end of *Surfacing* only confirms her continuing existence in a world where definition has been lost. Joe isn't one thing or the other, "he isn't anything." And what of the embryonic "time-traveller, the primaeval one who will have to learn" (S, p. 191)? Is it real ("even

that is uncertain" [S, p. 191]), and if it is, will it become "the first
true human" or will it, like its mother, find that what seems most
true is a lie? True lies. As in *The Edible Woman*, oxymoron
becomes an omnipresent principle of structure. Not only at the
end of the novel, but all through *Surfacing*, the apparent binary
distinctions are obliterated. What forms do these apparent distinctions take?

To answer this question it is necessary to return briefly to the
conventional interpretation of the novel which explains the
narrator's development in terms of the opposition between culture
and nature. Culture, in the broadest sense, is the present-day urban
world of commerce and American capitalism. Nature is the past,
the backwoods realm of innocence, community, heritage. In
culture, the individual is alienated and depersonalized; in nature,
the self remains whole, supported by ancestry, ritual, and myth.
The civilized world forces its inhabitants to adopt a prevailing
linguistic code; the natural world is speechless, uncodified, and
free. On the most apparent level, the narrator is involved in a
search for her father who has mysteriously disappeared from his
cottage on a wilderness island in the northern Quebec woods. As
she leaves the city behind, the narrator gradually becomes involved
in all that nature seems to represent: she rejects her stereotypical
female role, casts off her city clothes, and retreats from language.
She descends into the past, into dream and symbol. Finally, she
discovers her dead father's body and the purgation seems to be
complete: nature triumphs and the narrator affirms her essential
female identity as she allows Joe to make love with her, in the hope
of becoming impregnated.

The usual reading. But two factors serve to call it into
question. First, the fact that the ending of the novel is inconsistent
with the narrator's ostensible affirmation of nature over culture;
second, the realization that the narrator is never really able to distinguish between the polarities in the first place because her
personality is formed by their conjunction. This conjunction
either manifests itself through the narrator's perceptions of herself
as a being who lives between spatial and temporal antitheses
(between city and county, present and past), or in terms of ironic
inversions which suggest that there no longer is any difference
between nature and culture.

It is not only the narrator's physical and psychological perceptions of herself and her environment which tend to become

blurred; the metaphorical distinctions to which she reacts are also shown to be false-fronted constructs. For example, she assumes that by finding her father she will be able to establish a link with the past, with a communal heritage that will allow her to see her present as a meaningful link in a temporal continuum. But the ancestors are gone, and when the narrator finally comes face to face with the remains of her father, the message — for us — becomes clear: ancestry is decayed, the communal figurehead is drowned, and the patriarch is unmasked as an agent of mimesis, and, by extension, as the metaphorical originator of the mirrored lifestyle from which the narrator would like to escape: "His drawings were not originals then, only copies" (S, p. 103), and copies, she later tells us while describing Joe, are the signs of "Second hand," "garbled" identities (S, p. 152). And so the wilderness cabin with which she associates her father irrevocably turns into a symbol of imprisonment. Although she believed that the cabin from the past represented stability and security ("I always felt safe here, even at night" [S, p. 73]), she is forced to admit that *"that's a lie"* (S, p. 73). The cabin is a "cage," a "wooden rectangle" full of the "tin cans and jars" (S, p. 178) which are the forbidden fruits of culture. Not surprisingly, the narrator's father wanted little to do with the idea of community. He isolated himself on an island "in the most remote lake he could find" or enclosed himself in the city "in a succession of apartments" (S, p. 59), and so managed to leave his family divided: "he split us between two anonymities, the city and the bush" (S, p. 59). This is one of the splits which leave the narrator unnamed and unable to differentiate between the waste land and the garden.

When the novel opens we find the narrator on the boundary between culture and nature as she passes "near the city limits" on her way to the north. The city presents itself both as frontier and conquered territory, "as the last or first outpost depending on which way we were going" (S, p. 7). As the car moves further north, hints accumulate to suggest that the narrator's ability to see the city limits as both disease and potential marks her own fence-sitting nature — her own two-sidedness. She recalls the question Anna had asked after she had read her palm: "'Do you have a twin?' I said No. 'Are you positive,' she said, 'because some of your lines are double'" (S, p. 8). The double lines describe the narrator's life and life to come; they point to the fact that she is defined as being between opposing temporal and spatial planes. The journey into the wilderness becomes a mediating voyage which oscillates between the narrator's interpretation of the present and her blurring memories of the past. It is in keeping with this mediated perspective that when David turns on the car radio, the narrator observes that "he couldn't get anything, we were between stations" (S, p. 10). And even when the car approaches "home ground," the identification is cancelled by the admission that home ground is "foreign territory" (S, p. 11), and by the realization that the "old road" which symbolized the past is full of "ruts and traces already blurring with grass and saplings" (S, p. 14). Finally, we reach the lake which is not only seen as "blue and cool as redemption," but also "through tears and a haze of vomit" (S, p. 15). The paradox which ends the framing chapter in a conjoined image of sickness and salvation reflects the ambivalence of the closing chapter where we find that in order to be saved the narrator must re-enter the world which she has previously identified as diseased.

Apparently, one of the signs of this disease is language. The narrator's movement away from culture is usually seen as synonymous with a rejection of the linguistic codes which embody prevailing social codes and mores. To find silence is to find freedom from a world in which everything is named, tamed, and finally dominated (particularly, as the narrator sees it, by Americans). "Language," she complains, "divides us into fragments, I wanted to be whole" (S, p. 146). Hence the narrator unnames herself and the world around her, adopting "the other language" which links her with "the animals [who] learned what to eat without nouns" (S, p. 150). She reasons that "what will preserve [Joe] is the absence of words" (S, p. 159), and she vows that her baby will remain languageless: "I will never teach it any words" (S, p. 162). At this point, however, things once again become duplicitous, for the heroine uses the first person voice to tell a story about the value of remaining wordless. She cannot help but speak about her pressing need for speechlessness. The paradox should lead us to question the motives which prompt the narrator to speak about her need to retreat from language. Does she reject language because she associates it with the stultifying effects of contemporary society, or is her supposed flight from speech really another form of self-escape which plays out the narrator's initial thought to the effect that "To be deaf and dumb would be easier" than communicating through words (S, p. 11)? Although the unnaming movement (again ironically) at first seems to indicate a step toward discovering identity, in reality she finds that without language, the whole notion of self is jeopardized because for her, as for the Americans, "a language is everything you do" (S, p. 129). At the end, we can only assume that the narrator responds to the calling of her name, and returns to the world of words and labels that she seemed so intent upon rejecting. Despite her claims to the contrary, the narrator is constantly reminding herself that the absence of human communication puts her presence in doubt. No sooner have her friends departed from the island than she calls out "Here I am," as her voice rises "with the frustration and then the terror of hearing no answer," just as it did when as a child she played hide and seek "and I hid too well, too far away and they couldn't find me" (S, p. 172).

The hide-and-seek motif cannot be ignored, because it places the narrator in relation to the acts of self-disappearance which figure so prominently in *The Edible Woman* and *Lady Oracle*. Even the circumstances surrounding Joan Foster's mock-death on Lake Ontario actually seem to be foreshadowed in *Surfacing* when at one point the narrator rises "up out of the lake, leaving my false body floated on the surface, a cloth decoy" (S, p. 178). More obviously, Joan Foster's childhood experience of being tied up by her fellow brownies and released by a kindly passer-by is here as well. The narrator recalls that

> When the boys chased and captured the girls after school and tied them up with their own skipping ropes, I was the one they would forget on purpose to untie. I spent many afternoons looped to fences and gates and convenient trees, waiting for a benevolent adult to pass and free me; later I became an escape artist of sorts, expert at undoing knots. (S, p. 72)

Like Joan, the narrator is reminded at every turn about the futility of believing that self-definition is possible. Soon after she has arrived on the island, the narrator sets out by canoe in search of her father. She is accompanied by what she calls "My other shape," the "foreshortened" shadow in the water with its "outline blurred" (S, p. 141). In a symbolic attempt to learn more about the other self, she plunges into the water, but the water unfocuses her vision, and she returns to the canoe which is "hung split between water and air" and so appears as "mediator and liferaft" (S, p. 141). For the narrator, this experience is "like learning to walk after illness" (S, p. 141), and she soon realizes that she must transcend the ambivalence which has characterized her: "it was time for me to choose sides" (S, p. 154). In fact, she has always been trying to choose sides and define things; hence her preoccupation with borders ("this is border country" [S, p. 26], "I paused, checking the fence, the border" [S, p. 78]), measurements ("I was measuring myself against what she was saying" [S, p. 471]), and order ("I wanted to keep busy, preserve at least the signs of order" [S, p. 78]). But she can't define, because whatever she sees in incontrovertibly intermediate, a matter of "interlacing branches," "leaves overlapping leaves," and the "absence of defining borders" (S, p. 83). Even "the creature in me" is felt as being a "plant-animal" which must be ferried "between death and life" (S, p. 168). Although she still believes that she can escape this pervasive doubling and superimposition and reminds herself that "I must stop being in the mirror" (S, p. 175), she knows that the "reflection [is] intruding between my eyes and vision" (S, p. 175), and that her act of reversing the mirror so that it faces the wall and "no longer traps me" accomplishes nothing. Fifteen pages later the mirror has been turned around but the duplicitous image which it originally reflected is back again.

Some readers may also be back to wondering why Atwood would want to deny her heroine the pleasure of finding an identity. It seems to me that here, and in all of Atwood's novels, there is a parody of all of the conventions associated with "search for identity" literature, and the suggestion that self-realization, as the term goes, is often not the product of a descent into nature, myth, or preconsciousness. In Lady Oracle, the parody is explicit: Joan Foster drowns and surfaces, only to find that she is back to the duplicity which prompted her to begin her twice-told tale. Marian MacAlpin is also swallowed up, and then regurgitated as an "I" to be ingested once again. The motifs of descent and ascent, the emphasis on narrative circularity, the repeated images of being swallowed up: these reveal Atwood's interest in the conventions of romance, particularly as they emerge in Gothic literature, a subgenre of the romance mode. As Eli Mandel has observed, Surfacing is about a maiden in flight, a maiden who is surrounded by "a variety of dark threats, either psychological or hidden in the social structure,"[10] and confronted at every turn by omens, portents, masquerades, and self-reflexive doppelgängers. (The same description, it should be noted, applies to The Edible Woman.) Atwood's proposed Ph.D. thesis was on Gothic romance, and, for what it's worth, she herself has identified *Surfacing* as a ghost story.[11] However, there is an important difference between Atwood's Gothic romances and the conventional Gothic horror story: in the latter, the resolution of the narrative is usually signalled by the heroine's final escape from a fate worse than death; in Atwood's novels, the heroine remains in the realm of duplicity, and although she may believe that she has moved out of the underworld's mirror, her belief is ultimately shown to be the greatest sign of self-delusion.

When the putative resolution of a novel becomes a comment on the impossibility of resolving anything, and when the notion of self-discovery is repeatedly exposed as a hoax, we are also dealing with a tragic vision of life. While it is certainly possible to read *The Edible Woman* and *Lady Oracle* as comic novels, they must also be seen as partaking in the dark undercurrent which runs through *Surfacing*. Moreover, the happy outcome involving the restoration of community with which comedy is traditionally marked is distinctly — and I would suggest consciously — shown to be absent or corrupted in Atwood's novels. Joan Foster winds up away from home, away from Arthur, in a hospital room in Italy where she continues to fabricate her life; Marian divorces herself from Peter; the narrator of *Surfacing* goes back to Joe, but sensing that "we will probably fail," and that "That's normal, it's the way it happens now . . ." (*S*, p. 192).

Although each of Atwood's heroines remains divided, *Surfacing* seizes the causes of this division most dramatically. The narrator is under the illusion that both she and her country are gradually being infected with "the American disease." But Atwood suggests that the narrator mistakes the nature of the illness (the "Americans" turn out to be Canadians after all). It is not the sickness from the south so much as the dis-ease of modern man which infects the narrator: her alienation, her anxiety, her confrontation with the absurd and the irrational — all of these features mark her as the victim of a world in which the traditional faith in identity no longer holds. If it were true, as Roberta Rubenstein has argued, that "the narrator completes the journey to psychic and spiritual rebirth,"[12] it might be possible to interpret the book as a kind of gloss on Joseph Campbell's *The Hero with a Thousand Faces* or on Mircea Eliade's *The Myth of the Eternal Return* (a reading which has also been suggested by Josie P. Campbell[13]), but the fact remains that the nature of the rebirth and the affirmation of self-discovery remain ambivalent. What Atwood really seems to be saying is that the mythical pattern of separation, initiation, and return must itself be seen as a sham in a culture where rituals have lost their potency.

III

The only defence was flight, invisibility.   (S, p. 135)

As the mythical patterns through which man knows himself are undermined, and the expected release from a ghost story about misplaced identity never materializes, we can only begin to wonder if ghost story existence has, for Atwood's heroines, become a way of life. The question remains implicit in *Surfacing*, but it is explicitly explored in *Lady Oracle*, a novel in which every "I" is a lie. Although the first person voice which speaks in *Lady Oracle* seems to be Joan Foster's, it isn't hers at all. The story is told — with eminent appropriateness — by a *ghost writer* whose creation provides a metaphorical and ironic commentary on Joan's inability to tell the tale which would give form to her shifting sense of self. At the end of the novel, we recall, the solitude of Joan's reclusive life in Terremoto (and the anonymity that she hopes will accompany it) is disrupted when the reporter who has stalked her (for her story, for her life) finally tracks her down. She hits him over the head with a bottle and he ends up "in the hospital with no one to talk to" (*LO*, p. 344). Joan takes it upon herself to provide the reporter with conversation, and with a conversation piece — namely herself. She pours out her story at the bedside and soon realizes that "I talked too much" (*LO*, p. 344). In fact, she talks enough to give the reporter enough material to write a book about Lady Oracle, and so she feels that "he's the only person who knows anything about me" (*LO*, p. 345). It is the reporter who creates Joan's story, making her voice his own. "I guess it will make a pretty weird story, once he's written it," Joan admits, "and the odd thing is that I didn't tell any lies. Well, not very many" (*LO*, p. 344). Consider the distortions here and the labyrinthine sense of identity which they imply: Joan tells us that she is involved in a story about herself which someone else has told (and no doubt altered), which is based on the partially falsified information that Joan (whose life has become a fiction) has related. The twice-told tale becomes a thrice-told tale echoing on and on. And the distortions do not stop in the telling: the reader must deal with the realization that the story forces him to participate in the duplicity and become a sympathetic imposter. (I say "Joan says," but what I really mean is that the ghost writer has created a character who gives voice to what Joan *might* have said if she had in fact been the book's narrator.) The character we agree to call Joan Foster is also Lady Oracle and Louisa K. Delacourt, and to a certain extent she is Marian MacAlpin and the narrator of *Surfacing*, as well.

Like Atwood's previous heroines Joan is the confused product of her own fictions, but unlike the other characters she is intensely conscious of her ambivalent nature. For one thing, she has been schooled in the Shakespearean notion that life is like a play and all the people in it actors constantly changing roles. Joan's education in this regard is influenced primarily by her mother, who is seen as a kind of stage manager and director intent upon casting her offspring into stardom on the stage and screen:

> . . . my mother named me after Joan Crawford. This is one of the things that always puzzled me about her. Did she name me after Joan Crawford because she wanted me to be like the screen characters she played — beautiful, ambitious, ruthless, destructive to men — or because she wanted me to be successful? (*LO*, p. 38)

Joan never really comes to terms with this question, but one thing is clear. This relationship with her mother "was professionalized early. She was to be the manager, the creator, the agent; I was to be the product" (*LO*, p. 64). It is from her mother that Joan learns about the art of disguise and duplicity which haunts her for years to come. The trances which she eventually experiences before the three-sided mirror in her bedroom are partly prompted by the fact that as a child she watched her mother "put on her face" (*LO*, p. 63) before a similar mirror. As the repeated make-up scenes involving Joan's mother suggest, she is also an actress who has worn so many masks that her real self and her roles have become almost indistinguishable. The application of lipstick, for example, made her look like Bette Davis; it "gave her a curious double mouth, the real one showing through the false one like a shadow" (*LO*, p. 65).

Although Joan finds the mirrors and make-up fascinating, she is puzzled by the knowledge that the triplicate image is frequently one of pain. "Some of the things [her mother] did seemed to be painful" and "She often frowned at herself . . . as if she saw behind or within the mirror some fleeting image she was unable to capture or duplicate" (*LO*, p. 63). Ultimately Joan will come to experience the pain of removing masks as well, but as a child she remains entranced by the possibility of being able to act out several lives. Her imagination provides her with the most effective means of rising above the all-too-real grossness of her physical body. And so the course of Joan's life seems to be set: she will be the "escape artist" in search of a place "where I would be free not to be myself" (*LO*, p. 139). She will be the actor who "wanted to have more than one life" (*LO*, p. 141), and she will be the doppelgänger who knows that "I was two people at once" (*LO*, p. 214). During the course of the narrative we follow her as she increasingly seeks out relationships (first with others and finally with herself) that are defined by doubleness. Aunt Lou, with whom Joan develops her first rewarding relationship, leads a pseudonymous existence as the author of a booklet entitled *You're Growing Up*, published by a sanitary napkin firm; she introduces Joan to the escape provided by the screen and leads her toward display windows "full of the animals, fairies and red-cheeked dwarfs" (*LO*, p. 68) which populate the literature of fantasy. Gradually Joan realizes that her father, like Aunt Lou, is double-sided. Although he appears to be serious and tight-lipped, his ability to bring the dead back to life (which Joan sees as the "resurrectionist side of his personality" [*LO*, p. 70]) also marks him as an actor, as "a conjuror of spirits, a shaman with the voice of a dry detached old opera commentator in a tuxedo" (*LO*, p. 74). As Joan moves away from the circle of her immediate family she inevitably runs into others who are composed of more than one persona. She wonders whether the man who untied her on the bridge was "a rescuer or a villain" (*LO*, p. 61) and considers "an even more baffling thought: was it possible for a man to be both at once?" (*LO*, p. 61). The Royal Porcupine is Chuck Brewer, while Arthur is cast as both the modern-day revolutionary and the romantic knight who is supposed to (but never does) appear to rescue his damsel in distress. Joan soon discovers that "there were as many of Arthur as there were of me" (*LO*, p. 213). The Polish count is the Mavis Quilp who relentlessly churns out nurse novels. Joan finally confirms what we have suspected all along: "Every man I'd ever been involved with, I realized, had had two selves" (*LO*, p. 294). These men, of course, can be seen as figments of Joan's imagination. Their split personalities dramatize their creator's multisidedness. In this sense *Lady Oracle* becomes a meta-fictional exploration of a writer who writes about writing and a meta-theatrical story about a dramatist/actor who participates in and comments on the process of playing to an audience.

Joan Foster becomes involved in this exploration most obviously through the Costume Gothics which tend to comment on the meaning of her own costume-oriented lifestyle. When she is writing, Joan becomes the heroines of *Escape from Love, Stalked by Love,* and *Love, My Ransom.* It is not unusual for writers to experience this kind of intense identification with their imaginary characters during the course of writing. But unlike most writers Joan gets trapped in her novels, and the more she writes, the more she becomes the conglomeration of all the characters to which she has given voice. At first Joan seems to be able to separate herself from the situations in her fiction and to distinguish reality from art, although she often finds it necessary physically to rehearse the scenes she is describing and sometimes becomes so involved in these rehearsals that they seem to have become her reality. In *Love, My Ransom,* the heightened identification between Joan and her creation is suggested by the fact that Penelope, the Gothic heroine, begins to experience the same problems with mirrors that Joan has started to encounter. Penelope's *"own reflection disappeared . . . further into the mirror she went, and further, till she seemed to be walking on the other side of the glass, in a land of indistinct shadows"* (*LO,* p. 220). Penelope's fate obviously echoes, or reflects, Joan's own voyage into her triple mirror — the voyage which leaves her on the other side of the glass where the self is unshown, unknown. "I went into the mirror one evening," Joan says, "and I couldn't get out again" (*LO,* p. 225). By the end of the novel the bond between Joan and her visions is so complete that she finds herself able to stand in for Felicia in *Stalked by Love.* As Joan opens the door to the reporter she simultaneously opens it to Redmond as Arthur and the synthesis of teller and tale is made complete.

But is this the result she desired? True, she tried to follow Mavis Quilp's advice to the effect that "Escape literature . . . should be an escape for the writer as well as the reader" (*LO,* p. 155), but Joan also makes it clear that she wanted her fiction to provide the reader (and no doubt herself) with a happy resolution. Like Felicia, *"All she wanted was happiness with the man she loved"*

(*LO*, p. 321), or as she says more pointedly in what we imagine to be her own voice: "I longed for happy endings, I needed the feeling of release when everything turned out right and I could scatter joy like rice all over my characters and dismiss them into bliss" (*LO*, p. 321). Here Joan is referring to the conventional comic resolution, and her use of rice imagery suggests that she is well aware of the wedding rituals which traditionally accompany comic endings. But the point is that Joan is unable to resolve *Stalked by Love* at all, let alone comically, just as she is unable to mould her own story according to the theories of comedy with which she is so obviously conversant. And although she can claim at the beginning of the novel that "The truth was that I dealt in hope, I offered a vision of a better world, however preposterous" (*LO*, p. 32), it seems more accurate to say that the final vision Joan offers us is one of her despair at being caught in a world of artifice with no relief in sight. At the end of the novel Arthur has not come, and the "rescuer" that replaces him is a reporter who offers Joan the option, not of release, but of returning to square one. In the final analysis, then, *Lady Oracle* moves toward a rejection of precisely the comic structures upon which it is based. Joan tries to escape from reality through her fiction, but once she is in the fiction she discovers that the problems which she faced in the so-called real world are still present, albeit much more forcefully because they have been fictionally distilled. The circularity which describes the movement of the narrative also describes the novel's theme: reality and fantasy are one, and to believe that it is possible to escape from either is the greatest delusion.[14]

The dilapidation of the comic vision should not come as a surprise; it is foreshadowed at several points by the images of alienation and frustrated creativity which inform the novel's subtexts. The first of these subtexts is the dancing school play which is directed by Miss Flegg, a quasi-artist who has choreographed "The Butterfly Frolic" routine in which Joan wants so desperately to participate. "I had my eye," she tells us, "on the chief butterfly spot" (*LO*, p. 42). Joan wants to be the centre of attention, but much more importantly she wants to align herself with all that the butterfly costume symbolizes. For her, the wings that go with the outfit represent "magic transformations," and the ability to rise from mundane reality towards a heightened state of awareness. Predictably, Joan sees "The Butterfly Frolic" as an emphatically "*spiritual*" expression of Miss Flegg's inventiveness, and it is to this spiritual dimension of the butterfly dance that Joan is drawn. Here we see in embryo the need for imaginative release which comes to control Joan's adult life. But just as Joan ultimately fails to find the role which will release her from her fiction, so is her wish to become the central butterfly ruthlessly crushed. Joan ends up as a mothball bumping and thumping around the stage. The scene is funny for everyone but Joan, who "spun in circles" and improvised "a dance of rage and destruction" (*LO*, p. 47). Joan quickly senses that it was "as if this ridiculous dance was the truth about me and everyone could see it" (*LO*, p. 47). The truth to which Joan refers can be described in another way: the dancer and the dance have become inseparable; the circles which Joan spins as a pirouetting mothball are the circles which will define her future life and the fictional lives she will create in the days to come.

As the story develops, the mothball and butterfly motifs reappear, but the distinction between them is gradually cancelled out as Joan realizes that the butterfly consciousness in which she placed her faith is an illusory form of happiness. At the Jordan Chapel Joan listens to Mr. Stewart's message about the optimistic and the pessimistic caterpillars. The optimistic caterpillar knows that the darkness of his metaphorical cocoon is only temporary: "we will rest there for a time, and after that we will emerge with beautiful wings; we will be butterflies, and fly up toward the sun" (*LO*, p. 106). The allegorical message is clear: we must suffer the darkness of our life on earth as preparation for the revelations offered by an after-life in heaven, and Joan must believe that she will be released from the cocoon of her life, metamorphosized and free. Although Joan admits that "Most of the time I was on the side of the optimistic caterpillar," she is bothered by one thought: "So what if you turn into a butterfly? Butterflies die too" (*LO*, p. 144). By the end of the novel, Joan's doubt concerning the validity of the butterfly metaphor has hardened; she sees the butterfly as false, and as a symbol of her own false hopes. In *Stalked by Love*, the last novel Joan writes, Felicia arrives at the *"central plot"* (and by implication at the central truth) of the maze in which she has become lost. There she sees four women, the last of whom *"was enormously fat. . . . From her head sprouted two antennae, like a butterfly's, and a pair of obviously false wings was pinned to her back"* (*LO*, p. 341). The scene brings together the very images which Joan has been trying to separate all along. The fat lady, of course, is Joan — still very much the fat child who played the mothball but yearned for wings. The wings, however, like the distinctions between fat and thin, past and present, are, for Joan, "obviously false." She is left lost in the centre of a labyrinth made up of mirrors. It is not only at the conclusion of the novel that this self-reflecting maze appears: the whole story is full of stories about reflections. One of the most interesting of these centres on the Lady of Shalott, who becomes, inevitably, a replicated version of Joan. Like Tennyson's Lady in the tower, Joan is condemned to thrive on her art, and the tales she weaves wind her into an existence in which reality can only be seen as the reflection of a dream. The palace of art becomes a prison, but the prison itself is sustenance. To succumb to the temptation of bypassing artifice is to invite certain death. Joan realizes that "you could stay in the tower for years, weaving away, looking in the mirror, but one glance out the window at real life and that was that. The curse, the doom" (*LO*, p. 316). Yet for Joan, what is outside the window is more of the fiction that she wants: the vision of happiness with Arthur as the Arthurian knight who will rescue her from the tower and ride with her into the sunset to live happily ever after. The problem is that Arthur never makes it across the ocean, just as in Tennyson's poem the knight never crosses the river. When the Lady of Shalott escapes from *her* confinement, however, her death is a final release. She doesn't find her knight, but she does manage to crack the mirror which has enslaved her.

Joan, on the other hand, finds that she can never escape from the looking glass, or from the art which has become a life sentence that can only end when she is "killed by a surfeit of words" (*LO*, p. 315). Like the Lady of Shalott, Lady Oracle ends up "on the bottom of the death barge where I'd once longed to be, my name on the prow, winding my way down the river" (*LO*, pp. 315-16). The difference between the two heroines is that Joan is so busy watching herself watch the Lady of Shalott that she never really manages to sing her own song. The automatic writing which is the product of her trances actually plagiarizes, duplicates Tennyson's verse:

> She sits on the iron throne
> She is one and three
> The dark lady   the redgold lady
> the blank lady   oracle
> of blood, she who must be
> obeyed   forever

> *Her glass wings are gone*
> *She floats down the river*
> *Singing her last song   (LO, p. 228)*

When the publisher Morton says that the poem "reminds me of something" (*LO*, p. 228), he is obviously remembering the Lady of Shalott, who is also heard "singing her last song" as "She floated down to Camelot." Joan even manages to duplicate the situations presented in her own duplicitous works: the poem which the publisher quotes, for example, is taken from Part V of the poetry book entitled *Lady Oracle*, but the woman who is singing her last song also reappears in Part V of the novel as the Joan who is trying to bring her last Costume Gothic to completion.

But she doesn't manage to complete it, and this fact points to an important feature in *Lady Oracle:* structurally the novel is a failed romance in which the heroine goes through all the motions that should lead to her inevitable release, only to discover that the romance's promised return from the dream world never occurs. Like her heroines, Joan casts herself as the maiden in flight who must repeatedly disguise herself in order to survive her own flights of fancy. Her escape brings her to Italy, and to new romantic roles: she plays the part of Juliet on her balcony, waiting for a Romeo who never appears, and the loneliness turns her into a Mariana figure who knows that "he cometh not." The relentless disruption of the romance modes and conventions creates, on the one hand, an amusing parody of the genre. But on a more serious level, the disruption of traditional romance structures provides an implicit comment on the contemporary impossibility of ever finding the final sense of identity and completion or the ultimate vision of happiness which, as Joan well realizes, is usually offered by romance.

Joan's understanding of the structure of romance appears to be innate, but Atwood's conception of the genre seems to have been influenced, at least in part, by a good deal of critical reading and study. One of the problems of interpreting Atwood's novels stems from the frequently made assumption that Atwood has taken theoretical perspectives and converted them, lock, stock, and barrel, into fictional terms. Thus *Surfacing* is often seen as an application of Northrop Frye's theories as they have been filtered through *Survival,* or it is read as "a creative or poetic 'Meta-criticism' of [Joseph] Campbell's theories" of the "mythic heroic quest."[15] Similarly, *Lady Oracle* might be read as creative meta-criticism which takes Frye's *The Secular Scripture* as its base.

Would it not be more accurate to say, however, that when Atwood uses these theoretical patterns, she does so in order to suggest that their assumptions may in fact be false?[16] It is interesting to observe that in one form or another, all of the theories to which Atwood is said to be indebted are structurally theories of romance. Jung speaks about the need to descend into the collective unconscious, into archetypal awareness, in order for the integrated self to surface. He also speaks, as does Lady Oracle, about the need (and the difficulty) of merging self and shadow. Campbell and Eliade wrote about the ritualized isolation that the hero must experience before he can be initiated into his society. In a sense, Frye brings all of these perspectives together in *Anatomy of Criticism* and *The Secular Scripture,* where he argues that the structure of romance corresponds to the movement of the hero, who inevitably becomes involved in a search for identity which leads him away from a childlike, unaware existence into an archetypal underworld realm of dream, darkness, and loneliness. This descent comprises the hero's initiation into experience; only after the downward movement has been completed can the hero rise again, returning to life, safety, community, and most of all, self-identity. This is of course a gross oversimplification of Frye's analysis: the upper world, in Frye's model, evokes an extended range of meaning that is connected with the identification of myth and the individual's role in society. Similarly, the lower world becomes a metaphor for the unconscious, for the demonic, and for all the qualities associated with darkness and divorce. Moreover, the romance cycle as Frye describes it is the product of an involved interplay between the themes of death and rebirth, exile and return. For Frye, as for Jung, Campbell, and Eliade, the return is essential: without it there can be no affirmation of self because the initiation experience has not taken its full course.

Now if we look back at *Lady Oracle,* it is possible to see that the emphasis which is placed on themes of descent far outweighs that placed on the ascending side of the structure: Joan spends most of her narrative telling us about the labyrinths she is caught in, how she drowned, how she had been hiding, and about the ways in which she has tried to bury her identity. She does not complete the return to the upper world demanded by Frye's model; the end of the book only pulls her back to the story of her death by drowning. The reintegration with society that is supposed to materialize is not part of the final picture, and we sense that if and when Joan does return to the "real" world it will be for "all the publicity" (*LO*, p. 345). Although Joan insists that "I won't write any more Costume Gothics," she is ready to "try some science fiction" (*LO*, p. 345), which, we realize, is paradoxically built on the same structural principles as romance. Even in interstellar terms the labyrinth will remain.

* * *

In a sense, the story in which Joan has been involved is also about Atwood's other central characters. Both *The Edible Woman* and *Surfacing* corrupt the prototypical romance movement from descent to ascent by demonstrating that the upper world is merely a reflection of the lower world of darkness, ambiguity, and isolation. The end of *The Edible Woman* brings Marian back to the same problems that caused her descent into the netherworld of Part II. The narrator of *Surfacing* is also left with the impossible task of trying to ascend from the dreams which always place her between stations on a road full of lies and ghosts and phantoms, monsters from the deep. And then there is Joan, whose comical follies are also part of a modern fall from any meaningful sense of self or community. Atwood's novels are well-crafted and sometimes very funny; but most importantly they haunt us as stories about multi-faceted characters who are as fragmented and duplicitous as the times in which they live.

CATHY N. and ARNOLD E. DAVIDSON

Prospects and Retrospect in *Life Before Man*

> . . . *It is never difficult to demonstrate that as science and history mythology is absurd. When a civilization begins to reinterpret its mythology in this way, the life goes out of it, temples become museums.*
> — Joseph Campbell,
> *The Hero With a Thousand Faces*[1]

I

Set in the tomblike Royal Ontario Museum, Margaret Atwood's latest and most relentlessly serious novel describes a bleak age in which the temples have become museums of a lost future, the museums temples to a vanished past. All coherence gone, the present can anticipate only its own passing. Ritual, mythology, religion, love seem merely outworn artifacts, objects to be catalogued and exhibited along with the other shards of civilization in the ROM. The novel itself, with each section ostentatiously labelled as to day and date, unfolds as broken bits of time. Centering on two intertwined love-triangles singularly lacking in passion, *Life Before Man* also pivots on the wordplay in its title. Lesje, the apex of one triangle, yearns for the lost innocence of primordial existence, for life before man: before Nate, before William, before the first *homo erectus* thought to call itself a human being. She envisions a world of lush vegetation, ancient continents, Lesjeland, Aliceosauraus, the far Mesozoic — an imaginative world more real than most of the events of her unfocused life. Chris, the apex of the other triangle, is dead before the book begins. A suicide, he represents another lost life that stretches out before mankind — the prospect of a self-inflicted doom too banal to be termed apocalypse. The characters caught in these triangles look back to other generations for explanation, but their immediate progenitors provide merely more puzzles and more pain. They look darkly ahead to a future partly redeemed only in that it cannot be clearly foreseen.

The characters in *Life Before Man*, as well as the title, invoke the epigraph with which this essay began. Suffering, to a greater or lesser degree, from what Campbell sees as a peculiarly contemporary disease, they are all, in their separate narrative fragments, recorders of the quotidian and analysts of the obvious. They are also mostly hypocrites whose basic pose is early summed up in a representative phrase voiced by Elizabeth. Abandoned lover in one triangle, betrayed wife in the other, this character can contrapuntally "play" one role, one victimization, against the other, while also maintaining, with a bravely stiff (only slightly quivering) upper lip: "We might as well behave like reasonable adults."[2] As she later similarly observes, she "believe[s] in being civilized about these things" (p. 147). But adults, Atwood suggests, are rarely reasonable or civilized. Neither are reason or civilization necessarily virtues. The characters in the novel repress, divert, sublimate, withdraw and even die as ways to avoid their more basic responses: fear, anger, desire, hate. Unlike Lesje's envisioned dinosaurs who once lumbered about the earth unhindered by any naggings of self-consciousness, the protagonists in *Life Before Man* try to act "civilized" about such things as illicit love affairs, confused career choices, private and public power plays, national politics, and even the prospects of human annihilation.

"Civility," however, becomes a kind of funhouse mirror in which outer self-distortions conveniently obscure inner ones. Thus Lesje, seeking an uncomplicated childlike love in a confusing adult world, still feels called upon to defend, to her lover's former mistress, the "civilized" behavior of that same lover's wife. As the two discuss how well the wife has coped with both of them, they are not the women of the world whom they would see reflected in their worldly discourse. Behind their joint pose of poised sophistication is mostly a shared naiveté. This encounter between Lesje, Nate's present mistress, and Martha, his past one, also illustrates how the characters use one another as distorting mirrors. Lesje wishes to see herself in the image of Elizabeth's capability; not as a future Martha, a discarded mistress; and thereby misjudges both herself and the other two women.

She misjudges herself on still another level too. Waiting for an affair to begin, she at one point remembers how her woman's group waffled on the question of the morality of adultery: "What it boiled down to was that manstealing was out but personal growth was commendable. You had to have the right attitude and be honest with yourself" (p. 127). Lesje also waffles, first, by raising the question only in the abstract form of her group's earlier "convolutions" and, second, by immediately dismissing even their contradictory formulation. She will not decide on the honesty of what she might feel even as Nate — who is, at the time, surely more self-deceived — discourses upon the morality of what they are about to do:

> Elizabeth would give the seal of approval to what he's doing and may even be pleased for him, since in a way they [Elizabeth and Lesje] are good friends, [but] now is not the right time to tell her. Elizabeth has been making an adjustment. . . . He wants her to finish doing that before he gives her something new that she has to adjust to. It has something to do with the children.   (p. 128)

Despite their pretense to intelligence, maturity, and civilization, the adults in *Life Before Man* behave like naughty children engaged in a perverse game of spiritual hide-and-seek begotten upon sexual half-show and half-tell.

Complex deluding games, metaphoric tricks with mirrors, are essential features of Atwood's earlier fiction, particularly *Lady Oracle* in which Joan Foster everywhere sees thinner or fatter, more domesticated or more free versions of herself. *Life Before Man* is clearly connected to the author's earlier fiction. But the scope now is broader, the execution more complex. One is reminded of Atwood's own assessment of Margaret Laurence's *The Diviners:* "a huge, risky, ambitious book, the kind writers produce at a summing-up period in their careers, if they ever make it that far."[3] *Life Before Man* is that type of "summing up" book. Its larger implications are obvious even in its narrative method. An authorial preoccupation with a single self-preoccupied protagonist such as the obsessively introspective I-narrator of *Surfacing* has been superseded by a carefully controlled third-person narration which only rarely and unpredictably breaks into first person. Nor do those breaks produce an effect analogous to the alternating first and third person narration of *The Edible Woman* — different views of the same central character. Instead, we have similar views of different characters who are only occasionally allowed to speak in their own unreliable voice, as if to prove how closely the author, within the grammar of the third person narration, can still approximate the I-voices of Elizabeth, Lesje, and Nate.

This shifting, non-shifting point of view, produced by superimposing the authorial narrator's omniscience upon the limited consciousness of the different characters portrayed, along with the device of labelling each short chapter with the name of the particular protagonist whose tone is thus rendered, calls to mind William Faulkner's *As I Lay Dying*.[4] That connection is not fortuitous. In *Life Before Man*, as in Faulkner's absurdist epic quest novel, a main character is dead throughout most of the book. Chris also follows Addie in that he exerts a tremendous impact, as person and as metaphor, throughout the entire novel. The surviving characters try to live at least partly to negate his dying and see themselves differently imaged in both his life and his death. Furthermore, and more important, Atwood's novel, like Faulkner's, profits from the seeming discontinuity of its numerous sections. The reader must synthesize a whole, an overall vision, that is more than the sum of the various parts.

In this respect, Nate's function in the novel is particularly significant. His male voice adds a new note to the choruses which Marian MacAlpin, the unnamed surfacer, and Joan Foster had sung mostly in concert with themselves. Like these earlier characters, like Elizabeth and Lesje, Nate too is ambivalently motivated by various conflicting desires and doubts. But the counterpointing of male and female paeans and plaints makes *Life Before Man* a more complex, a more polyphonic work than its predecessors. We do not have so much an extended account of the battle of the sexes as seen only from one side. Instead, merging recitatives show both sexes defeated even as each manoeuvres for some advantageous ground upon which it can engage the other.

Victories are unlikely. Survival is problematic. The characters in the novel who endure do so through no inherent strengths of their own and, accordingly, receive little credit for their survival. Indeed, the fact of continuing life in *Life Before Man* is largely immaterial. Chris dead is as necessary, as relevant, and as real as Elizabeth, Lesje, or Nate alive. They are all described in similar terms, as problematic specimens to be classified on the basis of available morphological and behavioristic observations. Like

Lesje, the paleontologist, readers must formulate the individuals from the scattered record of the broken bones, the disconnected hints that underpin some construct of "is" or "was." Like Chris, the taxidermist, they must give to the dead body reconstructed an air of life. Like Elizabeth, the arranger of exhibits, they must create a context, a world in which the living creature had its being. And then they have only a simulacrum of the original. The living dinosaur does not stalk the museum corridors. The owl does not swoop at night from the diorama. Nevertheless, if the museum tropes in the novel suggest that reality eludes the narrow confines of the curator's display case, the author's novel, the reader's recreated tableau, they equally suggest that we must still attempt to delimit it. To that end we can turn now to an examination of the individual characters and appropriately begin with Chris who is at least partly fixed by the fact that he is dead throughout most of the novel.

II

Chris looms large in death just as he did in life, when, all shoulders and sinew, he was characterized chiefly by his imposing physical presence. But neither his brute strength nor his capability at such games of calculation as chess particularly served him when he was caught up in a still more complicated game, the rules of which he could not learn. He was undone by the niceties of contemporary courtship rituals, rituals which supposedly facilitate both the family and occasional adulteries. And if marriage à la mode defeated this massive man, just what mode of modern mammalian behavior brought about the extinction, metaphorically speaking, of a human dinosaur?

Eschewing old double standards, aware of the value of new experience, Nate and Elizabeth can accept both their own and their spouse's extra-marital entanglements. But what might pass as a frolicsome set of mixed doubles is actually a passionless divvying up of sexual services. When Elizabeth points out that the participants in a working *ménage à quatre* must be able to count on one another, she makes clear what she really means. To be counted on, one must never alter the schedule, never phone, never come to the house, never do anything that might disturb the children, disrupt the family. Elizabeth's rational arrangements — Thursdays for her and Chris, Saturdays for Nate and Martha — provide the rules that all "partners" are expected to follow. Thus Martha at one point in the novel resentfully insists to a characteristically obtuse Nate that she was more his wife's backstairs maid than his mistress. She should really have been paid, and paid by Elizabeth. Chris's revolt is much more graphic. The shot whereby he ends his function as discreet marital aid definitely disturbs Elizabeth's universe. Through his death he finally becomes emotionally real to her, a being that can obsessively possess her mind, instead of briefly — and only at the appointed hour — occupying her body.

The two flashbacks to the time when he was still alive (August 28, 1975, soon after he and Elizabeth began their affair and October 7, 1976, shortly after she has ended it and approximately two weeks before he commits suicide) emphasize Chris's single-minded desire for passion, commitment. He would have some claim on the woman with whom he has shared his bed, even if it is only a fight with her husband while the affair is in progress or a scene at her house after it is over. All along Chris was adverse to Elizabeth's attempts to maintain propriety and could act in opposition to her rules. He explains such indecorous behavior (indecorous, it should be noted, only according to her contradictory standards) by claiming a different heritage: "He let on to her at first, hinted, that he was part Indian and part French, Métis, that mythical hybrid; archaic, indigenous, authentic as she was not, his sense of grievance fully earned." Continuing her retrospective account of Chris's creation of that imagined past, Elizabeth turns his explanation into her own: "He sneered at her, the whiteness of her skin and presumably her blood, made love as if exacting payment, and she'd let herself be bullied. As she would otherwise have not" (p. 160). Yet both explanations have one feature in common. If he is part Indian, a "natural man," both he and she can be excused for not conforming to her civilized conventions. A projected history justifies them both. But when they exchange the sad facts of their actual antecedents, the novel reverses the process undergone by the unnamed protagonist of *Surfacing*. Abandoning the false justification of a made-up past brought the surfacer and Joe to the belated beginning of a real — and hence necessarily ambiguous — relationship. It drives Elizabeth and Chris apart. He can no longer be her version of Lesje's escape dinosaurland, "a dangerous country, swarming with ambushes and guerillas, . . . a demon lover" (p. 213), and she drops him.

With his subsequent suicide, Chris makes a final concession to the rituals of the civilized. He puts on a white shirt, a tie, a suit, and even polishes his shoes before he blows his head off, in bed, with a shotgun. As previously observed, he will become real to her in the finality of his death. But more is at issue. Rejected, he will retaliate, childishly, by removing himself completely from the scene. As he does so with the overdramatized suicide, he also demonstrates how little his strength serves him. He can punish Elizabeth for betraying him only by far more graphically punishing himself. Considering the Dickinsonian implications of his proper attire, we can reasonably surmise that he intends to betray her too through a solemn marriage with death. Elizabeth will be doubly abandoned and, indeed, she seems to rage that she cannot revenge a jilting far more than she mourns the passing of a recent lover. Finally, Chris's death might be his judgment on himself for trying to solve a crisis by thinking it through — the "rational" basis for his suicide — as opposed to living it through: "The head had been a troublemaker, which was probably why Chris had chosen to shoot at it instead of at some other part of himself. He wouldn't have wanted to mutilate his body" (p. 16).

It is more than slightly ironic that Nate is called upon to identify the torso of Chris who was so much identified with his torso while Nate mostly prefers to forget he has one. In other ways too, Nate is Chris's emotional and physical opposite. Ever befuddled and indecisive, he is tall, gawky, gangling, all Adam's apple and great length of bone. Whereas the dead man met challenges directly, "like a moose in heat" (p. 236), and confronted even death head-on, Nate prefers evasion. Significantly, his one physical accomplishment is his modest success as a runner, as if his long limbs can function properly only in flight. In other ways too Nate is most himself when engaged in evasive action. Chris, perhaps too aware of his own needs, might represent the ego as blind appetite. Nate, however, by hiding his desires behind a pretended proper concern for the feelings of others, gives us the ego as artful dodger:

> Occasionally . . . Nate thinks of himself as a lump of putty, help-
> lessly molded by the relentless demands and flinty disapprovals of
> women he can't help being involved with. Dutifully, he tries to
> make them happy. He fails not because of any intrinsic weakness
> or lack of will, but because their own desires are hopelessly
> divided.   (p. 41)

But this moving portrait of the good man as self-sacrificed victim of neurotic women who know not what they want is painted right after Nate returns from visiting his former mistress. After calling off their affair a month earlier, he now supposedly wants to talk things out. More accurately, as he admits only when Martha voices the unflattering truth, he was "running away from mother" and "wanted some other nice lady to give [him] a cookie and a tumble in the sack" (p. 33). In short, his gentility is pure sham. He does not recognize "desires," his own or those of others, but simply attributes to others what he wants them to want and is as selfish covertly as Chris was openly.

Another difference between the two is of particular thematic importance. Chris cannot survive in this world; Nate can. So Nate becomes the progenitor. He perpetuates his genes by fathering children with two women. His head resting on Lesje's belly, but preparing to return to his wife and family, he can observe: "'I want to have a child by you.'" The import is not altered by his immediate change of "by you" to "with you," and then to, "'I want us to have a child together'" (p. 208). At the end of the novel, Lesje carries his child. Prudent adherent to the principles of sociobiology, Nate triumphs, in his fashion. Yet one wonders what brave new world awaits his progeny, for he is, he admits, an "evolutionary mistake" (p. 48). At his height, he is "unbalanced" (p. 48), and in more ways than one. For example, too tall to make it through most doorways, he is also too abstracted to remember to duck: "Once or twice and a rat would learn to stoop" (p. 35).

Nate's nature is to run, but in flight, in any action, he is less than impressive. His first independent deed in the novel, calling Lesje and then hanging up as soon as he hears her voice, epitomizes his many indecisive gestures of escape. His attempts to flee the prison of his present and his self are, however, all futile. Incompleted phone calls only affirm his yearning isolation. The same condition continues, on a different level, when he finally brings Lesje to a seedy hotel room and, supposedly, the beginning of an affair. He looks long and longingly at her, and then remembers that he must call "home" to arrange to take "the kids" to dinner at his "mother's." "Hello love," he greets Elizabeth, and the words he uses all fix Lesje in an isolating vacuum: "it's as if she doesn't exist" (p. 128). Nor is she consoled when he reassures her, just before he rushes off, "There's lots of time, love. . . . Next time will be better" (p. 129). She is still left alone to contemplate how unworthy she apparently is when it comes to love, how unattractive if mere sex is the issue. Of course, neither postulate is valid. He retrospectively castigates himself for his ineptitude and consoles himself too with the promise that next time will be better. But Nate's next times are not better, only — sometimes — different. He leaves an unsatisfying and already dead relationship with Elizabeth to enter into one of the most depressing flings described in modern literature — an affair doubly dreary because he had foolishly dreamed that it would mean so much.

A break with his old past is not, for Nate, a new beginning. Even after he forces his wife to ask him to leave her, he cannot tolerate separation from her. Half hanging on to the defunct marriage, he becomes another contemporary dangling man. Caught between two women because he is really committed to neither, he proceeds to blame them both for his own painful sense of unbonded redundancy. Is this suspended condition another "life before man" alluded to in the book's title, a future for the modern world other than self-inflicted annihilation? The author suggests that it is. Consider Nate's obsessive interest in Quebec politics and his identification with René Lévesque. Atwood often invokes Québécois Separatism, and in time and event provincial politics parallels the breakup of Nate and Elizabeth's malfunctioning union. Thus Nate speaks for both himself and René Lévesque when, on November 25, 1977, he translates what he hears the political leader saying on the evening news: "Something about the economy, from what Nate can catch. *These days they're saying they never meant separation, not just like that*" (p. 274, italics added). But Nate's uncertain career is embued with more than just his nation's current political climate. A former would-be activist lawyer turned toymaker for the rich, turned, again, part-time legal aid worker who defends mostly the guilty, Nate recapitulates the changing social ethos of the last few decades. From political awareness and efforts at reform to narcissistic exercises in self-realization to disillusioned acquiescence to what was once called The System: one wonders, what comes next?

Never considering such large questions, Nate, like others in the novel, lives mostly in his fantasies. His fantasies, however, unlike those of such an accomplished fantasist as Lesje, are not recognized as fantasy. Indeed, with respect to Lesje, Nate prompts himself to action only by fancying that a dubious dream is real. Lesje must be the self-contained, cool, aloof, saving Madonna that he imagines her to be. Skittish, jumpy, self-conscious, insecure, socially maladroit, she is nothing of the sort. But it is also one of Atwood's ironies that fantasy draws one fantasist to another:

The fact is that she's addicted to Nate's version of her. Sometimes, when he touches her, she feels not naked but clothed, in some long unspecified garment that spreads around her like a shimmering cloud. She's realized with something close to panic that the picture he's devised of her is untrue. He expects her to be serene, a refuge; he expects her to be kind. . . . He ought to be able to tell by now that she isn't like this at all. Nevertheless she wants to be; she wants to be this beautiful phantom, this boneless wraith he's conjured up. (p. 267)

The conjurer becomes the conjured. Lesje in her own dream world had previously created pastel and even polka dotted dinosaurs. In fact, we first see her "wandering in prehistory" (p. 18), at play, as it were, in the field of her profession. As a paleontologist, she catalogues the bones of defunct forms of life. As a fantasist, she resurrects that dead life and sees, in her imagination, how she will be descended from it. Perched in a Mesozoic tree, "she watches an Ornithomimus, large-eyed, birdlike, run through the scrub, chasing a small protomammal. How many years to learn to grow hair, to bear young alive, to nurture them?" (p. 157). Her fantasy thus connects her with Chris even more than it does with Nate. Like Chris, she does not understand the powerplays, the emotional predations of contemporary civilized mammals, and, again like Chris, she seeks partial refuge in an invented past. How much simpler things would be in the state of nature, for the natural man. Caught up, as much as Chris was, in the disconnected world of the present, the "civilized" games played by Nate and Elizabeth, she finds herself undone by Nate's fantasy far more than she is saved by her own and — a final connection with Chris — almost commits suicide: "On the spur of the moment she'd decided to kill herself. . . . at last she could see why Chris did it: it was this anger and the other thing, much worse, the fear of being nothing. . . . Chris hadn't died for love. He'd wanted to be an event, and he's been one" (pp. 292-93). But Lesje cannot bring herself to saw away at her wrists with a grapefruit knife, so she flushes her birth control pills down the toilet, pretends to have forgiven Nate for offences that he, with his usual awareness, cannot see he has committed, and then, as "the only way she could stop being invisible" (p. 293), becomes pregnant by him.

The stark dichotomy on which the novel here turns — life or death, suicide forestalled through prospective motherhood — suggests *Surfacing*, which, on its deepest levels, opposes the surfacer's unresolved abortion along with similar despoilments

and choices for death against her second almost mythic conception. But if the two novels turn on the same dichotomy, they turn
with an obvious difference. In *Surfacing*, the unnamed protagonist anticipates bearing an animal god or, at the very least, "the
first true human."[5] In *Life Before Man*, Lesje looks fearfully
forward to a child that will be a "throwback, a reptile, a mutant
with some kind of scales and a little horn on the snout" (p. 293).
"How many years to learn . . . to bear young alive, to nurture
them." But Lesje has not "learned." Enceinte as the result of an
impulsive act of vengeance, this "pregnant paleontologist" (p.
308) sees herself as embodying the life from which she had earlier
seen herself evolving. And pregnancy, a natural condition, does
not make her relationship with Nate natural, manageable. In
short, Lesje, at the end of *Life Before Man*, like the title itself,
extends two ways. Since ontology at least in part recapitulates
phylogeny, the fetus within her ties her to ancient forms of life. It
ties her to Nate too and, consequently, to an at best difficult future.

Elizabeth also embodies, late in the novel, time past and time
to come. Time past is the world of her childhood, dominated by
her own dinosaur, her "Auntie Muriel." A brontosaurus of a
woman, immovably self-righteous in her ponderous certainty that
she was always right, the aunt took two children away from their
mother, her own alcoholic younger sister, and raised them with a
grim determination to do right, and no more than right, by those
unfortunate nieces. Doing so drove one of the children to insanity
and suicide; affirmed in Elizabeth, the older and stronger of the
two, a determination never to forgive the aunt. And there was
much not to forgive. But at her aunt's incongruous funeral, particularly during the Bible reading which deals, as the deceased did
not, with fornication and secret sinful pleasures, Elizabeth begins
to question her view of the woman who raised her. Auntie Muriel,
controlling as usual all that fell within her purview, had dictated
the terms of her own funeral. So the unlikely reading seems an
even more unlikely posthumous practical joke — as if a dinosaur,
though dead, should suddenly begin to dance a jig. Elizabeth
understandably wonders if she has "invented" her Auntie Muriel.
She also wonders, quite reasonably, why she would invent an aunt
who had already invented herself as far more "devastating" than
anything the niece could imagine.

Balancing, at the aunt's graveside, her own certainties and
uncertainties about her childhood, Elizabeth then senses, in a
sudden blackout, the onslaught of her certain and uncertain

future. That faint is her first clear intimation of mortality and, she suspects, a subconscious half-answer to the call of suicide: "How close has she come," she asks herself, "how many times, to doing what Chris did?" (p. 301). In other words, when Lesje once conjoins the future and the past, she does so through the possibility of life, through the unborn child that she, with some doubts, decides to bear. But the second conjunction recorded in the novel comes through the inescapable fact of death. At the grave of a pseudomother whose passing she will not mourn, Elizabeth nevertheless realizes that Auntie Muriel cannot be simply "dirted over and done with" (p. 300). Auntie Muriel, like Chris, lives on in her just as surely as she will die. Lesje embodies the possibility of birth; Elizabeth recognizes the reality of death; each woman thereby achieves a transcendence of time.

In neither case is the vision particularly promising. Indeed, Elizabeth's epiphany returns her immediately to the ongoing world of the quotidian — to, more specifically, peanut butter sandwiches. "She has two children" and they are hungry. So as the past and future briefly conjoined crash apart, "despite the rushing of wind, the summoning voices she can hear from underground, the dissolving trees, the chasms that open at her feet," Elizabeth is held by the fact of her modestly "crumbling" house ("most noticeably the front porch") and the tasks to be accomplished therein. "She has built a dwelling over the abyss, but where else was there to build it? So far, it stands" (pp. 301-02). We must take that understated conclusion at more than face value because, in this strikingly effective passage, Atwood sets a pentecost within an apocalypse and then, with appropriate homey details — the dilapidated porch — passes it off as realism.

Elizabeth's dwelling is appropriately located. Her capable manipulation of others does not save her from her own disasters. Quite the opposite. Much of the novel charts "the chasms that open at her feet," chasms that gape all the wider in that she helped to dig them. We first see her, for example, reacting to Chris's suicide with helpless grief and futile rage. "I don't know how I should live" (p. 11), she laments, in the first words of the book. Nor is she living. "Not in" in several senses — "somewhere between her body, which is lying sedately on the bed, . . . and the ceiling with its hairline cracks" (p. 12) — she originally appears as another version of the earlier Atwood dissociated heroine and seems as self-divided as Marian MacAlpin, the surfacer, or Joan

Foster at their most diffuse. Behind a mask of pained civility, she mechanically performs only those duties as mother and wife that cannot be passed on to the reluctantly mothering husband, Nate. That emotional paralysis lasts throughout the Halloween celebration of their children and the suddenly personalized message of All Soul's Day, the posturings of costumed mortals taunting the beckoning dead.

But even in her initial, passive, helpless role, we see that Elizabeth possesses an almost indomitable strength that soon separates her from the earlier heroines. She is not just a survivor. She is a fighter too, and as a fighter she displays, for an Atwood heroine, a different duality. She can defend herself, her territory, in two styles, two languages: "The genteel chic she's acquired, which is a veneer but a useful one: insinuating, flexible, accommodating. And another language altogether, older, harder, left over from those streets and schoolyards on the far edge of gentility where she fought it out after each one of her parents' quick decampments" (p. 148). Thus, through her "haute WASP" exterior and superior tone — "we must be reasonable about these things" — she can thoroughly cow a Martha who, indeed, is cowy as compared to Elizabeth's polished façade. But before the enforced gentility of Auntie Muriel, Elizabeth also learned the harsh lesson of the streets — to fight in whatever style necessary to take care of herself: "If pushed she'll stop at nothing" (p. 150). So she is too capable to be, later in the novel, when Nate engineers his inconclusive leaving, simply the abandoned wife whose defeat affirms the victory of the new lovers' new beginning: "Lesje knows that when Nate moved completely in, or as completely as he's going to, Elizabeth should have felt deserted and betrayed and she herself should have felt, if not victorious, at least conventionally smug. Instead it seems to be the other way around" (p. 238). In fact, "sometimes she thinks Nate is an obscure practical joke being played on her by Elizabeth" (p. 267).

Perhaps a joke is also being played on the empiricist reader by the fabulist author. Elizabeth is originally presented as a helpless victim. But she is, as the other characters in the novel soon attest, a most capable victimizer too. But that reversal is itself countered by a second reversal. Elizabeth is also first seen as a woman who has brought on herself her obvious suffering — who deserves the bed in which she cannot lie. At the end of the novel, however, she is a woman whose fortitude in the face of still another mundane abandonment merits the reader's sympathy. Her father left his wife and children; her mother, losing herself in drink, left her daughters to the not-so-tender care of their Auntie Muriel; her husband leaves Elizabeth for a younger woman. Yet Elizabeth endures and does so through an admirable strength that is more than the obverse of her bitchy calculation. We have then, in these two reversals, different versions of an evolving Elizabeth who is herself the product of contradictions in the past of her family — for example, the loving mother who sold her children for a regular allowance to spend on alcohol and then could not completely renounce those children — and the ongoing present of her own confused life — for example, the love/hate relationship with Nate, which leads to a different love/hate relationship with Chris, which further complicates the one with Nate.

III

Elizabeth, as a self-contradictory product of contradictions, embodies what she herself saw in her aunt, what the museum tropes in the novel along with certain key scenes clearly imply. Imperfect constructs of a past and/or present unfolding life (the dinosaur as displayed in the museum, Elizabeth as first seen in the novel) are not approximate renderings of some final reality nor are they simply another relative reality — one more way of looking at that particular blackbird. What can seem a final point of view might better serve as a beginning point for vision. Any resultant illumination, such as Elizabeth's graveside epiphany or Nate's belated realization that he was not the center and circumference of his widowed mother's universe, does not necessarily redeem life or change it or substantially alter the way it is seen. The characters who briefly achieve some moment of heightened awareness cannot thereby escape even the personal bias that allows them to distort self-servingly their view of their own past and present. Yet these flickers of illumination still attest to truths beyond history and science, truths that cannot be empirically validated. In short, there is always, Atwood suggests, more to fact — or to realistic fiction — than meets the eye of the objective observer.

Which, to return to a point with which we began, is why Atwood provides us with the different points of view of different observers, none of whom is the least bit objective. So, to repeat another earlier observation, readers must synthesize their own point of view based on the disparate fragments that comprise *Life Before Man*. Various events are described by different characters.

Those different characters are cast in, or cast themselves into, conflicting roles. Thus we encounter such seeming contradictions as strong Chris succumbing to suicide, as unassertive Lesje catching her man, as inept Nate achieving his half-successes with different women. But the very terms of these apparent contradictions — Chris *strong*? Chris *succumbing* to suicide? — are themselves misleading constructs, simplifications whereby the complexities of human nature are partially misperceived by others of different natures who still reveal something of their own nature in both what they do and do not see. The careful reader must therefore attend to the intricate interplay of actions reacted to and assessments reassessed delineated throughout the novel. Through this extended interplay the limited characters portrayed are both rendered fully human and, as individual specimens and representatives of the species, caught up in a complex dance to the music of time. In this respect, a thread that keeps the book from being a mere calendar of occurrences is the very humanness inherent in even the names that are given equal billing with the day and date at the beginning of each narrative fragment. Character gives time coherence, just as time threatens the existence of each character — a new twist to the old cliché that character unfolds in time.

Atwood also gives a new twist to what is by now a convention of twentieth-century literature, the "open ending" that supposedly reflects the "unreduced and irreducible" nature of twentieth-century experience.[6] *Life Before Man* could well have concluded with such a non-conclusion: Elizabeth contemplating her lonely future at her aunt's graveside; Lesje hoping, before Nate's divorce from Elizabeth, for the "miracle" that might save her future marriage with Nate; Nate still suspended between the two women. The surviving characters would all be at some psychological crossroads, facing an uncertain future that bodes both promise and pain. Atwood, in her three previous novels, has relied on such indefinite endings that give us, in Friedman's terms, "the design of life in . . . open form . . . as an endlessly expanding process."[7] Marian eating her cake, the unnamed surfacer leaning towards Joe and Toronto, Joan Foster visiting the reporter she has clubbed with the Cinzano bottle, each of these final actions hints at a decision not yet fully decided which will only require a still more difficult decision. At the end of *Life Before Man*, however, decisions have been made and hanging issues have been resolved. The result is an old-fashioned closed ending. But it is a closed ending with a difference and does not promise either a reestablished proper social order or the continued happiness for the deserving that were the chief postulates of the traditional closed ending.

The open ending countered the cozy view of life advanced in the fairy-tale conclusions — "and they lived happily ever after" — of many eighteenth- and nineteenth-century novels. Atwood's closed ending similarly counters the promise or at least the possibilities implicit in twentieth-century fictional indefiniteness, and does so so effectively that the sentimental reader might well yearn for a little less resolution. Had the novel ended some seventy pages earlier, there would have been room for hope. Perhaps Lesje and Nate in some concluding continuance could negate Chris's opening end. The novel, however, provides no hint of better or different things to come. Nate remains the same Nate. His relationship with Lesje recapitulates his marriage to Elizabeth. Elizabeth embodies much of what seemed worst in Auntie Muriel and also recognizes the same qualities in her eldest daughter. Disastrous closes, like promising beginnings — suicide or separation, new love or conception — may temporarily alter the flow but they do not really end or enhance existence as long as it continues. They are simply the givens of life, and the novel could end or begin with one such given as well as another. No obvious change in significance would be effected if *Life Before Man* opened with Lesje's pregnancy and terminated with Chris's suicide.

Confronting a flux that must inexorably sweep him away, man seeks solace and seeming stability in terminology. "Why is it called the Mesozoic," Lesje at one point asks, paraphrasing a student who wants a homework question answered by an expert:

> The correct answer, the one the teacher wants, is on the fact sheet. *Meso*, middle, *zoos*, life. . . . But does the Mesozoic exist? When it did it was called nothing. The dinosaurs didn't know they were in the middle. . . . They didn't intend to become extinct; as far as they knew they would live forever. (p. 290)

But if the Mesozoic is "the middle" then what comes after? Are we now near "the end"? If so, *Life Before Man*, decidedly closed, has a more "mimetic" conclusion than any of Atwood's other novels.

Nevertheless, and "nevertheless" does seem to be a key word in this work, there are glimmerings of hope. Chris, Elizabeth, Nate, Lesje — living, and dying, their dreary lives — are artificers: taxidermist, creator of exhibits, palaeontologist, toymaker. Despite the tawdriness of their personal affairs, they still exhibit an urge to order and create. Joseph Campbell would maintain that this urge is corrupted in the contemporary world in which rituals have become habits and iconography reduced to toymaking. Indeed, in *Life Before Man*, the traditional holidays and holydays are mainly unwelcome ties to a personal history that most of the characters would prefer to forget, occasions for another depressing encounter with some "Auntie Muriel." Religion past — Christmas, Hanukkah, Easter, Passover — evokes memories of wars, religious rivalries, the Holocaust. The secular present is no less bleak, as one successful and numerous contemplated suicides attest. The novel is replete with violence and death, and images of extinction abound. "Instead of synagogue Lesje attended the Museum, which at first did look to her a little like a church or a shrine, as if you were supposed to kneel" (p. 95). The temples have become museums, because the museum, a mausoleum of lost life forms, better represents the time it serves.

Nevertheless — and here the image turns — the museum by design *commemorates* what has died, is dying, is doomed to extinction. The dead, the defunct, the never-living artifact are all linked to the living and even to the as yet unborn. The museum thereby *implies* a future, even as it re-collects the past. As the sign soliciting contributions to the museum rebuilding fund proclaims: "ROM wasn't built in a day." Lesje, looking at the various brontosaurus and tyrannosaurus skeletons, shouts, "Live again!" And in a sense they do, for her and the other museum visitors who can see them. Similarly, fiction — which must, even when open-ended, end — comes to life with each new reader who thereby opens even closed endings. For Atwood, life and fiction wheel in strange circles. Chris, dead, becomes a kind of fossil. But to alter slightly Atwood's two epigraphs, as an "extinct animal in action," he still manages, for those who survive him, "to breathe in every quiver of [their] hand."[8] Which may just be why the too-real characters in the novel can fall in love and make love even among the dinosaurs of the Royal Ontario Museum, and why those dead dinosaurs preserved are Atwood's ambivalent icon of the life before man and her multi-valent symbol for the life of man.

GEORGE WOODCOCK

Bashful But Bold:

Notes on Margaret Atwood as Critic

One sets out on a study of Margaret Atwood as critic in the face of repeated warnings on her part that her critical writings are not to be weighed too heavily. Claiming that she started writing *Survival* to provide "a short, easy-to-use guide to Canadian literature," she insists, "I'm a writer rather than an academic or an expert." And in the first sentences of a paper on "Canadian Monsters" which she delivered at a Harvard symposium in 1976, she remarked that "unlike my compatriots here assembled, I am not a professional academic and my collecting and categorizing of monsters must be ascribed to an amateur, perverse and private eccentricity. . . ."[1]

Anyone who knows Atwood's career can be forgiven for attributing a certain disingenuousness to such statements. For not only did she study in that special sanctuary of Canadian academic criticism, Victoria College at Toronto, where she was Northrop Frye's student; not only did she pursue postgraduate studies at Harvard. She also taught English at four different Canadian universities before a modicum of fame and fortune released her to become a professional writer, and even then she returned to the academic ambience to serve for a year (1972-73) as a writer in residence at the University of Toronto.

Yet when one considers what Atwood has actually written as a critic, it is evident that in such work the literary imagination is always more ascendant than the scholarly urge to analyze and dissect. This, it seems to me, is in accordance with the development of Canadian criticism, which has been far less academically dominated than the American criticism of recent decades. Whole schools of American criticism, like the New Critics, were manned (even if a few of their officers were practicing poets) by professional academics whose interest in literature was scholarly rather than creative. But in Canada, despite the prominence achieved by Northrop Frye, most good critics — even when they have earned their livings teaching in universities — have been practicing poets, and, I believe, the poetic insights have been more important to their criticism than the academic formalities. It is historically true that poets are more likely than novelists to become good critics (the examples of Dryden and Coleridge, Baudelaire and Mallarmé and Eliot show this as clearly for the past as Canadian poet-critics do for the here-and-now). I am convinced, as I have said elsewhere, that this is because "Poetry is a craft which demands more intense and meticulous intellectual disciplines than fiction, and it does so by very reason of the irrationality of its sources."[2] It is practice in such disciplines at shaping the intuitive with the blade of the intellect that develops in so many poets the critical insights which they apply first to their own work and then to the work of others.

I am not necessarily suggesting that Margaret Atwood is a critic because she is a poet, since by no means all poets take up criticism, but I do suggest there is a link between the kind of poetry she writes and the inclination to observe literature critically, and, perhaps more important, I consider that her criticism is not separate from her fiction and her poetry; it is another facet of the same whole, and it constantly inter-reflects with them. Thus we can find clues that illuminate her critical insights in novels like *Surfacing* and *Lady Oracle* and in a great deal of her poetry, while her criticism, which rarely even mentions her own writings, gives us immensely illuminating insights into her fiction and her poetry even when she is discussing with accurate judgment the work of other writers.

Once one has accepted Atwood's disclaimer of being an academic or a formal critic it is, paradoxically, easier to find the essential patterns in her critical writing, even though at first sight it seems a curiously heterogeneous body of work that might well be given a secondary status, as literary journalism, in comparison with her novels and her poems, which do in fact present a greater appearance of formal discipline than her discursive non-fictional prose.

Among the work we may draw together under the heading of

criticism there are sharply intelligent book reviews of contemporary poets and novelists in student journals like *Acta Victoriana,* in literary magazines like *Canadian Literature* and *Open Letter,* in newspapers like the *Globe and Mail* and the *New York Times.* There are a few long and formally critical pieces (though even here the manner tends to be personal and informal in tone) like her essay on "MacEwen's Muse" in *Canadian Literature,* her Rider Haggard dissertation, "Superwoman Drawn and Quartered," and her "Canadian Monsters" essay which is subtitled "Some Aspects of the Supernatural in Canadian Fiction."[3] These are the only pieces in which Atwood carefully observes the scholarly practices, to the extent in some cases of providing a formidable and unneeded *chevaux-de-frise* of footnotes. And there are such frankly journalistic ventures as the *Maclean's* profiles of Margaret Laurence and Marie-Claire Blais,[4] and Atwood's occasional excursions into the frontierland between literature and feminist politics, such as the essay on "Paradoxes and Dilemmas: The Woman as Writer," which she wrote for Gwen Matheson's symposium, *Women in the Canadian Mosaic.*[5] And there is, finally, *Survival.*

The levels vary, as they do in the work of any man or woman of letters who follows the two basic rules of the craft: never turn down an assignment that interests you, and never do less than your best in the circumstances! Inevitably there are pieces bearing her name which neither Atwood nor her judicious readers would want perpetuated beyond a single printing. But there remain, in my view, enough critical and quasi-critical pieces to form an acceptable volume, a miscellany that would not only supplement *Survival* by revealing a variety of approach not evident in her best-known piece of critical writing, but also by showing a suppleness of mind and mood which is needed to modify the rather self-conscious single-mindedness that makes *Survival* such a stirring literary polemic.

Let me reserve *Survival* as the astringent *pièce de résistance* of this study, to be approached through the intermediate courses of Atwood's physically smaller critical works. It is an approach which I think can offer its rewards, since the smaller pieces not only display Atwood's critical talents operating on specific and restricted targets with an intensive concentration that is rarely present in the rather diffuse structure of *Survival,* but they also reflect certain recurrent elements in her poetry and fiction. They display as well her concern with the role of the artist, especially of the woman artist, and with the tendency of the public — even the relatively intelligent public that reads books — to confuse the artist with his or her creation.

One finds this concern perhaps most strongly expressed in Atwood's *Maclean's* profiles of Margaret Laurence and Marie-Claire Blais. Here we confront not so much the literary work itself as the psychology of creation (seen by a creator facing other creators) and the sociology of public response, both of which are pertinent to any critical approach that seeks to view the work of literary art within its actual progression from impulse to artifact to object of appreciation.

I suspect that Margaret Laurence is, among the two, the writer to whom Margaret Atwood feels the closer affinity, at least in terms of the actual working process (for their writing is tonally far apart). So it is that, after the customary character sketch and biographical summary which any magazine profile has to include, and after what in the early 1970s was still a necessary ritual reference to the relationship of women writers to the feminist cause, she zeroes in on what in any searching encounter between writers is always the main subject: the writing process and the relationship established during that process between the writer and her creation. Talking about Margaret Laurence, Atwood at this point is in fact uttering general truths about the process of literary creation, but also, one feels certain, particular truths that apply to herself as well as to Margaret Laurence. For example:

> *Work,* for her, is a key word and an honoured one and writing is hard work, emotionally as well as physically; when she's writing a book she feels she is "living" the character, taking on the personality she is simultaneously creating. "I lead a double life," she says, "theirs and mine." But she emphasizes that the relationship between author and character is far from a simple one-to-one equation; none of the characters in her books is "her."

Yet — and this is the perilous paradox of any kind of fictional creation — there is a sense in which, with time, the author and her creations grow more alike, rather as old married couples tend in behaviour if not always in physical appearance to resemble each other. At first, as Atwood points out, Laurence picked African settings remote enough from her own past — if not from her experience as a travelling observer — for her characters in books like *This Side Jordan* and *The Tomorrow Tamer* to seem remote from their creator. (Though how remote they were, given the ability of the literary imagination to conceal its sources, it is not so easy to determine as Atwood seems to assume.) But then Laurence turned resolutely to the world of her own past in rural Manitoba, and here, as Atwood hastens to emphasize, she moved into shifting terrain where the distinction between creation and creator became much more tenuous:

> With *The Stone Angel* she moved into her own locale, the Canadian Prairies, and each of her successive heroines — Rachel, Stacey, Vanessa — was a step closer, in age, experience and interests, to something that might be identified by the careless as herself. The central character in *The Diviners* is, in fact, a woman writer in her forties who is living in an isolated farmhouse and writing a novel. "I know it's bloody difficult, it's one of the most difficult things to do," she says, "writing about a writer. But I had to. At first I had her as a painter, but what the hell do I know about painting."
>
> *The Diviners*, which took her three years of writing time, is a huge, risky, ambitious book, the kind writers produce at a summing-up period in their careers, if they ever make it that far. . . .

It is hard, of course, to believe that a great summing-up book contains nothing of its author, and in fact Morag Gunn is in many details close enough to her creator for the resemblance to be haunting for those who know them both. Margaret Laurence has of course admitted in *Heart of a Stranger* that in retrospect she had to accept one of her Manawaka books, *Bird in the House*, in which the girl Vanessa was the central character, as being semi-autobiographical, dominated by her own relationship with her maternal grandfather. Atwood does not mention this admission, and this reluctance on her part to grant the existence of a shifting frontier between fiction and autobiography emerges again in her essay on Marie-Claire Blais.

The reasons why Atwood was attracted to Blais are evident, for in Blais, a writer exactly her own age, she found an example of the Gothic imagination which has always fascinated her. Her profile, "Marie-Claire Blais Is Not for Burning," in fact begins with her reading, when it first appeared in 1959, *La Belle Bête* in its English translation (*Mad Shadows*):

The book made me very uneasy, for more than the obvious reasons: the violence, the murders, suggestions of incest and the hallucinatory intensity of the writing were rare in Canadian literature in those days, but even scarier was the thought that this bloodcurdling fantasy, as well as its precocious verbal skill, were the products of a girl of 19. I was 19 myself, and with such an example before me I already felt like a late bloomer.

Atwood gives no hint that the reading of *La Belle Bête* actually influenced her own writing, and her use of Gothic and mock-Gothic motifs in books like *Surfacing* and *Lady Oracle* is quite different in character from that of Blais, who is not using motifs so much as recreating ancestral Quebec as a self-consistent world of Gothic horror. But even if Atwood herself has never written consistently Gothic novels, the interest in the grotesque and the monstrous is a constant element in her critical purview, emerging in the elaborate study of Rider Haggard's mysteries in "Superwoman Drawn and Quartered" and in her essay on "Canadian Monsters," with its discussion of the supernatural and the pseudo-supernatural as elements in Canadian novels, and attracting her to poets like James Reaney whose work, in what she calls its "unprecedented weirdness," is generally remote from her own both technically and emotionally.

But once we are embarked on the profile of Marie-Claire Blais, we encounter again that abrasive Atwood sensitivity over the identification of the author with his or her creation. She describes her meeting with Blais, and the astonishment that betrayed her expectations of encountering someone resembling a character in *La Belle Bête:*

Still, when it comes to so-called serious fiction, the autobiographical fallacy rears its head sooner or later, and we project onto the author, and take as literal truth, those imaginary images he or she has created. I've had this done to me so often that I should have been well aware of the difference between fictions and those who make them; still, I must have been expecting the waif of the early press coverage or the romantic demon-ess of the more *outré* of the novels. Otherwise I would not have been quite so surprised by the reality.

And after the customary profile sketch of her subject's career she comes back to this insistent theme, to the misunderstandings Blais — and by implication Atwood — have experienced, and to the final remark in which Blais seems to be summing the matter up for both of them:

More seriously, she said, "Surely it is not impossible to project your imagination into the mind of some one else" — a very succinct definition of the art of fiction writing.

Appearing in a popular magazine, such statements, which vastly over-simplify the relationship between the novelist and her creations, appear to be warning off the readers from the even more simplistic tendency to seek the author in her characters, of which Atwood readily assumes the general reading public to be recurrently guilty. What, of course, she does not say in either essay is that the public speculates on such matters only if authors are presented to it as interesting personalities, and it is therefore possible to see her vehement denials of characters resembling their authors as being linked with those ambiguities of her own public persona which Robert Fulford has well exposed in his essay on "The Images of Atwood":

> The media are not usually creative enough to invent a myth; they must be supplied with at least the raw materials of hagiography. This is what Atwood supplies, not only through the densely personal character of her work — exemplified most obviously in *Power Politics* — but through the elusiveness of her public stance, her half-shy and half-assertive public manner. When she says that she has become a Thing and is appalled by it, she is expressing the essentially shy individual's horror of her own public self-creation.
>
> . . . She shows us, by her work and her utterance, that there is something important about her; but she shields from us the essence of what it is. Then, whenever disclosure of the essence seems a possibility, she changes it.[6]

But even when we have granted the justice of Fulford's remarks, the fact remains that Atwood is taking a legitimate critical stance, if a somewhat purist one, in her denunciation of the autobiographical fallacy as it applies to fiction, just as in her essay on "The Woman as Writer" in *Women in the Canadian Mosaic* she is taking a somewhat different but equally legitimate stance when she sharply delimits the extent to which writers should become involved in politics, even feminist politics: "their involvement may be good for the movement, but it is yet to be demonstrated that it's good for the writer."

She views with evident alarm the possibility of the kind of feminist-oriented criticism in which "reviewers will start demanding that heroines resolve their difficulties with husband, kids or themselves by stomping out to join a consciousness-raising group or get a job, which will be no more satisfactory from the point of view of literature than the legendary Socialist Realist romance with one's tractor." Nor, she goes on to suggest, is it any more satisfactory than the various types of masculine reviewing which use the fact that writers happen to be women as a special factor in critical judgments. In such criticism — however chivalrous it may appear — women become stereotypes, as Atwood remarks in a passage which comes near to an attempt to counter the kind of comment on her public persona like that by Fulford which I have just quoted:

> The point about these stereotypes is that attention is focused not on the actual achievements of the authors, but on their lives, which are distorted and romanticized; their work is then interpreted in the light of the distorted version. Stereotypes like these, even when the author cooperates in their formation and especially when the author becomes a cult object, do no service to anyone or anything, least of all the author's work. Behind all of them is the notion that authors must be more special, peculiar or weird than other people, and that their lives are more interesting than their work.

Later on in the same essay Atwood argues, quite justly, that "no good writer wants to be merely a transmitter of somebody else's ideology, no matter how fine that ideology may be," and at this point she circles back to give a sharper definition of her idea of the difference between the propagandist and the writer:

> The aim of propaganda is to convince and to spur people to action; the aim of fiction and poetry writing is to create a plausible and moving imaginative world, and to create it with words. Or, to put it another way, the aim of any political movement is to improve the quality of people's lives on all levels, spiritual and imaginative as well as material (and any political movement that doesn't have this aim is worth nothing). Imaginative writing, however, tends to concentrate more on life not as it ought to be, but as it is, as the writer feels it, experiences it. Writers are eye-witnesses, I-witnesses.

And it is precisely, she suggests, in abandoning both stereotypes and idealized images of their sex, and in striving to portray life and women as they are, that the serious women writers in Canada recently have defined themselves:

> Women in their books are no longer relegated to the shadow-lands
> of either/or. They proclaim, if anything, their right to be fully
> human, to nurture without being Earth Mothers, to curse without
> being witches, to suffer without being Little Nell the loveable
> victim, to copulate without being the Scarlet Woman. *Woman* as
> a homogeneous gender has become obsolete; women as human
> beings, on and off the page, are flourishing as never before.

Anti-autobiographical and anti-political stances of this kind
are of course conceived to counter anything that seems to diminish
the role and the autonomy of the writer's imagination, and as
defences against takeover by publicists and politicians they have
their purpose. Yet they are simplistic. While it is obviously foolish
to expect to find the origins of what happens in a novel in the
events of its author's life (though some novelists freely mine their
personal experiences without harming their fictional achieve-
ments) or the motives of a character in the author himself, the fact
remains that nothing an author produces (unless he borrows
slavishly from another) comes from anywhere but within, and
thus there must be one among his personae — even if not the everyday one — whose life is in fact being written in his novels. At some
level everything we produce is part of our life, and the denial of the
autobiographical becomes merely an argument for the defence in
the court of critical judgment. The same applies to the denial of
the political, for, as Orwell said, "no book is genuinely free from
political bias. The opinion that art should have nothing to do
with politics is itself a political attitude." So, in a curious, inverted
way, is Atwood's view that politics is concerned with life as it
ought to be, whereas imaginative literature is concerned with life
as it is. This, of course, says too much for politics, which usually
all too sordidly concerns itself with the here-and-now, and too
little for imaginative literature, which by definition is an act of
creation as well as an act of witnessing. "Life as it is," is the subject
of classic realism, but even fiction, certainly in Canada, has been
veering away from realism for a long time now.

It seems to me that in *Survival*, the critical book by which she
is best known, Atwood recognizes these complexities. As I shall
later show, even if she avoids considering Canadian books as the
autobiographies of individuals, she considers Canadian literature
as the autobiography of a people, a collective consensus on the
part of many writers concerning the common meanings to be
found in their individual lives. And if her roughly thematical

approach in this way tends to emphasize collective as against individual psychology, it also tends to stress the mythical, in the sense of generalized collective concepts of our national destiny, as against the historical, which deals in terms of precise events. In this way the political seems to be avoided, but in fact nobody can really say that *Survival* is not a political book, since the predicament its arguments delineate is that of a national culture, and the solutions to that predicament, even though they are no more than implied, cannot be other than political. If, even as poets and novelists, we must raise ourselves out of colonialism in order to achieve artistic maturity, then the achievement of artistic maturity is a political act performed by non-politicians, and for that reason all the purer politically.

But before I go on to examine *Survival*, which is a frankly polemical book with much of the provocativeness and calculated exaggeration of a good political pamphlet, I would like to test Atwood's ability in the "pure" and unpolemical kind of criticism which her arguments about the unbiographical and unpolitical nature of literature seem to suggest. Can she really produce the clear, sharp analysis of a work of writing that will please the critic and the creator as easily as she can produce the thematic overview that seems so easily appropriate to its time that, as *Survival* did, it becomes — with or without the consent of its creator — something approaching a manifesto of nationalist cultural theory?

The answer is, I believe, an emphatic Yes. As I have suggested, Atwood's shorter pieces are varied in their emphasis, and some of them, like "Canadian Monsters" and "Eleven Years of *Alphabet*," tend to be historical in approach, the first tracing a particular genre in Canadian writing from early to modern times and the second following the brief history of James Reaney's very original literary magazine, *Alphabet*.[7] Both reflect Atwood's ability to utter bold and convincing generalizations about her subjects and to relate particular examples to them, and here a paragraph in "Eleven Years of *Alphabet*," comparing English, American, and Canadian habits of mind, tells us not only a great deal about our collective way of looking at things, but even more about how Atwood sees herself within the critical spectrum. She begins by remarking that the English habit of mind is empirical, sees reality embodied in the social hierarchy, and values "taste." The American habit of mind is abstract and analytical, sees reality in how things work, and values "technique":

The Canadian habit of mind for whatever reason — perhaps a history and a social geography which both seem to lack coherent shape — is synthetic. 'Taste' and 'Technique' are both of less concern to it than is the ever-failing but ever-renewed attempt to pull all the pieces together to discover the whole of which one can only trust one is a part. The most central Canadian literary products, then, tend to be large-scope works like *The Anatomy of Criticism* and the *Gutenberg Galaxy* which propose all-embracing systems within which any particular bit of data may be placed. Give the same poem to a model American, a model English and a model Canadian critic: The American will say "This is how it works;" the Englishman "How good, how true to life!" (or, "How boring, tasteless and trite"); the Canadian will say "This is where it fits into the entire universe." It is in its love for synthesis that *Alphabet* shows itself peculiarly Canadian.

And so does Margaret Atwood — even though she grants in "Canadian Monsters," after categorizing the forms of unnatural beings that exist in Canadian fiction, that "such a critical pattern exists in the mind of the critic rather than in the external world." Even in the shorter pieces of criticism which are clear and sharp in their perceptions, one is always aware that Atwood is going beyond particular works, and particular aspects of a writer's whole body of work, to find the clue out of which a synthetic view of the writer's significance can be created.

This is shown admirably in her essay on "MacEwen's Muse." In a single opening sentence she acknowledges and at the same time dismisses the questions of taste and technique which, as she argues, might concern English and American critics, and then she goes on immediately to the real unifying concept (or symbol if you wish) in MacEwen's poetry:

In reading Gwendolyn MacEwen's poetry it is a temptation to become preoccupied with the original and brilliant verbal surfaces she creates, at the expense of the depths beneath them. But it is occasionally instructive to give at least passing attention to what poets themselves say about their work, and MacEwen has been insisting for some time that it is 'the thing beyond the poem,' the 'raw material' of literature, that above all concerns her. There is, of course, more than one thing beyond the poems, but there is one figure whose existence is hinted at throughout her work and who acts as a key to much of it. This is the Muse, often invoked and described but never named; and in MacEwen's poetry the Muse, the inspirer of language and the formative power in Nature, is

male. Ignore him or misinterpret him and her 'muse' poems may
be mistaken for 'religious' ones or reduced to veiled sexuality.
Acknowledge him, and he will perform one of the functions Mac-
Ewen ascribes to him: the creation of order out of chaos.

What Atwood tells us is that we should not look for the
moving inspiration of MacEwen's poetry in sources of energy that
lie outside the literary imagination. MacEwen, she argues, has in
fact created her own myth, rather than accepting it from the
circumambient culture. "The informing myth, developed
gradually but with increasing clarity in her poetry, is that of the
Muse, author and inspirer of language and therefore of the ordered
verbal cosmos, the poet's universe." In translating this myth into
poetry, MacEwen also translates it into life. Proceeding by way of
the poet's expressed intent, and by a lengthy analysis of the
appearances and functions of mysterious male figures in Mac-
Ewen's poems, Atwood supports her insight in a critically
impeccable way, with careful attention both to the text *and* to the
intention. Quite evidently, she does not subscribe to that curious
American cultural aberration, the doctrine of the "intentional
fallacy," which supposes that the writer's intent can tell us
nothing about his finished work. And in this she fits her own
definition of the Canadian critic as one who is willing to use any
piece of data that may have relevance to the synthesis he is creating.

An example of a somewhat less tightly unified kind of critical
writing is Atwood's long review article, "Reaney Collected," on
Germaine Warkentin's 1973 edition of James Reaney's *Poems*.[8]
This is by intent a different kind of piece from "MacEwen's
Muse." It does not seek to explore a single dominant myth, but to
set back in his proper place in critical attention a poet whose
reputation at the time of writing Atwood felt had slumped unjus-
tifiably, largely because critics had not been reading the poems for
themselves but "reading into them various philosophies and
literary theories which the poet is assumed to have." Read the
poems again, as they actually are, she suggests, and "one of your
first reactions will almost certainly be that there is nothing else
like them."

"First reactions" are important to Atwood even critically. It is
characteristic of her "Canadian" method that she does not try to
interest us in the poems by elaborate discussions of taste and technique. All she says about such matters does indeed tend to have the
impulsive immediacy of personal reaction:

Reaney's best poems come from a fusion of 'personal' and 'mythic' or 'universal': when they lean too far towards either side, you get obscurity or straight nostalgia at one end or bloodless abstraction at the other. And at times, reading his work, I feel the stirrings of that old Romantic distinction between the Fancy and the Imagination, though I try hard to suppress it; I even hear a voice murmuring 'Whimsy,' and it murmurs loudest when I come across a concrete image linked arbitrarily and with violence to a 'universal' meaning. If you can see a world in a grain of sand, well, good; but you shouldn't stick one on just because you think it ought to be there.

But the way she reaches into Reaney's imaginative world is one that, as with MacEwen, aims to bring the whole poet before our eyes rather than merely the poet as technician or the poet as eccentric philosopher. She does it through a rather obvious device, picking up the familiar critical cliché about Frye's influence over Reaney. She does not deny that there was a kind of influence, but she suggests that it was a "catalyst" rather than an "ingredient," and she continued to what — with her routine gesture of modesty about her critical pretensions — she calls "a little deductive speculation."

She first shows the early Reaney creating a world that fails to work, a world of bored and destructive people, filled with objects "lacking in all but personal significance," presenting instead of love "sex observed through a child's eye, foreign and monstrous." It is, despite the verbal richness with which it is presented, a world of "sin with no possibility of redemption, a fallen world with no divine counterpart."

Atwood "guesses" that Frye's literary theories offered Reaney the religion in which he had lost faith "in a different, more sophisticated, acceptable form: The Bible might not be *literally* true, but under the aegis of Frye it could be seen as metaphorically, psychically true." This did not mean that Frye's mind altered Reaney's mind, or even added anything to what was already latent in the poet's imagination. It was neither forms nor potential material that Frye changed, but the "kind of resolutions" that were possible to the poet. Such altered resolutions released his imagination, his memory, his "verbal magic" to function as redemptive agents, bring about the paradox that "in Reaney's work the Songs of Innocence come *after* the Songs of Experience." Not that even now every poem Reaney produced achieved its resolution; Atwood suggests this is because Reaney is a magic, Coleridgean kind of poet rather than a meditative Wordsworthian poet:

> The trouble with being a magic poet is that when you fail, you fail
> more obviously than the meditative or descriptive poet; the rabbit
> simply refuses to emerge from the hat.

All this, I felt when Atwood sent her article to me for *Canadian Literature* in 1973, explained the problems everyone feels about Reaney's poetry — its division between early and late periods, its progression from complexity towards an often disconcerting simplicity (even at times simple-mindedness) and the whole question of influences — more convincingly than any other critical explanation I had encountered. It seemed to be practical-mediational criticism — as distinct from the academic-theoretical kind — at its most vital level, and re-reading it has made me regret, as I have often done before, that Atwood has not more often turned her penetrating combination of insight and intelligence to the examination of individual figures in Canadian writing. She would have made a fine professional critic, but for obvious reasons she has chosen not to be so.

Indeed, she has tended to preserve with a certain quiet obstinacy her amateur position, discussing her fellow writers with personal informality more often than with critical formality, and in *Survival* she has produced one of the oddest-looking critical books ever written in Canada.

The genesis of the book, which seems to have been put together quite quickly before its publication in 1972 as a fattish tract for the nationalistic times, appears to have lain in Atwood's period of literary missionary work, when she became so concerned over the absence of Canadian books and authors in schools and colleges that she would travel around the southern Ontario countryside giving talks and readings at schools and lugging suitcases full of books by Canadian poets which she tried to sell for the cause. At this time she decided to write what she called "a teacher's guide to the many new courses in Canadian literature."

By now — I write in 1979 — we have a number of such guides, and usually "in the kingdom of the blind the one-eyed man is king." When Margaret Atwood gets to work on such a project, it seems to be a case of third-eye not quite fitting into the local situation but nevertheless telling one-eye to keep no-eye out of the mire.

Survival ended up being a curious hybrid of a book, for the mechanical features of the course guide are retained: the lists of recommended texts, the feature of "fifteen useful books," the appendices relating to research resources are all there, and while this may be informative to the uninformed, it is plaguily condescending to anyone who has even a rudimentary knowledge of Canadian books and the literature concerning them. The serious reader who does not wish to be biased against Atwood's conclusions must ignore these intrusions which seem like a kind of survival course to test the reality of one's interest in the book or its subject. This means refusing to read (or reading on a shallower level of one's mind) perhaps a quarter of the book in order to arrive at the real core of *Survival,* the work that eventually emerged but was not intended.

For *Survival* is one of those mildly exasperating books in which a brilliant intelligence has been unable to put the brakes on its activity and has run far ahead of the task undertaken, so that all readers get more than they bargain for, and the disappointed are perhaps as numerous as those who are gratefully surprised. The body of the work is a sophisticated and challenging exposure of the Canadian psyche as revealed through our literature, an exposure that is double-edged since it also reveals that the born writer who attempts to popularize usually ends up producing something whose real meaning can be appreciated only by her peers. I suspect most students on any level of the educational ladder below the postgraduate (unless perhaps they attend Victoria College, Toronto) will be confused when they are faced with *Survival* and will never emerge from their bewilderment.

Yet Margaret Atwood presents very plausibly and supports with shrewdly chosen examples from the work of Canadian writers the argument that our literature is still scarred and distorted by the mental condition that emerges from a colonial past. It is, she suggests, essentially a literature of failure. Our greatest triumphs as a nation were achieved by blind collective urges; the "heroes" we name in connection with them turn out to be at best outward successes, and often not even that. Our literature reflects this situation.

All Canadian attitudes, in Atwood's view, can be related to the central fact of victimization imposed or at least attempted, and she lists and grades these attitudes, from *"Position One: To deny the fact that you are a victim"* (which objectively considered is the ultimate in victimization), to *"Position Four: To be a creative non-victim,"* the position of those — among whom the reader hopefully includes himself — whom Atwood tells "You are able to accept your own experience for what it is, rather than having to distort it to make it correspond with others' versions of it (particularly those of your oppressors)."

Such a literature, Atwood suggests, whether it expresses a denial or a recognition of experience, reflects an attitude to life that aims no higher than survival. French Canadians turned this fact into a self-conscious way of life, with *La Survivance* as a motto but also a national aim; the English Canadians recognized it explicitly in their pioneer literature and implicitly in their literary identification with animals, whom they see as quintessential victims and whose triumph can be no more than to live on to face another danger and, if they are fortunate, another survival.

It is a thesis that admirably fits many of the facts about our life and our literature, and in presenting it Atwood has condensed into a sharp focus the scattered insights which many other critics have recorded about the Canadian condition. We have no heroes; only martyrs. We pride ourselves with Calvinist or Jansenist smugness on our ironic modesty. With an inverted Pharisaism, we stake what claims we may propose to moral superiority, not on our successes, but on our failures. The main difference between Atwood and the others, like Frye and D.G. Jones who have explored the same territory, is that their maps are descriptive, charts for explorers; hers are tactical, tools in a campaign, charts to help us repel a cultural invasion and arise, foursquare in Position Four, consciously manifesting our true identities.

There is some truth in Malcolm Ross's contention that Atwood "offers us a rhetoric not a poetic."[9] The propagandist urge which we have seen her repudiating seems here to be turned towards the very heart of the world of literary creation, and writers' works are interpreted as records of the experience of being colonialized in such a way that one cannot see them as other than autobiographical, even if the final effect is a collective rather than an individual one.

There are, of course, other limitations to Atwood's thesis. There are many Canadian writers whom it does not fit, like Robertson Davies and Irving Layton and Ethel Wilson. On the other hand obsessions with failure and survival are not especially Canadian. Survival as a recurrent mythic pattern is exemplified in world literature from the *Epic of Gilgamesh* and the *Odyssey* down to the novels of such colonizing (rather than colonized)

writers as Kipling and (more ambiguously) Orwell, who by
Atwood's criteria looks like a pretty good candidate for Canadian
cultural naturalization, given his famous remark that every life,
viewed from the inside, is a failure.

Yet even if we must deny that Atwood's thesis identifies a
peculiarly or universally Canadian condition, we have to agree
that our poets and novelists of failure and survival have been too
numerous and too compelling not to give a special flavour to our
literature. It is no accident that to be dubbed "a survivor" is a
compliment among Canadians. The more generalized criticism
becomes, the more tentative inevitably it is, and certainly no
critical map of the literary terrain of any land or period should be
accepted as more than a useable frame of reference, a hypothesis
that holds the facts together. *Survival* performs both functions.

But — bearing in mind Atwood's own admission that most
critical schemata are creations of the critics' minds — we can
perhaps at this point relate the various facets of her creativity and
remark that the prime importance of *Survival* — to the reader if
not necessarily to the writer — may well be not its remarks about
Canadian books (many of which have been made in other ways by
other people) but the fact that it gives another form to themes and
insights that can be found in her poetry and her fiction.

In fact, when we try to distill the real spirit that inspires
Survival we go down below the ephemeral level of polemics and
come to the persons inspiring the book. And here — I must shift to
the singular since I am discussing personal identifications — one
finds a kind of mental toughness and resilience which call up a
poem from *Power Politics* that has always seemed to me to project
a poetic as well as an ethical stance so far as Atwood was concerned:

> Beyond truth,
> tenacity: of those
> dwarf trees & mosses,
> hooked into straight rock
> believing the sun's lies & thus
> refuting/gravity
>
> & of this cactus, gathering
> itself together
> against the sand, yes tough
> rind & spikes but doing
> the best it can

It seems to me that the tenacity, the defensive strength, the "doing/
the best it can," characterize Atwood's own poetry but characterize
also her view of Canadian literature. But beyond the recognition of
being and hence survival, beyond the mere will to continue, there
is the journey of self-discovery that begins from the simplest levels
and which at the end of *Survival* Atwood offers for Canadian
literature and, through it, for Canadian self-awareness. It is a
journey with bleak beginnings, but the start has been made:

> When I discovered the shape of the national tradition I was depres-
> sed, and it's obvious why: it's a fairly tough tradition I was saddled
> with, to have to come to terms with. But I was exhilarated too:
> having bleak ground under your feet is better than having no
> ground at all. Any map is better than no map as long as it is accu-
> rate, and knowing your starting points and your frame of reference
> is better than being suspended in the void.

Thus, in *Survival* one finds transmuted into logical terms
many of the ideas one absorbs almost osmotically from reading
Atwood's poems, and perhaps in more direct ways from her novels,
which also are reflected in some of her critical essays, like
"Canadian Monsters," where there are echoes of the heroine's preoccupation with Gothic novels in *Lady Oracle* (itself a splendid
fictional critique of the genre and those who write it) and in the
grotesque incidents that propel *Edible Woman* and *Surfacing* at
times over the edge into fantasy.

But *Surfacing* has perhaps a more central role in one's view of
Atwood as critic than the other novels, since it was written just
before *Survival,* which, as Eli Mandel has remarked, can almost be
read as a "gloss" on that novel. Certainly *Surfacing* concerns
survival, and it is also so obsessed with Canadian victims that one
can find therein a majority of the types of victims described in *Survival's* various chapters. There are animal victims, victim Indians
(but not Eskimos since it is too far south), victim children, victim
women, victim French Canadians, a victim artist, and victim sham
pioneers, since it is too late in history for real ones. The other
victim types — explorers, immigrants, heroes, and jail breakers —
are not directly represented, but in a sense the narrator is all of
them, since in searching for her dead father she explores her own
past, she migrates into a new self, she breaks the jail of her
imprisoned old self, and she is as much the heroine as the tone of
the novel admits.

More than that, *Surfacing* like *Survival* portrays Canada as a victim of the sickness of colonialism, and, while one should not over-stress the didactic elements in these aspects of the novel, there is enough to show that the novel and *Survival* were inspired by related impulses. Each in its own way is a book about self-realization, hence life-realization; *Surfacing* appears to concern an individual and *Survival* a people, but the allegory of the novel is collective and the emotion inspiring the critical polemic is personal. The difference may be that the novel contains an extra element of criticism, self-criticism, in the form of a self-mockery, that writers on Atwood have been slow to recognize. Let us take her seriously, but not too seriously. She has never claimed to be a systematic critic. But in her mutable way she has been a good and important one at this crucial time in the development of our sense of a literary culture.

ALAN J. HORNE

Margaret Atwood

A Checklist of Writings
By and About Margaret Atwood[1]

Part 1   Works by Margaret Atwood

    A   Books: Poetry

    B   Books: Fiction and Other Prose Writings

    C   Poetry Contributed to Periodicals, Books
        and Anthologies

    D   Prose Contributed to Periodicals, Books
        and Anthologies

Part 2   Works on Margaret Atwood

    E   Books, Articles, Theses and Interviews

    F   Selected Reviews: Poetry

    G   Selected Reviews: Prose

Part I: Works by Margaret Atwood

A Books: Poetry

A1   *Double Persephone.*
(Market Book Series, Book 1.) Toronto: Hawkshead Press, 1961. 16 pp.

A2   *The Circle Game.*
Bloomfield Hills, Mich.: n.p., 1964. 18 leaves (incl. 8 plates.) Printed in a limited edition of 15 copies designed, printed and illustrated by Charles Pachter.

A3   *Talismans for Children.*
Bloomfield Hills, Mich.: n.p., 1965. 6 leaves. col. illus. Printed at the Cranbrook Academy of Art in a limited edition of 20 copies, with coloured illustrations by Charles Pachter.

A4   *Kaleidoscopes Baroque: A Poem.*
Bloomfield Hills, Mich.; n.p., 1965. 15 pp. col. illus. Printed at the Cranbrook Academy of Art in a limited edition of 20 copies, with coloured illustrations by Charles Pachter.

A5   *Speeches for Doctor Frankenstein.*
Bloomfield Hills, Mich.: n.p., 1966. 29 pp. col. illus. Printed at the Cranbrook Academy of Art in a limited edition of 15 copies, designed, illustrated and printed by Charles Pachter.

A6   *Expeditions.*
Bloomfield Hills, Mich.: n.p., 1966. 10 leaves. col. illus. Printed in a limited edition of 15 copies, with lithographs by Charles Pachter.

A7   *The Circle Game.*
Toronto: Contact Press, 1966. 80 pp.
Toronto: House of Anansi, 1967. 80 pp. (100 copies of this House of Anansi edition were published in cloth with a slipcase, signed by Atwood.)
Toronto: House of Anansi, [1978]. 95 pp. Reprinted with an introduction by Sherrill Grace.

A8   *The Animals in That Country.*
Toronto: Oxford University Press, 1968. 69 pp.
Boston: Little, Brown [1968]. 69 pp.

A9   *What Was in the Garden.*
      Santa Barbara, Ca.: Unicorn Press, 1969. A broad-
      side with col. illus. by Charles Pachter. (One of
      twelve broadsides by Canadian poets in *Unicorn
      Folio Series 3 No. 1, A Canadian Folio.)*

A10   *Dreams of the Animals.*
      n.p., n.d. [1970?] A broadside. (The poem, later pub-
      lished in *Procedures for Underground,* is here
      printed from an original drawing by Atwood.)

A11   *The Journals of Susanna Moodie.*
      Toronto: Oxford University Press, 1970. 64 pp. illus.
      ("The collages and cover design are by Margaret
      Atwood.")

A12   *Procedures for Underground.*
      Toronto: Oxford University Press, 1970. 79pp.
      Boston: Little, Brown, [1970]. 79 pp.

A13   *Power Politics.*
      Toronto: Anansi, 1971. 58 pp.
      New York: Harper & Row, [1973?] 56 pp.

A14   *You Are Happy.*
      Toronto: Oxford University Press, 1974. 96 pp.
      New York: Harper & Row, [1974]. 96 pp.

A15   *Selected Poems.*
      Toronto: Oxford University Press, [1976]. 240 pp.
      New York: Simon and Schuster [1978]. 240 pp.
      (Contains a selection from six books of poetry: *The
      Circle Game, The Animals in That Country, Pro-
      cedures for Underground, The Journals of Susanna
      Moodie* (in full), *Power Politics* and *You Are
      Happy.)*

A16   *Marsh, Hawk.*
      Toronto: Dreadnaught, [1977]. A broadside, illus-
      trated by Suzanne Mogensen. (One of 52 broadsides
      printed as a collection — 52 pickup.)

A17   *Up in the Tree.*
      Toronto: McClelland and Stewart, [1978]. 28 pp.
      (Written and illustrated for children by Atwood.)

A18   *Two-Headed Poems.*
      Toronto: Oxford University Press, 1978. 112 pp.

B   Books: Fiction and Other Prose Writings

Fiction

B1   *The Edible Woman.*
Toronto: McClelland and Stewart, 1969. 281 pp.
London: Andre Deutsch, 1969. 281 pp.
Boston: Little, Brown, 1969. 281 pp. An Atlantic
Monthly Press Book.
New Canadian Library, No. 93. Toronto: McClel-
land and Stewart, 1973. 281 pp.
New York: Popular Library, 1976. 287 pp.
La Donna da Mangiare. Trans. Mario Manzari.
Milan: Longanesi, 1976. 295 pp.
Toronto: Seal Books, 1978. 294 pp. (Plus 15 pp. from
Lady Oracle).
London: Virago, 1980. 281 pp. With an introduction
by Atwood.

B2   *Surfacing.*
Toronto: McClelland and Stewart, 1972. 192 pp.
London: Andre Deutsch, 1973. 192 pp.
London: Wildwood House, 1973. 192 pp.
New York: Simon & Schuster, 1973. 224 pp.
Don Mills, Ontario: Paperjacks, 1973. 192 pp.
New York: Popular Library, 1974. 224 pp.
Vancouver: Taped Books Project, 1974. Audiotape;
7 hours duration.
Faire Surface. Trans. Marie-France Girod. Mon-
treal: Editions L'Etincelle, 1978. 231 pp.
Der Lange Traum. Trans. Reinhild Böhnke. Düssel-
dorf: Classen, 1979.
London: Virago, 1979. 192 pp. With an introduction
by Francine du Plessix Gray.

B3   *Lady Oracle.*
Toronto: McClelland and Stewart, 1976. 345 pp.
New York: Simon & Schuster, 1976. 345 pp.
London: Andre Deutsch, 1977. 345 pp.
Toronto: Seal Books, 1977. 345 pp.
New York: Avon Books, 1978. 380 pp.

B4   *Dancing Girls.*
Toronto: McClelland and Stewart, 1977. 256 pp.
Toronto: Seal Books, 1978. 245 pp.

B5   *Life Before Man.*
Toronto: McClelland and Stewart, 1979. 317 pp.
New York: Simon and Schuster, 1979. 317 pp.
London: Jonathan Cape, 1980. 317 pp.
Toronto: Seal Books, 1980. 291 pp.

Criticism

B6   *Survival.*
Toronto: House of Anansi, 1972. 287 pp.

Drama

B7   *Grace Marks.*
Unpublished typescript, 1974. 85 pp.
Produced on CBC television in January 1974, as *The Servant Girl.*

C   Poetry Contributed to Periodicals, Books and Anthologies
Note: Poems which have been subsequently collected and reprinted in one of Atwood's books are omitted from this listing.

Poems in Periodicals

C1   "The First Brush-Cut." *Clan Call* (Leaside High School), 1, No. 6 (1954-55), 29.

C2   "The Mind." *Clan Call,* 2, No. 1 (1956-57), 37.

C3   "The Conversation." *Acta Victoriana,* 83, No. 1 (November 1958), 11.

C4   "Spratire." *Acta Victoriana,* 83, No. 2 (December 1958), 22.
(This poem is one of several contributions by "Shakesbeat Latweed" which, according to Margaret Atwood, is the "joint author" pseudonym under which Atwood and Dennis Lee wrote while students at Victoria College.)

C5   "Knell and Nativity." *Acta Victoriana,* 83, No. 4 (February 1959), 19.

C6   "Fruition." *Canadian Forum,* 39 (September 1959), 130.

C7   "Confessional." *Acta Victoriana,* 84, No. 1 (December 1959), 8.

C8   "Small Requiem." *Canadian Forum*, 39 (December 1959), 202.

C9   "Paeon." *The Sheet*, 1, No. 1 (January 1960), 7.

C10   "Hanging Garden." *Acta Victoriana*, 84, No. 2 (March 1960), 10. — Also in *Canadian Forum*, 40 (August 1960), 114.

C11   "Small Colossus." *Acta Victoriana*, 84, No. 2 (March 1960), 10. — Also in *Canadian Forum*, 40 (August 1960), 114.

C12   "Sculpted Zeus." *Acta Victoriana*, 84, No. 2 (March 1960), 11. — Also in *Canadian Forum*, 40 (August 1960), 114.

C13   "Temple of Artemis." *Acta Victoriana*, 84, No. 2 (March 1960), 11. — Also in *Canadian Forum*, 40 (August 1960), 114.

C14   "Mausoleum." *Acta Victoriana*, 84, No. 2 (March 1960), 12. — Also in *Canadian Forum*, 40 (August 1960), 115.

C15   "Pharos." *Acta Victoriana*, 84, No. 2 (March 1960), 12. — Also in *Canadian Forum*, 40 (August 1960), 115.

C16   "Pyramid at Sunrise." *Acta Victoriana*, 84, No. 2 (March 1960), 13. — Also in *Canadian Forum*, 40 (August 1960), 115.

C17   "Inscription." *Acta Victoriana*, 84, No. 2 (March 1960), 13. — Also in *Canadian Forum*, 40 (August 1960), 115.

C18   "The Bottled Woman." *Varsity*, 79, No. 68 (18 March 1960), 6. — Also in *Tamarack Review*, No. 21 (Autumn 1961), p. 21.

C19   "The Expelled." *Varsity*, 79, No. 68 (18 March 1960), 6.

C20   "The Triple Goddess: a Poem for Voices." *Acta Victoriana*, [84], No. 3 (April 1960), 8-13.

C21   "Harvesters." *Canadian Forum*, 40 (June 1960), 60.

C22   "Towered Woman." *Canadian Forum*, 40 (June 1960), 60.

C23 "The Girl Too Early." *The Sheet,* No. 2 (September 1960), p. 3.

C24 "Reflection." *The Sheet,* No. 2 (September 1960), p. 3.

C25 "The Kollege Koffee Krowd . . . a Pome." (By Shakesbeat Latweed, *pseud.*) *The Strand* (Victoria College), 14 October 1960, p. 3.

C26 "A Hymn to VCU." (By Shakesbeat Latweed, *pseud.*) *The Strand,* 11 November 1960, pp. 3-4.

C27 "To The Strand, on Demand." (By Shakesbeat Latweed, *pseud.*) *The Strand,* 25 November 1960, p. 3.

C28 "From the Island: Three Small Songs." *Acta Victoriana,* [85], No. 1 (November 1960), 13.

C29 "Seaweedy." (By Shakesbeat Latweed, *pseud.*) *The Strand,* 10 March 1961, pp. 2-3.

C30 "Childhood Under Glass." *Acta Victoriana,* [85], No. 4 (March 1961), 1.

C31 "Eye." *Acta Victoriana,* [85], No. 4 (March 1961), 1.

C32 "Island, Fall." *Acta Victoriana,* [85], No. 4 (March 1961), 1.

C33 "The Field of Souls." *Acta Victoriana.* [85], No. 4 (March 1961), 2.

C34 "We and Our Lost Souls." *Acta Victoriana,* [85], No. 4 (March 1961), 2.

C35 "The Triple Woman." *Jargon,* No. 2 (Spring 1961), p. 3.

C36 "Wind in Weeds." *Jargon,* No. 2 (Spring 1961), p. 4.

C37 "Proserpine." *Jargon,* No. 2 (Spring 1961), p. 4.

C38 "Woman By the Water." *Canadian Forum,* 41 (April 1961), 5.

C39 "Invasion." *Delta,* No. 15 (August 1961), p. 19.

C40 "Woman on the Subway." *Tamarack Review,* No. 21 (Autumn 1961), p. 20.

C41 "Lover." *Tamarack Review,* No. 21 (Autumn 1961), p. 21.

C42   "Etc." *Alphabet,* No. 3 (December 1961), p. 74.

C43   "Event." *The Sheet,* No. 3 [1961?], p. 3.

C44   "News From Nowhere." *The Sheet,* No. 3 [1961?], p. 3.

C45   "Pastoral Elegy." *The Sheet,* No. 3 [1961?], p. 4.

C46   "Garden." *Canadian Forum,* 42 (July 1962), 92.

C47   "The Interior Decorator." *The Sheet,* No. 5 (September 1962), p. 7. — Also in *Tamarack Review,* No. 27 (Spring 1963), p. 33.

C48   "The Witch and the Nightingale." *Alphabet,* No. 5 (December 1962), pp. 44-45.

C49   "The Whore and the Dove." *Alphabet,* No. 5 (December 1962), pp. 48-49.

C50   "The Kings." *Fiddlehead,* No. 55 (Winter 1963), p. 10.

C51   "Recollections of Vivien." *Fiddlehead,* No. 55 (Winter 1963), p. 10.

C52   "The Betrayal of Arthur." *Fiddlehead,* No. 55 (Winter 1963), p. 11.

C53   "Elaine in Arcadia." *Fiddlehead,* No. 55 (Winter 1963), p. 11.

C54   "The Rider." *Fiddlehead,* No. 55 (Winter 1963), p. 12.

C55   "The Apotheosis of Guinivere." *Fiddlehead,* No. 55 (Winter 1963), pp. 12-13.

C56   "The King." *Fiddlehead,* No. 55 (Winter 1963), p. 13.

C57   "The Little Sister." *Tamarack Review,* No. 27 (Spring 1963), p. 29.

C58   "The Cold Philosopher." *Tamarack Review,* No. 27 (Spring 1963), p. 30.

C59   "What Happened to the Idiot Boy." *Tamarack Review,* No. 27 (Spring 1963), p. 31.

C60   "The Dwarf." *Tamarack Review,* No. 27 (Spring 1963), p. 32. — Also in *Manitoba Law School Journal,* 1, No. 2 (1963) 146.

C61   "The Orphan from Alberta." *Alphabet,* No. 6 (June 1963), p. 51.

C62   "Poor Tom." *Alphabet,* No. 6 (June 1963), p. 52.

C63   "Mad Mother Ballad." *Alphabet,* No. 6 (June 1963), p. 53. — Also in *Canadian Forum,* 43 (June 1963), 70.

C64   "Little Nell." *Alphabet,* No. 6 (June 1963), p. 54.

C65   "The Mad Mother." *Canadian Forum,* 43 (June 1963), 70.

C66   "My Leper Lover." *Canadian Forum,* 43 (June 1963), 71.

C67   "The Idiot Boy Unborn." *Evidence,* No. 7 (Summer 1963), p. 90.

C68   "Pig-Girl." *Delta,* No. 22 (October 1963), p. 28.

C69   "Exhibition Rides." *Volume 63,* No. 1 (December 1963), pp. 59-60.

C70   "Fall and All." *Fiddlehead,* No. 59 (Winter 1963), p. 58.

C71   "The Acid Sibyl." *Fiddlehead,* No. 59 (Winter 1963), p. 59.

C72   "The Siamese Twins." *Fiddlehead,* No. 59 (Winter 1963), p. 60.

C73   "The Revelation." *Fiddlehead,* No. 59 (Winter 1963), pp. 60-61.

C74   "The Double Nun." *Fiddlehead,* No. 59 (Winter 1963), pp. 61-62.

C75   "The Witch's House." *Fiddlehead,* No. 59 (Winter 1963), pp. 62-63.

C76   "The City Girl." In *Poesie/Poetry 64.* Eds. Jacques Godbout and John Robert Colombo. Montreal: Les Editions du Jour; Toronto: Ryerson Press, 1963. pp. 107-108.
      (Note: Items C76-C80 have been found only in the anthologies as listed, and not in periodicals or reprinted in one of Atwood's books.)

C77   "The Lifeless Wife." In *Poesie/Poetry 64.* Eds. Jacques Godbout and John Robert Colombo. Montreal: Les Editions du Jour; Toronto: Ryerson Press, 1963. p. 110. — Also in *The Blasted Pine.* Eds. F.R. Scott and A.J.M.

Smith. Revised ed. Toronto: Macmillan of Canada, 1967. p. 72. — and in *Listen! Songs and Poems of Canada*. Ed. Homer Hogan. (Methuen Canadian Literature Series.) Toronto: Methuen, 1972. p. 57.

C78   "The Somnambulist." In *Poesie/Poetry 64*. Eds. Jacques Godbout and John Robert Colombo. Montreal: Les Editions du Jour; Toronto: Ryerson Press, 1963. pp. 110-111.

C79   "The Slideshow." In *Poesie/Poetry 64*. Eds. Jacques Godbout and John Robert Colombo. Montreal: Les Editions du Jour; Toronto: Ryerson Press, 1963. p. 111.

C80   "Houses." In *Poesie/Poetry 64*. Eds. Jacques Godbout and John Robert Colombo. Montreal: Les Editions du Jour; Toronto: Ryerson Press, 1963. p. 113.

C81   "A Failure of Spells in the Necropolis." *Canadian Poetry*, 27, No. 2 (February 1964), 29-30.

C82   "Voices: Ancestors." *Canadian Poetry*, 27, No. 2 (February 1964), 30-31.

C83   "Descent As Dissection." *Canadian Forum*, 43 (March 1964), 280.

C84   "Willow Pattern Plate." *Canadian Forum*, 44 (April 1964), 23.

C85   "He/She/It." *Queen's Quarterly*, 71 (Spring 1964), 40-41.

C86   "Office Lady." *Canadian Forum*, 44 (September 1964), 131.

C87   "The Commuters." *Edge*, No. 4 (Spring 1965), p. 83.

C88   "The Mountain Climbers." *Edge*, No. 4 (Spring 1965), p. 84.

C89   "Talismans for Children." (*See* A3) *Canadian Forum*, 45 (July 1965), 86-87.

C90   "Gardens." *Literary Review*, 8, No. 4 (Summer 1965), 513-514.

C91   "Descents." *English*, 15, No. 90 (Autumn 1965), 216-217.

C92   "Pink Lady (Sea Anenome, Stanley Park)." *Evidence,* No. 9 (1965), pp. 11-12.

C93   "Epithalamion." *Evidence,* No. 9 (1965), pp. 12-13.

C94   "Boar." *Evidence,* No. 9 (1965), p. 14.

C95   "The Stamps." *Kayak,* No. 4 (1965), pp. 45-46.

C96   "A Pair of Complements." *Kayak,* No. 4 (1965), pp. 46-47.

C97   "The Impossibility." *Kayak,* No. 4 (1965), pp. 48-49.

C98   "Camera." *Kayak,* No. 4 (1965), pp. 49-50.

C99   "Private Life of Mr. Z the Detective." *Quarry,* 15, No. 3 (March 1966), 6-7.

C100   "The Listener." *Quarry,* 15, No. 3 (March 1966), 7-8.

C101   "Where Are You." *Kayak,* No. 9 (1966), p. 13.

C102   "The Soldiers." *Kayak,* No. 9 (1966), p. 14.

C103   "National Film Board: Shorts Before Features." *Saturday Night,* 83 (October 1968), 30.

C104   "Closet." *Pluck,* 2, No. 1 (Fall 1968), 4-5. — Also in *Spectrum: The Richmond Tri-Annual Review,* 5, No. 2 (Winter 1969-70), 45-46.

C105   "Even Here in the Cupboard." *Canadian Author & Bookman,* 44, No. 3 (Spring 1969), 23.

C106   "3 Moons." *Maclean's Magazine,* 82 (August 1969), 8.

C107   "Ancestors." *Spectrum: The Richmond Tri-Annual Review,* 5, No. 1 (Fall 1969), 19-20.

C108   "Time Trap." *Spectrum: The Richmond Tri-Annual Review,* 5, No. 1 (Fall 1969), 21.

C109   "Automatic Pension." *Duel,* No. 1 (Winter 1969), p. 66.

C110   "Death of an Unidentified Insect; Atonement and Apotheosis." *Kayak,* No. 18 (1969), p. 61.

C111   "Earth Dances in a Bad Area." *Kayak,* No. 18 (1969), p. 62.

C112   "Hypothesis: City." *Kayak,* No. 18 (1969), p. 63.

C113 "Poem: Nov. 22." *Merry Devil of Edmonton*, No. 2 (January 1970), broadside.

C114 "Magician As Junkman." *Tamarack Review*, No. 54 (Winter 1970), pp. 43-44.

C115 "Descent." *New Yorker*, 46 (June 27, 1970), 50.

C116 "Christmas Tree Farm: Oro Township." *Malahat Review*, No. 15 (July 1970), pp. 97-98.

C117 "You Mean You Can't Fly and See." *First Encounter* (1970), p. 36.

C118 "Fragments: Beach." *Imago*, No. 13 (1970?), pp. 27-29.

C119 "Oratorio for Sasquatch, Man and Two Androids." In *Poems For Voices*. By Al Purdy and others. Toronto: Canadian Broadcasting Corporation, 1970. pp. 14-28. (Note: the first eleven lines are not by Atwood; the CBC later produced an erratum slip apologising for this.)

C120 "It Is a Trap." *Tuatara*, No. 4 (March 1971), p. 17.

C121 "He Discovers It Is No Longer a Dignified Profession." *Seven* [1971?] p. 23.

C122 "Singing and Dancing: Near Lake Ontario." *Toronto Life* (June 1972), p. 12.

C123 "You Try Undressing Me." *Edge* (New Zealand), No. 4 (August 1972).

C124 "First Element." *Blackfish*, No. 3 (Summer 1972), pp. 24-28. — Also in *Vanderbilt Poetry Review*, 1, No. 2 (Fall-Winter 1972), 21-22.

C125 "Last Prayer." *Unmuzzled Ox*, 1, No. 3 (Summer 1972), 57.

C126 "I Knew What I Wanted." *Unmuzzled Ox*, 1, No. 4 (Autumn 1972), 21.

C127 "Near the High Bridge With Traffic." *Moving Out*, 2, No. 2 (1972), p. 84.

C128 "A Return." *Northern Journey*, No. 2 (1972-73), pp. 77-78.

C129 "Paradigm #3." *Applegarth's Folly*, No. 1 (Summer 1973), p. 104.

C130   "Audience." *Ariel*, 4, No. 3 (July 1973), 38-39.

C131   "Fishbowl." *New*, Nos. 22 & 23 (Fall/Winter 1973-74), p. 30.

C132   "War Movie II." *Times Literary Supplement*, No. 3738 (26 October 1973), p. 1294.

C133   "Chaos Poem." *Branching Out*, Preview Issue (December 1973), p. 22.

C134   "Life Mask." *Branching Out*, Preview Issue (December 1973), p. 23.

C135   "Variations for the Termite Queen." *Kayak*, No. 32 (1973), p. 3.

C136   "Love Is Not a Profession." *Branching Out*, 1, No. 1 (March/April 1974), 13.

C137   "I Am Not A Saint Or a Cripple." *Branching Out*, 1, No. 1 (March/April 1974), 13.

C138   "Too Much Rain This Year." *Mademoiselle*, 78 (May 1974), 136.

C139   "For G. Making a Garden." *Craft Horizons*, 34, No. 3 (June 1974), 14.

C140   "Paradigm #1." *Craft Horizons*, 34, No. 3 (June 1974), 17.

C141   "Silence." *Craft Horizons*, 34, No. 3 (June 1974), 31.

C142   "The Santa Claus Trap." *Weekend Magazine*, 26, No. 52 (25 December 1976), 7-9.

C143   "Threes." *Malahat Review*, No. 41 (January 1977), p. 152.

C144   "Once I Could Move." *Mademoiselle*, (July 1977), p. 142.

C145   "Dust." *Field*, No. 18 (Spring 1978), pp. 80-81.

C146   "Another Night Visit." *Canadian Forum*, 58, No. 681 (June-July 1978), 20.

C147   "Lunch." *This Magazine*, 14, No. 2 (March-April 1980), 14.

C148   "A 'Women's Issue.'" *Canadian Forum*, 60, No. 698 (April 1980), 12.

C149 "Trainride, Vienna-Bonn." *Canadian Forum*, 60, No. 698 (April 1980), 12.

C150 "Torture." *Canadian Forum*, 60, No. 698 (April 1980), 13.

C151 "The Arrest of the Stockbroker." *Canadian Forum*, 60, No. 698 (April 1980), 13.

C152 "A Conversation." *Canadian Forum*, 60, No. 698 (April 1980), 13.

C **Selected Anthologies containing Atwood's Poems**

C153 *Modern Canadian Verse in English and French.* Ed. A.J.M. Smith. Toronto: Oxford University Press, 1967.
Contains: "The Explorers"; "The Settlers"; "Eventual Proteus"; "August Still Life"; "Bring with You"; "Returning to the Room"; and "Summer Again", pp. 401-11.

C154 *New Voices of the Commonwealth.* Ed. Howard Sergeant. London: Evans Brothers, 1968.
Contains: "The City Planners" and "Descents," pp. 42-44.

C155 *15 Canadian Poets.* Ed. Gary Geddes and Phyllis Bruce. Toronto: Oxford University Press, 1970.
Contains: "Some Objects of Wood and Stone"; "The Islands"; "The Animals in That Country"; "A Night in the Royal Ontario Museum"; "Progressive Insanities of a Pioneer"; "Further Arrivals"; "Death of a Young Son By Drowning"; "The Immigrants"; "Game After Supper"; "Procedures for Underground"; and "Younger Sister Going Swimming," pp. 163-80.

C156 *Five Modern Canadian Poets.* Ed. Eli Mandel. Toronto: Holt, Rinehart & Winston, 1970.
Contains: "This Is a Photograph of Me"; "After the Flood, We"; "Playing Cards"; "Journey to the Interior"; "A Night in the Royal Ontario Museum"; "Backdrop Addresses Cowboy"; "At the Tourist Center in Boston"; "The Animals in That Country"; "Elegy for the Giant Tortoises"; "The Green Man"; "The Landlady"; and "Astral Traveller," pp. 56-71.

C157   *Live Poetry.* Ed. Kathleen Sunshine Koppell. New York: Holt, Rinehart & Winston, 1971.
     Contains: "It Is Dangerous To Read Newspapers"; "Man with a Hook"; and "The City Planners," pp. 7-10.

C158   *New American and Canadian Poetry.* Ed. John Gill. Boston: Beacon Press, 1971.
     Contains: "I Can Change My —"; "In Restaurants We Argue"; "After the Agony in the Guest"; "You Want To Go Back"; "Your Back Is Rough All"; "You Refuse To Own"; "This Year I Intended Children"; "We Are Standing Facing Each Other"; and "Lying Here, Everything In Me," pp. 9-16.

C159   *40 Women Poets of Canada.* Ed. Dorothy Livesay. Montreal: Ingluvin Publications, [1972?].
     Contains: "Eden Is A Zoo"; "A Dialogue"; "Dream: Bluejay as Archeopteryx"; "He Is Last Seen"; and "The Accident Has Occurred," pp. 15-20.

C160   *Poets of Contemporary Canada 1960-1970.* Ed. Eli Mandel. New Canadian Library No. 7. Toronto: Mc-Clelland and Stewart, 1972.
     Contains: "This Is a Photograph of Me"; "After the Flood, We"; "On the Streets Love"; "Journey to the Interior"; "A Place: Fragments"; "The Animals in That Country"; "The Landlady"; "At the Tourist Center in Boston"; "A Night at the Royal Ontario Museum"; "The Gods Avoid Revealing Themselves"; "Backdrop Addresses Cowboy"; "Further Arrivals"; "Departure from the Bush"; "Girl and Horse, 1928"; "Procedures for Underground"; "Younger Sister, Going Swimming"; and "They Eat Out," pp. 85-105.

C161   *The Oxford Anthology of Canadian Literature.* Ed. Robert Weaver and William Toye. Toronto: Oxford University Press, 1973.
     Contains: "The Animals in That Country"; "Three Desk Objects"; "Dream 1: The Bush Garden"; "Dream 2: Brian the Still-Hunter"; "Death of a Young Son by Drowning", and "They Travel by Air," pp. 7-13.

C162   *Psyche, The Feminist Poetic Consciousness: An Anthology of Modern American Women Poets.* Ed.

Barbara Segnitz and Carol Rainey. New York: Dial Press, 1973.

Contains: "Game After Supper"; "Stories in Kinsman's Park"; "It Is Dangerous To Read Newspapers"; "The Landlady"; "Midwinter, Presolstice"; "The Revenant"; "They Eat Out"; "Their Attitudes Differ"; and "After All You Are Quite," pp. 217-25.

C163   *Lobsticks.* Ed. Clare MacCulloch. Guelph: Alive Press, [1974].

Contains: "Owl Song"; "Bull Song"; "Crow Song"; "Rat Song"; "Song of the Fox"; "Song of the Hen's Head"; "Pig Song"; "Marsh, Hawk"; "Siren Song"; and "Late August," pp. 9-28.

C164   *Canadian Poetry: The Modern Era.* Ed. John Newlove. Toronto: McClelland and Stewart, 1977.

Contains: "Journey to the Interior"; "The Animals in That Country"; "Chronology"; "Procedures for Underground"; "Dreams of the Animals"; "They Eat Out"; "You Refuse To Own"; and "There Is Only One of Everything," pp. 21-31.

Audio and Audio-Visual Recordings

C165   *The Journals of Susanna Moodie.* Canadian Poets 2. Toronto: Canadian Broadcasting Corporation, 1969.

A 12-inch phonodisc, 33 r.p.m. Read by Mia Anderson.

C166   *The Twist of Feeling.* Toronto: Canadian Broadcasting Corporation, 1971.

An audio-tape, cassette and reel-to-reel, 30 minutes duration. Margaret Atwood discusses the ideas and emotions behind her poems in *Power Politics* and reads some of the poems.

C167   *Margaret Atwood.* Toronto: High Barnet, 1973.

A cassette audio-tape, 60 minutes duration. Atwood reads from *The Circle Game, The Animals in That Country,* and *Procedures for Underground.*

C168   *Progressive Insanities of a Pioneer.* Willowdale, Ontario: Universal Education & Visual Arts, n.d.

A 16 mm. colour film, duration 5 minutes. A film interpretation of the poem.

C169   *The Journals of Susanna Moodie.* Willowdale, Ontario: Universal Education & Visual Arts, n.d.
 A 16 mm. black and white film, duration 15 minutes. A film interpretation of the volume of poetry.

C170   *The Poetry and Voice of Margaret Atwood.* New York: Caedmon, 1977.
 A 12-inch phonodisc, 33 r.p.m. Atwood reads a selection from *The Animals in That Country, Procedures for Underground, Power Politics,* and *You Are Happy.*

D Prose Contributed to Periodicals, Books and Anthologies

Short Stories

D1   "The Glass Slippers." *Acta Victoriana,* 82, No. 3 (March 1958), 16-18.

D2   "The Pilgrimage." *Acta Victoriana,* 83, No. 2 (Dec. 1958), 34-36.

D3   "A Cliché for January." *Acta Victoriana,* 83, No. 4 (Feb. 1959), 7-9.

D4   "The Child Is Now." *The Sheet,* 1, No. 1 (Jan. 1960), 10-12.

D5   "Insula Insularum." *Acta Victoriana,* [85], No. 3 (Feb. 1961), 6-11.

D6   "Going To Bed." *Evidence,* No. 9 (1965), pp. 5-10.

D7   "Testament Found in a Bureau Drawer." *Prism International,* 5, No. 2 (Autumn 1965), 58-65.

D8   "Encounters with the Element Man." *Impulse,* 1, No. 2 (Winter 1972), 24-31.

D9   "Betty." *Chatelaine,* 51, No. 2 (Feb. 1978), 41, 84, 86-88, 90, 92-94.

Articles and Book Reviews

D10   "Diminutive Dramatics." *Clan Call* (Leaside High School), 1, No. 6 (1954-55), 24-25.

D11   "Portrait of a Pet." *Clan Call,* 2, No. 1 (1956-57), 34.

D12   "Apocalyptic Squawk from a Splendid Awk." Rev. of *The Cruising Auk,* by George Johnston. *Acta Victoriana,* 84, No. 1 (Dec. 1959), 25-26.

D13   "The Face Behind the Eyes." Rev. of *Eyes Without a Face*, by Kenneth McRobbie. *Acta Victoriana*, [85], No. 1 (Nov. 1960), 22.

D14   "Some Sun for This Winter." Rev. of *Winter Sun*, by Margaret Avison. *Acta Victoriana*, [85], (Jan. 1961), 18-19.

D15   "Narcissus: Double Entendre." Rev. of *Alphabet*, No. 1 and *Mad Shadows*, by Marie-Claire Blais. *Acta Victoriana*, 83 (sic) 85, (Feb. 1961), 14-16.
     Includes a line drawing by Atwood.

D16   "Art in Alumni." *Acta Victoriana*, [85], No. 4 (March 1961), 8-10.
     An article "collected and edited by Margaret Eleanor Atwood and Ian Cameron."

D17   "Kangaroo and Beaver." Rev. of *Tradition in Exile*, by J.P. Matthews. *Alphabet*, No. 5 (Dec. 1962), pp. 78-79.

D18   Rev. of *Alexsandr Blok: Between Image and Idea*, by F.D. Reeve. *Alphabet*, No. 6 (June 1963), pp. 70-71.

D19   "Superwoman Drawn and Quartered: The Early Forms of *She*." *Alphabet*, No. 10 (July 1965), pp. 65-82.
     An article on the works of Rider Haggard.

D20   "Four Poets from Canada." Rev. of *Phrases from Orpheus*, by D.G. Jones; *The Absolute Smile*, by George Jonas; *An Idiot Joy*, by Eli Mandel; and *North of Summer* and *Wild Grape Wine*, by Al Purdy. *Poetry*, 114, No. 3 (June 1969), 202-207.

D21   "Some Old, Some *New*, Some Boring, Some Blew, and Some Picture Books." *Alphabet*, No. 17 (Dec. 1966), pp. 61-64.
     A review of some Canadian little magazines.

D22   "MacEwen's Muse." *Canadian Literature*, No. 45 (Summer 1970), pp. 24-32. Rpt. *Ellipse*, No. 7 (Spring 1971), pp. 83-93, in French translation. Rpt. in *Poets and Critics: Essays from "Canadian Literature": 1966-1974*. Ed. George Woodcock. Toronto: Oxford University Press, 1974, pp. 215-24.

D23   Rev. of *On the Street*, by Pat Lane. *Blewointmentpress*, Occupation Issue (Aug. 1970) p. 109.

D24   "The Messianic Stance." Rev. of *West Coast Seen*, ed. Jim Brown and David Phillips. *Canadian Literature*, No. 47 (Winter 1971), pp. 75-77.

D25   "Nationalism, Limbo and the Canadian Club." *Saturday Night*, 86 (Jan. 1971), 10-11.

D26   "Poetic Process?" *Field*, No. 4 (Spring 1971), pp. 13-14.

D27   "Eleven Years of *Alphabet*." *Canadian Literature*, No. 49 (Summer 1971), pp. 60-64.

D28   "Love Is Ambiguous ... Sex Is a Bully." Rev. article on *Love in a Burning Building*, by A.W. Purdy. *Canadian Literature*, No. 49 (Summer 1971), pp. 71-75.

D29   "Sang des Betes." Rev. of *The Broken Ark, a Book of Beasts*, ed. Michael Ondaatje. *Books in Canada*, 1, No. 4 (Nov. 1971), 12-13.

D30   "The Books I Enjoyed Most in 1971. . . ." *Financial Post*, 11 Dec. 1971, pp. 33-34.

D31   "First People; an Extract from *Survival*." *Northern Journey*, No. 2 (1972-73), pp. 18-30.

D32   "Introduction." *Incisions*, by Robert Flanagan. Toronto: House of Anansi, 1972 pp. ii-v.

D33   Rev. of *Great Canadian Short stories*, ed. Alex Lucas. *World Literature Written in English*, 11, No. 1 (April, 1972), 63-64.

D34   "Getting Out from under." *Empire Club of Canada: Addresses 1972-1973*. Toronto: Empire Club Foundation, 1973, pp. 353-67.
       An address given to the Empire Club on 5 April 1973, in which Atwood describes her present situation as a "thing" rather than a celebrity and gives her views on nationalism.

D35   "Introduction." *The Sun and the Moon and Other Fiction*, by P.K. Page. Toronto: House of Anansi, 1973, pp. iii-v.

D36   Letter. *Harvard Advocate*, 106, Nos. 2/3 (Winter 1973), p. 17.
        A letter about "feminine sensibility."

D37   "Travels Back." *Maclean's*, 86 (Jan. 1973), 28, 31, 48.
        An article on nationalism, subtitled "Refusing to Acknowledge Where You Come From Is an Act of Amputation."

D38   "How Do I Get Out of Here: The Poetry of John Newlove." *Open Letter*, 2nd Series, No. 4 (Spring 1973), pp. 59-70.

D39   "Notes on *Power Politics*." *Acta Victoriana*, 97, No. 2 (April 1973), 6-19.
        First broadcast on the CBC programme "Ideas."

D40   "Surviving the Critics: Mathews and Misrepresentation." *This Magazine*, 7, No. 1 (May-June 1973), 29-33.
        A reply to Robin Mathews' review of *Survival* in the Winter 1972-73 issue of *This Magazine Is About Schools* (see E8).

D41   "Reaney Collected." *Canadian Literature*, No. 57 (Summer 1973), pp. 113-17. Rpt. *Poets and Critics: Essays from "Canadian Literature" 1966-1974.* Ed. George Woodcock. Toronto: Oxford University Press, 1974. pp. 151-58.

D42   "What Nationalism Is All About." *Financial Post*, 11 Aug. 1973, p. 6.

D43   "Poetry in the Buffer Zone." *Times Literary Supplement*, 26 Oct. 1973, pp. 1305-06.
        An article on Canadian poetry.

D44   "Diving into the Wreck." Rev. of *Poems 1971-1972*, by Adrienne Rich. *New York Times Book Review*, 30 Dec. 1973, pp. 1-2.

D45   Rev. of *Half-Lives*, by Erica Jong. *Parnassus: Poetry in Review*, 2, No. 2 (Spring/Summer 1974), 98-104.

D46   "Face to Face: Margaret Laurence As Seen by Margaret Atwood." *Maclean's*, 87 (May 1974), 38-39, 43-46.

D47   Rev. of *In the Springtime of the Year*, by Susan Hill, and *The Half-Sisters,* by Cynthia Propper Seton. *New York Times Book Review,* 5 May 1974, p. 7.

D48   "Into the Bell Jar World of Unreality." Rev. of *Mundome,* by A.G. Mojtabai. *New York Times Book Review,* 12 May 1974, p. 6.

D49   "Masterful. A Game of Musical Beds in a House of Mirrors." Rev. of *The Sacred and Profane Love Machine,* by Iris Murdoch. *The Globe and Mail,* 1 June 1974. p. 23.

D50   "Picking up the Pieces of the Battered Kate Millett — After the Trashing." Rev. of *Flying,* by Kate Millett. *The Globe and Mail,* 27 July 1974, p. 30.

D51   "What's So Funny? Notes on Canadian Humour." *This Magazine,* 8, No. 3 (Aug.-Sept. 1974), 24-27.

D52   Rev. of *St. Lawrence Blues,* by Marie-Claire Blais. *New York Times Book Review,* 29 Sept. 1974, pp. 4-5.

D53   "Don't Expect the Bear To Dance." *Maclean's,* 88, No. 6, (June 1975), 68-71.
        About the new Toronto Zoo.

D54   "Marie-Claire Blais Is Not for Burning." *Maclean's,* 88, No. 9 (Sept. 1975), 26-29.

D55   "Un Petit Rat Heureux." *Le Maclean,* Sept. 1974, pp. 19-21, 43.
        An interview with Marie-Claire Blais.

D56   "It's Seminal. A Landmark. The Struggle of Woman on Almost Every Possible Level." Rev. of *Poems, Selected and New,* by Adrienne Rich. *The Globe and Mail,* 6 Dec. 1975, p. 35.

D57   "Introduction." *St. Lawrence Blues,* by Marie-Claire Blais. Toronto: Bantam Books, 1976, pp. vii-xvi.

D58   "Paradoxes and Dilemmas: the Woman As Writer." *Women in the Canadian Mosaic.* Ed. Gwen Matheson. Toronto: Peter Martin Associates, 1976, pp. 256-73.
        Gives some details of discrimination in reviewing and in interviews, and examples of rivalry of male writers.

D59   "A Reply." *Signs: Journal of Women in Culture and Society*, 2, No. 2 (1976), 340-41.

        A comment by articles in the same issue of *Signs* by Christ (see E37) and Plaskow (see E38). Atwood's view is that *Surfacing* is neither a feminist/ecological treatise as reviewed in the USA nor a nationalist one as reviewed in Canada, but a novel.

D60   "Of Woman Born." Rev. of *Motherhood As Experience and Institution*, by Adrienne Rich. *The Globe and Mail*, 11 Nov. 1976, p. 41.

D61   "Canadian Monsters: Some Aspects of the Supernatural in Canadian Fiction." *The Canadian Imagination: Dimensions of a Literary Culture*. Ed. David Staines. Cambridge, Mass.; London: Harvard University Press, 1977, pp. 97-122.

D62   Letter. *Saturday Night*, 92, No. 1 (Jan.-Feb. 1977), 3.

        Claims that the Royal Porcupine in Lady Oracle is a character in a novel and does not represent any real person.

D63   "Why Annie Got Her Gun." Rev. of *A Harvest Yet To Reap: A History of Prairie Women*, ed. Linda Rasmussen and others. *Books in Canada*, 6, No. 2 (Feb. 1977), 9-10.

D64   Rev. of *Ten Green Bottles and Ladies & Escorts*, by Audrey Thomas. *The Globe and Mail*, 16 April 1977, p. 25.

D65   "Uncle Dennis' Hat-Trick." *The Canadian*, 10 Sept. 1977, pp. 16-19.

        Pages from Dennis Lee's book for children, *Garbage Delight*, introduced by Atwood.

D66   "Courage and Passion." Rev. of *Report on the Death of Rosenkavalier*, by Jan Drabek. *Essays on Canadian Writing*, Nos. 7/8 (Fall 1977), pp. 97-100.

D67   "Monument for a Dead Self." Rev. of *A Self-Portrait*, by Anne Sexton. *New York Times Book Review*, 6 Nov. 1977, p. 15.

D68   "An Important Book, for Many Reasons." Rev. of *The Wars,* by Timothy Findley. *Financial Post,* 12 Nov. 1977, p. 6. Rpt. *Book and Periodical Development Council Newsletter,* No. 2 (Dec. 1977), pp. 4-6.

D69   "Atwood Among the Ozzies." *Saturday Night,* 93, No. 5 (June 1978), 45-47, 49-50.
       An article about a visit to Australia for *Writers' Week.*

D70   "Unfinished Women." Rev. of *The Dream of Common Language: Poems 1974-1977,* by Adrienne Rich. *New York Times Book Review,* 11 June 1978, pp. 7, 42-43.

D71   "Obstacle Course." Rev. of *Silences,* by Tillie Olsen. *New York Times Book Review,* 30 July 1978, pp. 1, 27.

D72   "Timeless in Afghanistan: Observations on Antiquity under Moonlight in Kabul." *Toronto Life,* Aug. 1978 (Travel Guide), pp. 12-15, 28-31.

D73   "Split-Level Life in New Zealand." Rev. of *Living in the Maniototo,* by Janet Frame. *New York Times Book Review,* 16 Sept. 1979, p. 13.

D74   "Introduction." *To See Our World,* by Catherine M. Young. New York: William Morrow, 1980, pp. 9-23.

D   Selected Anthologies containing Atwood's Short Stories

D75   *72: New Canadian Stories.* Ed. David Helwig and Joan Harcourt. Ottawa; Oberon Press, 1972.
       Contains: "The Grave of the Famous Poet."

D76   *The Story So Far/2.* Ed. Matt Cohen. Toronto: Coach House, 1973.
       Contains: "Encounters with the Element Man."

D77   *Modern Canadian Stories.* Ed. John Stevens. New York: Bantam, 1975.
       Contains: "The Grave of the Famous Poet."

D78   *Toronto Short Stories.* Ed Morris Wolfe and Douglas Daymond. Toronto: Doubleday, 1977.
       Contains "Rape Fantasies."

Part 2: Works on Margaret Atwood

E   Books, Articles, Theses and Interviews

Books

E1   Sandler, Linda, ed. *Margaret Atwood: A Symposium.* (*The Malahat Review*, No. 41, Jan. 1977). Victoria: University of Victoria, 1977. 228 pp.

Contents: Linda Sandler. "Interview with Margaret Atwood," pp. 5-27; Rosemary Sullivan. "Breaking the Circle," pp. 30-41; Jane Rule. "Life, Liberty and the Pursuit of Normalcy — The Novels of Margaret Atwood," pp. 42-49; George Woodcock. "Transformation Mask for Margaret Atwood," pp. 52-56; Rick Salutin. "A Note on the Marxism of Atwood's 'Survival,'" pp. 57-60; Al Purdy. "An Unburnished One-Tenth of One Per Cent of an Event," pp. 61-64; Margaret Atwood. "An Album of Photographs," pp. 65-88; Tom Marshall. "Atwood under and above Water," pp. 89-94; Robert Fulford. "The Images of Atwood," pp. 95-98; John Hofsess. "How To Be Your Own Best Survival," pp. 102-06; Robin Skelton. "Timeless Constructions — A Note on the Poetic Style of Margaret Atwood," pp. 107-20; Margaret Atwood. "Worksheets," pp. 121-33; Rowland Smith. "Margaret Atwood: The Stoic Comedian," pp. 134-44; Margaret Atwood. "Threes," p. 152; Eli Mandel. "Atwood Gothic," pp. 165-74; Margaret Atwood. "The Resplendent Quetzal," pp. 175-88; Jerome H. Rosenberg. "On Reading the Atwood Papers in the Thomas Fisher Library," pp. 191-94; Alan J. Horne. "A Preliminary Checklist of Writings by and about Margaret Atwood," pp. 195-222.

E2   Grace, Sherrill. *Violent Duality: A Study of Margaret Atwood.* Montreal: Véhicule Press, 1980. 154 pp.

Articles

E3   Dawe, Alan. "Introduction." *The Edible Woman.* By Margaret Atwood. New Canadian Library, No. 93. Toronto: McClelland and Stewart, 1969, [pp. 2-7].

E4   Marshall, Tom. "Les Animaux de Son Pays: Notes sur la Poesie de Margaret Atwood." *Ellipse,* No. 3 (Spring 1970), pp. 81-86.

E5   Brown, Rosellen. "The Poetry of Margaret Atwood." *Nation,* 212 (28 June 1971),824-26.

E6   Woodcock, George. "Margaret Atwood." *Literary Half-Yearly,* 13, No. 2 (July 1972), 233-42.

E7   Ayre, J. "Margaret Atwood and the End of Colonialism." *Saturday Night,* 87 (Nov. 1972), 23-26.

E8   Mathews, Robin. "Survival and Struggle in Canadian Literature." *This Magazine Is about Schools,* 6, No. 4 (Winter 1972-73), 109-24.

E9   Onley, Gloria. "Margaret Atwood: Surfacing in the Interests of Survival." *West Coast Review,* 7, No. 3 (Jan. 1973), 51-54.

E10   French, William. "Icon and Target: Atwood As Thing." *The Globe and Mail,* 7 April 1973, p. 28.

E11   Davey, Frank. "Atwood Walking Backwards." *Open Letter,* 2nd Series, No. 5 (Summer 1973), pp. 74-84.
      A critical article about *Surfacing* and *Survival.*

E12   Webb, Phyllis. "Letters to Margaret Atwood." *Open Letter,* 2nd Series, No. 5 (Summer 1973), pp. 71-73.
      A personal response to Atwood and her work.

E13   Woodcock, George. "Surfacing to Survive: Notes of the Recent Atwood." *Ariel,* 4, No. 3 (July 1973), 16-28.

E14   Gutteridge, Don. "Surviving the Fittest: Margaret Atwood and the Sparrow's Fall." *Journal of Canadian Studies,* 8, No. 3 (Aug. 1973), 59-64.
      On *Survival.*

E15   Piercy, Marge. "Margaret Atwood: Beyond Victimhood." *American Poetry Review,* 2, No. 6 (Nov.-Dec. 1973), 41-44.

E16   Davey, Frank. "Margaret Atwood." In his *From There to Here.* Erin, Ontario: Press Porcépic, 1974, pp. 30-36.

E17   Page, Sheila. "Supermarket Survival: A Critical Analysis of Margaret Atwood's 'The Edible Woman.'" *Sphinx,* No. 1 (Winter 1974), pp. 9-19.

E18   MacLulich, T.D. "The 'Survival' Shoot-Out." *Essays on Canadian Writing*, No. 1 (Winter 1974), pp. 14-20.

E19   Onley, Gloria. "Breaking Through the Patriarchal Nets to the Peaceable Kingdom." *West Coast Review*, 8, No. 3 (January 1974), 43-50.
       On Atwood's poetry, in particular on *Power Politics*.

E20   Onley, Gloria. "Power Politics in Bluebeard's Castle." *Canadian Literature*, No. 60 (Spring 1974), pp. 21-42.
       A study of the sexual politics evidenced in Atwood's work.

E21   Rogers, Linda. "Margaret the Magician." *Canadian Literature*, No. 60 (Spring 1974), pp. 83-85.

E22   Ross, Gary. "The Circle Game." *Canadian Literature*, No. 60, (Spring 1974), pp. 51-63.

E23   Glicksohn, Susan Wood. "The Martian Point of View." *Extrapolation*, 15, No. 2 (May 1974), 161-73.
       This article claims that Atwood's poetic vision is that of a contemporary individual trying to comprehend an alien world and of an unworldly creature revealing the reality beneath the civilized surface of this world.

E24   Morley, Patricia. "Survival, Affirmation and Joy." *Lakehead University Review*, 7, No. 1 (Summer 1974), 21-30.

E25   Jones, D.G. "Cold Eye and Optic Heart: Marshall McLuhan and Some Canadian Poets." *Modern Poetry Studies*, 5, No. 2 (Autumn 1974), 170-87.

E26   Macri, F.M. "Survival Kit: Margaret Atwood and the Canadian Scene." *Modern Poetry Studies*, 5, No. 2 (Autumn 1974), 187-95.

E27   Schaeffer, Susan Fromberg. "'It Is Time That Separates Us': Margaret Atwood's 'Surfacing'" *Centennial Review*, 18, No. 4 (Fall 1974), 319-37.

E28   Brady, Elizabeth. "Towards a Happier History: Women and Domination." In *Domination*. Ed. Alkis Kontos. Toronto: University of Toronto Press, 1975, pp. 17-31.

E29   French, William. "The Women of Our Literary Life."
       Imperial Oil Review, 59, No. 1 (1975), 2-7; rpt. *Cana-
       dian Author and Bookman*, 51 (Spring 1976), pp. 1-6.

E30   McLay, Catherine. "The Divided Self: Theme and Pat-
       tern in Margaret Atwood's 'Surfacing.'" *Journal of
       Canadian Fiction*, 4, No. 1 (1975), 82-95. Rpt. *The
       Canadian Novel: Here and Now*. Ed. John Moss.
       Toronto: NC Press, 1978, pp. 32-44.

E31   Woodcock, George. "Margaret Atwood: Poet As
       Novelist." In *The Canadian Novel in the Twentieth
       Century*. Ed. George Woodcock. New Canadian Lib-
       rary, No. 115. Toronto: McClelland and Stewart, 1975,
       pp. 312-27.

E32   Norris, Ken. "Survival in the Writings of Margaret
       Atwood." *CrossCountry*, No. 1 (Winter 1975), pp. 18-29.

E33   Frankel, Vivian. "Margaret Atwood: A Personal
       View." *Branching Out*, 2, No. 1 (Jan.-Feb. 1975), 24-26.

E34   Conlon, Patrick. "Margaret Atwood: Beneath the Sur-
       face." *Toronto Life*, Feb. 1975, pp. 44-51.
       A journalistic, biographical article.

E35   Ladousse, Gillian. "Some Aspects of the Theme of
       Metamorphosis in Margaret Atwood's Poetry." *Etudes
       Canadiennes*, No. 2 (1976), pp. 71-77.

E36   Northey, Margot. "Sociological Gothic: 'Wild Geese'
       and 'Surfacing.'" In her *The Haunted Wilderness: The
       Gothic and Grotesque in Canadian Fiction*. Toronto:
       University of Toronto Press, 1976, pp. 62-69.

E37   Christ, Carol P. "Margaret Atwood: The Surfacing of
       Women's Spiritual Quest and Vision." *Signs: Journal
       of Women in Culture and Society*, 2, No. 2 (1976), 316-30.

E38   Plaskow, Judith. "On Carol Christ on Margaret At-
       wood: Some Theological Reflection." *Signs: Journal
       of Women in Culture and Society*, 2, No. 2 (1976), 331-39.

E39   Sweetapple, Rosemary. "Margaret Atwood: Victims
       and Survivors." *Southern Review* (University of Ade-
       laide), 9, No. 1 (March 1976), 50-69.
       An essay on *Surfacing*.

E40   Bjerring, Nancy E. "The Problem of Language in Margaret Atwood's 'Surfacing.'" *Queen's Quarterly,* 83, No. 4 (Winter 1976), 597-612.

E41   Gerson, Carole. "Margaret Atwood and Quebec: A Footnote on 'Surfacing.'" *Studies in Canadian Literature,* 1, No. 1 (Winter 1976), 115-19.

E42   Gerstenberger, Donna. "Conceptions Literary and Otherwise: Women Writers and the Modern Imagination." *Novel: A Forum on Fiction,* 9, No. 2 (Winter 1976), 141-50.
       Deals with *Surfacing* at some length as the best example she knows of "a contemporary novel by a woman with feminist concerns which confronts the problem of myth and language."

E43   Sullivan, Rosemary. "Surfacing and Deliverance." *Canadian Literature,* No. 67 (Winter 1976), pp. 6-20.

E44   Garebian, Keith. "'Surfacing': Apocalyptic Ghost Story." *Mosaic,* 9, No. 3 (Spring 1976), 1-9.

E45   Davey, Frank. "Surviving the Paraphrase." *Canadian Literature,* No. 70 (Autumn 1976), pp. 5-13.
       A critical review of the thematic criticism of Frye, Jones, Moss, and Atwood.

E46   Rubenstein, Roberta. "'Surfacing': Margaret Atwood's Journey to the Interior." *Modern Fiction Studies,* 22, No. 3 (Autumn 1976), 387-99.

E47   MacGregor, Roy. "Mother Oracle." *The Canadian,* 25 September 1976, pp. 15-18.
       An interview-style article.

E48   Moss, John. "Strange Bedfellows: Atwood and Richler." In his *Sex and Violence in the Canadian Novel: The Ancestral Present.* Toronto: McClelland and Stewart, 1977. pp. 123-46.
       A detailed interpretation and comparison of Atwood's *Surfacing* and Richler's *St. Urbain's Horseman.*

E49   Nodelman, Perry. "Trusting the Untrustworthy." *Journal of Canadian Fiction,* No. 21 (1977-78), pp. 73-82.
       A review article on *The Edible Woman.*

E50 Dilliott, Maureen. "Emerging from the Cold: Margaret Atwood's 'You Are Happy'." *Modern Poetry Studies,* 7, No. 1 (Spring 1977), 73-90.

E51 Allen, Carolyn. "Margaret Atwood: Power of Transformation, Power of Knowledge." *Essays on Canadian Writing,* No. 6 (Spring 1977), pp. 5-17.
"One of the major themes in Atwood's poetry is transformation."

E52 Davey, Frank. "Atwood's Gorgon Touch." *Studies in Canadian Literature,* 2, No. 2 (Summer 1977), 146-63. Rpt. *Brave New Wave* Ed. Jack David. Windsor: Black Moss Press, 1978, pp. 171-196.
Davey maintains that Atwood's poetry is preoccupied with a struggle between time and space.

E53 King, Bruce. "Margaret Atwood's 'Surfacing.'" *Journal of Commonwealth Literature,* 12, No. 1 (Aug. 1977), 23-32.

E54 Davidson, Cathy N. "Canadian Wry: Comic Vision in Atwood's *Lady Oracle* and Laurence's *The Diviners.*" *Regionalism and the Female Imagination,* 3, No. 2 (Fall 1977), 50-56.

E55 Foster, John Wilson. "The Poetry of Margaret Atwood." *Canadian Literature,* No. 74 (Autumn 1977), pp. 5-20.

E56 Stevens, Peter. "Explorer/Settler/Poet." *The University of Windsor Review,* 13, No. 1 (Fall-Winter 1977), 63-74.
A discussion of the poetry of Atwood, Newlove, Purdy and McNeil which uses the figures of early pioneers to construct a sense of a Canadian literary consciousness.

E57 Cameron, Elspeth. "Margaret Atwood: A Patchwork Self." *Book Forum,* 4, No. 1 (1978), 35-45.
A review article of *Lady Oracle* and *Dancing Girls.*

E58 Cude, Wilfred. "Bravo Mothball! An Essay on 'Lady Oracle.'" In *The Canadian Novel: Here and Now.* Ed. John Moss. Toronto: N.C. Press, 1978, pp. 45-50.

E59   Grace, Sherrill E. "Introduction." *The Circle Game.* By Margaret Atwood. New edition. Toronto: House of Anansi, 1978, pp. 9-15.

E60   Lauber, John. "Alice in Consumer-Land: The Self-Discovery of Marian MacAlpin." In *The Canadian Novel: Here and Now.* Ed. John Moss. Toronto: N.C. Press, 1978, pp. 19-31.

E61   Mathews, Robin. "Margaret Atwood: Survivalism." In his *Canadian Literature: Surrender or Revolution.* Toronto: Steel Rail Educational Publishing, 1978, pp. 119-30.
      A slightly edited version of the essay which appeared in *This Magazine Is About Schools* (see E8).

E62   Steele, James. "The Literary Criticism of Margaret Atwood." In *In Our Own House: Social Perspectives on Canadian Literature.* Ed. Paul Cappon. Toronto: McClelland and Stewart, 1978. pp. 73-81.

E63   Mallinson, Jean. "Ideology and Poetry: An Examination of Some Recent Trends in Canadian Criticism." *Studies in Canadian Literature,* 3, No. 1 (Winter 1978), 93-109.
      An examination of three separate instances of ideological criticism of Canadian poetry. After a brief mention of Davey's criticism of *Power Politics* — "the flashily contrived wit of most of the poems parallels the 'castrating bitch' manipulativeness of the persona" — Mallinson concentrates on Amabile's review of *You Are Happy* in *CV/II* (see F51).

E64   Rosenberg, Jerome H. "Women As Everyman in Atwood's 'Surfacing': Some Observations on the End of the Novel." *Studies in Canadian Literature,* 3, No. 1 (Winter 1978), 127-32.

E65   Allen, Carolyn. "Failures of Word, Uses of Silence: Djuna Barnes, Adrienne Rich, and Margaret Atwood." *Regionalism and the Female Imagination,* 4, No. 1 (Spring 1978), 1-8.

E66   Campbell, Josie P. "The Woman As Hero in Margaret Atwood's 'Surfacing.'" *Mosaic,* 11, No. 3 (Spring 1978), 17-28.

E67   Lyons, Bonnie. "'Neither Victims Nor Executioners' in Margaret Atwood's Fiction." *World Literature Written in English*, 17, No. 1 (April 1978), 181-87.

E68   Quigley, Theresia. "'Surfacing': A Critical Study." *Antigonish Review*, 34 (Spring 1978), 77-87.

E69   Bilan, R.P. "Margaret Atwood's 'The Journals of Susanna Moodie.'" *Canadian Poetry*, No. 2 (Spring/Summer 1978), pp. 1-12.

E70   Davidson, Arnold E. and Cathy N. "Margaret Atwood's 'Lady Oracle': The Artist as Escapist and Seer." *Studies in Canadian Literature*, 3, No. 2 (Summer 1978), 166-77.

E71   Hutcheon, Linda. "Atwood and Laurence: Poet and Novelist." *Studies in Canadian Literature*, 3, No. 2 (Summer 1978), 255-63.

E72   MacLulich, T.D. "Atwood's Adult Fairy Tale: Levi-Strauss, Bettleheim, and 'The Edible Woman.'" *Essays in Canadian Writing*, No. 11 (Summer 1978), pp. 111-29.

E73   Mansbridge, Frances. "Search for Self in the Novels of Margaret Atwood." *Journal of Canadian Fiction*, No. 22 (1978), pp. 106-17.

E74   Rigney, Barbara Hill. "'After the Failure of Logic': Descent and Return in 'Surfacing'." In her *Madness and Sexual Politics in the Feminist Novel: Studies in Bronte, Woolf, Lessing and Atwood*. University of Wisconsin Press, 1978, pp. 91-127.

E75   Colman, S.J. "Margaret Atwood, Lucien Goldmann's Pascal, and the Meaning of 'Canada.'" *University of Toronto Quarterly*, 48, No. 3 (Spring 1979), 247-60.

E76   Ross, Catherine Sheldrick. "Calling Back the Ghost of the Old-Time Heroine: Duncan, Montgomery, Atwood, Laurence and Munro." *Studies in Canadian Literature*, 4, No. 1 (Winter 1979), 43-58.

E77   Sillers, Pat. "Power Impinging: Hearing Atwood's Vision." *Studies in Canadian Literature*, 4, No. 1 (Winter 1979), 59-70.

E78   Davidson, Arnold E. and Cathy N. "The Anatomy of Margaret Atwood's 'Surfacing." *ARIEL: A Review of International English Literature*, 10, No. 3 (July 1979), 38-54.

E79   Weir, Lorraine. "'Fauna of Mirrors': The Poetry of Hebert and Atwood." *ARIEL: A Review of International English Literature*, 10, No. 3 (July 1979), 99-113.

Theses

E80   Yeo, Margaret E. "The Living Landscape: Nature Imagery in the Poetry of Margaret Atwood and Other Modern Canadian Lyric Poets." M.A. Thesis Carleton University, 1969.

E81   Power, Linda Laporte. "The Reality of Selfhood: A Study of Polarity in the Poetry and Fiction of Margaret Atwood." M.A. Thesis McGill 1973.

E82   Robertson, Esther. "The Politics of Relationships: An Examination of Margaret Atwood's 'The Edible Woman,' 'Surfacing,' and 'Survival.'" M.A. Thesis British Columbia 1974.

E83   Regan, Nancy. "The Geography and History of the Mind: An Analysis of the works of Margaret Atwood." M.A. Thesis Rhode Island, 1975.

E84   Parks, Claudia Susan (now Ingersoll). "The Solitary Dancer: Isolation and Affirmation in the Poetry of Margaret Atwood." M.A. Thesis Memorial University of Newfoundland, 1976.

E85   Gronvigh, Joanne. "Thematic Development in the Work of Margaret Atwood." M.A. Thesis Dalhousie, 1977.

E86   Packer, Miriam. "Beyond the Garrison: Approaching the Wilderness in Margaret Laurence, Alice Munro and Margaret Atwood." Diss. Montreal, 1978.

Interviews

E87   Halpenny, Francess: "A Dialogue with Margaret Atwood." Toronto: University of Toronto, Faculty of Library Science, 1972.
       A cassette audio-tape, 45 minutes duration. Not

published. A general interview before a class at the
Faculty, 18 Oct. 1972.

E88   Levenson, Christopher. "Interview with Margaret
Atwood." *Manna*, No. 2 (1972), pp. 46-54.

E89   Gibson, Graeme. "Margaret Atwood." In his *Eleven
Canadian Novelists*. Toronto: House of Anansi, 1973,
p. 1-31.

E90   Miner, Valerie. "Atwood in Metamorphosis: An Authentic Canadian Fairy Tale." In *Her Own Woman: Profiles of Ten Canadian Women*. Ed. Myrna Kostash.
Toronto: Macmillan of Canada, 1975, pp. 173-94; rpt.
(abridged) "The Many Facets of Margaret Atwood."
Chatelaine, 48, No. 6 (June 1975), 32-33, 66-70.

E91   Swan, Susan. "Margaret Atwood: The Woman As
Poet." *Communique*, No. 8 (May 1975), pp. 8-11, 45-46.

E92   Van Varsveld, Gail. "Talking with Atwood." *Room of
One's Own*, 1, No. 2 (Summer 1975), 66-70.
    Deals with Atwood's attitude towards feminism in
literature.

E93   Kaminski, Margaret. "Interview with Margaret Atwood." *Waves*, 4, No. 1 (Autumn 1975), 8-13.

E94   *The Education of Mike McManus: Margaret Atwood*.
Ontario Educational Communications Authority, 1976.
    Videotape, colour, 30 minutes duration. A television
interview.

E95   Gibson, Mary Ellis. "A Conversation with Margaret
Atwood." *Chicago Review*, 27, No. 4 (Spring 1976),
105-13.
    Atwood describes what she attempted to do with *Sur-
vival* and how the literary and publishing scene in
Canada has changed drastically over recent years.

E96   Slopen, Beverley. "Margaret Atwood." *Publisher's
Weekly*, 210, No. 8 (23 Aug. 1976), 6-8.
    An interview given just after publication of *Lady
Oracle*. Provides some interesting biographical details
including those which relate to incidents in the novel.

E97   Slinger, Helen. "Interview with Margaret Atwood."
Maclean's, 89, No. 15 (6 Sept. 1976), 4-7.
    Fairly superficial.

E98   Schiller, William. "Interview with Margaret Atwood."
       PWP, 2, No. 3 (Fall 1976), 2-15.
       An interesting interview which concentrates on
       Atwood's poetry.

E99   Struthers, J.R. (Tim). "An Interview with Margaret
       Atwood." *Essays on Canadian Writing*, No. 6 (Spring
       1977), pp. 18-27.
       A stimulating interview which touches on many
       topics; serious but not solemn. It deals both with the
       poetry and the fiction, with some emphasis on *Lady
       Oracle*.

E100   Oates, Joyce Carol. "An Interview with Margaret
       Atwood." *New York Times Book Review*, 21 May
       1978, pp. 15, 43-45.
       Provides some biographical background informa-
       tion. Atwood explains her interest in the Gothic and in
       supernatural fantasy, and gives her views on writing.

E101   Davidson, Jim. "Margaret Atwood." *Meanjin*, 37,
       No. 2 (July 1978), 189-205.

E102   Hammond, Karla. "An Interview with Margaret
       Atwood." *American Poetry Review*, 8, No. 5 (Sept.-
       Oct. 1978), 27-29.

E103   Hancock, Geoff. "Interview." *Books in Canada*, 9,
       No. 6 (June-July 1980), 30-31.
       Atwood on being an international literary success.

F   Selected Reviews: Poetry

Double Persephone

F1   Scott, Peter Dale. "Turning New Leaves." *Canadian
       Forum*, 41 (February 1962), 259-60.

F2   Mandel, Eli. "Seedtime in Dark May." *Alphabet*, No. 4
       (June 1962), pp. 69-70.

F3   Wilson, Milton. Review of *Double Persephone*. *Uni-
       versity of Toronto Quarterly*, 31 (July 1962), 448-49.

The Circle Game (A2)

F4   MacCallum, Hugh. Review of *The Circle Game*. *Uni-
       versity of Toronto Quarterly*, 35 (July 1965), 383.

The Circle Game (A7)

F5   Gibbs, Robert. Review of *The Circle Game. Fiddle-head*, No. 70 (Winter 1967), pp. 69-71.

F6   Harrison, Keith. Review of *The Circle Game. Tamarack Review*, No. 42 (Winter 1967), pp. 73-74.

F7   Ondaatje, Michael. Review of *The Circle Game. Canadian Forum*, 47 (April 1967), 22-23.

F8   Stevens, Peter. "On the Edge, on the Surface." *Canadian Literature*, No. 32 (Spring 1967), pp. 71-72.

F9   MacCallum, Hugh. Review of *The Circle Game. University of Toronto Quarterly*, 36 (July 1967), 357-59.

F10   Seaman, Roger. Review of *The Circle Game. Quarry*, 16, No. 4 (Summer 1967), 40-42.

F11   Rutsala, Vern. "An Authentic Style." *Kayak*, No. 12 (1967), pp. 63-65.

F12   Thompson, Eric. Review of *The Circle Game. Fiddle-head*, No. 75 (Spring 1968), pp. 76-77.

F13   Moon, Samuel. "Canadian Chronicle." *Poetry*, 112 (June 1968), 204-05.

F14   Garnet, Eldon. "For the Poets, the Landscape Is the Great Canadian Myth." *Saturday Night*, 85, No. 2 (February 1970), 31-33.

The Animals in That Country

F15   Gasparini, Len. Review of *The Animals in That Country. Canadian Forum*, 48 (December 1968), 212.

F16   Barbour, Douglas. Review of *The Animals in That Country. Dalhousie Review*, 48 (Winter 1968-69), 568-70.

F17   Purdy, Al. "Poet Besieged." *Canadian Literature*, No. 39 (Winter 1969), pp. 94-96.

F18   Helwig, David. Review of *The Animals in That Country. Queen's Quarterly*, 76 (Spring 1969), 161-62.

F19   MacCallum, Hugh. Review of *The Animals of That Country. University of Toronto Quarterly*, 38 (July 1969), 343-44.

F20   Marshall, Tom. Review of *The Animals of That Country. Quarry,* 18, No. 3 (Spring 1969), 53-54.

F21   Van Duyn, Mona. "Seven Women." *Poetry,* 115 (March 1970), 432-33.

The Journals of Susanna Moodie

F22   Bowering, George. "To Share the World or Despair of It." *Globe and Mail,* 2 May 1970, p. 16.

F23   Barbour, Douglas. Review of *The Journals of Susanna Moodie. Canadian Forum,* 50 (September 1970), 225-26.

F24   Skelton, Robin. Review of *The Journals of Susanna Moodie. Malahat Review,* No. 17 (January 1971), pp. 133-34.

F25   Purdy, Al. "Atwood's Moodie." *Canadian Literature,* No. 47 (Winter 1971), pp. 80-84.

F26   Doyle, Mike. "Made in Canada?" *Poetry,* 119 (1972), 360-62.

F27   Stephen, Sid. Review of *The Journals of Susanna Moodie. White Pelican,* 2, No. 2 (Spring 1972), 32-36.

Procedures for Underground

F28   Maddocks, Melvin. "That Consuming Hunger." *Time,* 96 (26 October 1970), 116 (p. 82 in Canadian edition).

F29   Barbour, Douglas. Review of *Procedures for Underground. Dalhousie Review,* 50, No. 3 (Autumn 1970), 437, 439.

F30   Gibbs, Jean. Review of *Procedures for Underground. Fiddlehead,* No. 87 (November-December 1970), pp. 61-65.

F31   Wainwright, Andy. "Margaret Atwood's Drowned World." *Saturday Night,* 85 (December 1970), 33, 35.

F32   Harcourt, Joan. Review of *Procedures for Underground. Quarry,* 20, No. 1 (Winter 1971), 52-53.

F33   Hornyansky, Michael. Review of *Procedures for Underground. University of Toronto Quarterly,* 40 (Summer 1971), 378-79.

F34   Stevens, Peter. "Dark Mouth." *Canadian Literature,* No. 50 (Autumn 1971), pp. 91-92.

Power Politics

F35   Stevens, Peter. "Deep Freezing a Love's Continual Small Atrocities." *Globe and Mail Magazine,* 24 April 1971, p. 16.

F36   Jonas, George. "Cool Sounds in a Minor Key." *Saturday Night,* 86 (May 1971), 30-31.

F37   Harcourt, Joan. Review of *Power Politics. Quarry,* 20, No. 4 (1971), 70-73.

F38   Bowering, George. "Getting Used to It." *Canadian Literature,* No. 52 (Spring 1972), pp. 91-92.

F39   Allen, Dick. "Shifts." *Poetry,* 120 (July 1972), 239-40.

F40   Hornyansky, Michael. Review of *Power Politics. University of Toronto Quarterly,* 41 (Summer 1972), 334-35.

F41   Larkin, Joan. "Soul Survivor." *Ms.,* 1 (May 1972), 33-35.

F42   Vendler, Helen. "Do Women Have Distinctive Subjects, Roles and Styles?" *New York Times Book Review,* 12 August 1973, pp. 6-7.

F43   Pritchard, William H. Review of *Power Politics. Hudson Review,* 26 (Fall 1973), 586-87.

F44   McCombs, Judith. "'Power Politics': The Book and Its Cover." *Moving Out,* 3, No. 2 (1973), 54-69.

You Are Happy

F45   Fulford, Robert. "Atwood's New Poetry an Exhilarating Trip." *Toronto Star,* 14 September 1974, p.H7.

F46   Pearson, Alan. "A Skeletal Novella in Plain Diction. A Bestiary under Iron Grey Skies." *Globe and Mail,* 28 September 1974, p. 33.

F47   Lauder, Scott. "We Are Not So Happy." *Canadian Forum,* 54 (November-December 1974), 17-18.

F48   Sandler, Linda. "Gustafson and Others." *Tamarack Review,* No. 64 (November 1974), pp. 92-93.

F49   Jacobs, Anne. Review of *You Are Happy. Dalhousie Review,* 54, No. 4 (Winter 1974-5), 790-92.

F50   Matson, Marshall. "Seize the Day and the Axe." *Books in Canada,* 4, No. 2 (February 1975), 24.

F51   Amabile, George. "Consciousness in Ambush." *CV/II,* 1, No. 1 (Spring 1975), 5-6.

F52   Scott, Andrew. "The Poet As Sorceress." *Essays on Canadian Writing,* No. 3 (Fall 1975), pp. 60-62.

F53   Trueblood, Valerie. "Conscience and Spirit." *American Poetry Review,* 6, No. 2 (March/April 1977), 19-20.

Selected Poems

F54   Colombo, John Robert. "There Is a Delight in Exposing Little Secrets." *Globe and Mail,* 24 April 1976, p. 39.

F55   Fulford, Robert. "Atwood's Poems Show Strength and Anger." *Toronto Star,* 24 April 1976, p. H6.

F56   Geddes, Gary. "Now You See It . . . Now You Don't: an Appreciation of Atwood and MacEwen, Two Grand Illusions." *Books in Canada,* 5, No. 7 (July 1976), 4-6.

F57   Sandler, Linda. "The Exorcisms of Atwood." *Saturday Night,* 91, No. 5 (July-August 1976), 59-60.

F58   Bobak, E.L. Review of *Selected Poems. Dalhousie Review,* 56, No. 2 (Summer 1976), 404-06.

F59   Woodcock, George. "Playing with Freezing Fire." *Canadian Literature,* No. 70 (Autumn 1976), pp. 84-86.

F60   Struthers, J.R. (Tim) "Margaret Atwood Has Surfaced: the Fist Is Now a Hand." *London Free Press,* 22 January 1977, p. 31.

F61   Forsche, Carolyn. Review of *Selected Poems. New York Times Book Review,* 21 May 1978, pp. 15, 42.

F62   Wood, Gayle. "On Margaret Atwood's *Selected Poems." American Poetry Review,* 8, No. 5 (September-October 1979), 30-32.

Up in the Tree

F63   Landsberg, Michele. "A Gentle Plot with Good Humored Charm in Red, White and Blue." *Globe and Mail,* 1 April 1978, p. 36.

Two-Headed Poems

F64   Mays, John Bentley. Review of *Two-Headed Poems.* *Globe and Mail,* 16 September 1978, p. 39.

F65   Matson, Marshall. "Yoked By Violence." *Books in Canada,* 8, No. 1 (January 1979), 12-13.

F66   Barbour, Douglas. Review of *Two-Headed Poems.* *Fiddlehead,* No. 121 (Spring 1979), pp. 139-42.

F67   Hornyansky, Michael. Review of *Two-Headed Poems.* *University of Toronto Quarterly,* 48, No. 4 (Summer 1979), 341-42.

G Selected Reviews: Prose

The Edible Woman

G1   Woodcock, George. "Are We All Emotional Cannibals?" *Toronto Star,* 13 Sept. 1969, p. 13.

G2   "Self-Deprecating." *Times Literary Supplement,* 2 Oct. 1969, p. 1122.

G3   Montagnes, Anne. "Two Novels That Unveil, Maybe, a Coming Phenomenon, the Species Torontoensis." *Saturday Night,* 84 (Nov. 1969), pp. 54, 56, 58.

G4   Jonas, George. "A Choice of Predators." *The Tamarack Review,* No. 54 (Winter 1970), pp. 75-77.

G5   Skelton, Robin. Rev. of *The Edible Woman. Malahat Review,* No. 13 (Jan. 1970), pp. 108-09.

G6   Stedmond, John. Rev. of *The Edible Woman, Canadian Forum,* 49 (Feb. 1970), 267.

G7   Marshall, Tom. Rev. of *The Edible Woman. Quarry,* 19, No. 3 (Spring 1970), 55-56.

G8   Roper, Gordon. Rev. of *The Edible Woman. University of Toronto Quarterly,* 39 (July 1970), 341.

G9   Bell, Millicent. "The Girl on the Wedding Cake." *New York Times Book Review,* 18 Oct. 1970, p. 51.

Surfacing

G10   Newman, Christina. "In Search of a Native Tongue." *Maclean's,* 85 (Sept. 1972), 88.

G11   Dobbs, Kildare. "Canadian's Second Novel Even Better Than Her First." *Toronto Star*, 12 Sept. 1972, p. 31.

G12   French, William. "Exhilarating: An All-Purpose Novel." *The Globe and Mail*, 16 Sept. 1972, p. 30.

G13   MacSween, R.J. Rev. of *Surfacing. Antigonish Review*, No. 11 (Autumn 1972), pp. 113-14.

G14   Clery, Val. "A Plea for the Victim." *Books in Canada*, 1, No. 12 (Nov. 1972), 45-46.

G15   Davis, Frances. Rev. of *Surfacing. Dalhousie Review*, 52 (Winter 1972-73), 680-82.

G16   Grosskurth, Phyllis. "Victimization or Survival." *Canadian Literature*, No. 55 (Winter 1973), pp. 108-10.

G17   Godfrey, Ellen. Rev. of *Surfacing. Canadian Forum*, 52 (Jan. 1973), 34.

G18   Davidson, Jane. "The Anguish of Identity." *Financial Post*, 24 Feb. 1973, p. C5.

G19   Delany, Paul. "Clearing a Canadian Space." *New York Times Book Review*, 4 March 1973, p. 5.

G20   Maddocks, Melvin. "Out of the Woods." *Time*, 101 (19 March 1973), 77-78 (pp. 66, 70 in Canadian ed.).

G21   Coleman, Margaret. Rev. of *Surfacing. Descant*, No. 6 (Spring 1973), pp. 70-73.

G22   Laurence, Margaret. Rev. of *Surfacing. Quarry*, 22 (Spring 1973), 62-64.

G23   Weeks, Edward. Rev. of *Surfacing. Atlantic*, April 1973, p. 127.

G24   Larkin, Joan. "Soul Survivor." *Ms.*, 1 (May 1973), 33-34.

G25   Mahon, Derek. "Message in the Bloodstream." *Listener*, 89 (24 May 1973), 696.

G26   "Ways of the Wild." *Times Literary Supplement*, 1 June 1973, p. 604.

G27   Harcourt, Joan. "Atwood Country." *Queen's Quarterly*, 80, No. 2 (Summer 1973), 278-81.

G28   Bessai, Diane. "Surfaces." *Lakehead University Review*, 6, No. 2 (Fall/Winter 1973), 255-57.

G29   Galt, George. "'Surfacing' and the Critics." *Canadian Forum*, 54 (May-June 1974), 12-14.

G30   Fraser, D.M. "Margaret Atwood's 'Surfacing.'" *3¢ Pulp*, 2, No. 7 (1 May 1974), 1-4.

G31   French, William. "Resurfacing. At Once the Worst and Best of Books." *The Globe and Mail*, 25 June 1974, p. 14.

Survival

G32   Sutherland, Fraser. "Fast and Loose." *Books in Canada*, 1, No. 11 (Oct. 1972), 10-11.

G33   Grosskurth, Phyllis. "Truth — and a Major Talent." *The Globe and Mail*, 28 Oct. 1972, p. 33.

G34   Fulford, Robert. "A Clever and Effective Analysis of the Literature of Canada." *Toronto Star*, 4 Nov. 1972, p. 79.

G35   Pickersgill, Alan. "Survival for Whom?" *Alive*, 3, No. 6 (1973), 12-14.

G36   Wolfe, Morris. "Atwood's Guide to the Geography of Survival." *Saturday Night*, 88 (Jan. 1973), 32-33.

G37   Ross, Malcolm. Rev. of *Survival*. *Dalhousie Review*, 53 (Spring 1973), 159-60.

G38   Geddes, Gary. Rev. of *Survival*. *Malahat Review*, No. 26 (April 1973), pp. 233-34.

G39   Gutteridge, Don. Rev. of *Survival*. *Canadian Forum*, 53 (May 1973), 39-41.

G40   Sonthoff, Helen. "The Long Will To Be in Canada." *Quarry*, 22, No. 3 (Summer 1973), 75-77.

G41   Watt, Frank. Rev. of *Survival*. *University of Toronto Quarterly*, 42 (Summer 1973), 440-41.

G42   Jonas, George. "Maggie Is a Thing Apart." *Maclean's*, 86 (Aug. 1973), 11, 14.

G43   Grosskurth, Phyllis. "Survival Kit." *New Statesman*, 86 (24 Aug. 1973), 254-55.

G44   Harrison, Richard T. "The Literary Geography of Canada." *Lakehead University Review*, 6, No. 2 (Fall/Winter 1973), 274-76.

G45   Swayze, Walter E. "Survey and Survival." *Journal of Canadian Fiction*, 3, No. 1 (Winter 1974), 112-13.

G46   Driver, Christopher. "Hastings Owl." *Listener*, 91 (14 March 1974), 342-43.

Lady Oracle

G47   Richler, Mordecai. Rev. of *Lady Oracle*. *Book-of-the-Month Club News*, Aug. 1976, pp. 1-3.

G48   Jackson, Marni. "Atwood As a Satirist Is Too Self-Assured." *Toronto Star*, 28 Aug. 1976, p. H7.

G49   Duffy, Dennis. "Read It for Its Gracefulness, for Its Good Story, for Its Help in Your Fantasy Life." *The Globe and Mail*, 4 September 1976, p. 32. Rpt. Cana-Reader, 17, No. 9 (Sept. 1976), 2-4.

G50   Owen, I.M. "Queen of the Maze." *Books in Canada*, 5, No. 9 (Sept. 1976), 3-5.

G51   Sandler, Linda. "Atwoodian Parody of the 1950s." *Saturday Night*, 91, No. 6 (Sept. 1976), 59.

G52   Waller, G.F. "New Fiction: Myths and Passions, Rivers and Cities." *Ontario Review*, No. 3 (Fall-Winter 1976-77), pp. 93-97.

G53   Pollitt, Katha. Rev. of *Lady Oracle*. *New York Times Book Review*, 26 Sept. 1976, pp. 7-8.

G54   Stimpson, Catharine R. "Don't Bother Me, I'm Dead." *Ms.*, 5, No. 4 (Oct. 1976), 36, 40.

G55   Struthers, J.R. (Tim). "Tale of Multiple Identities Has More Than One Identity of Its Own." *London Free Press*, 2 Oct. 1976, p. 28.

G56   Brophy, Brigid. "A Contrary Critic Takes a Crack at 'Lady Oracle.'" *The Globe and Mail*, 9 Oct. 1976, p. 33.

G57   Miller, Karl. "Orphans and Oracles." *New York Review of Books*, 23, No. 17 (28 Oct. 1976), 30-32.

G58   Rosengarten, Herbert. "Urbane Comedy." *Canadian Literature*, No. 72 (Spring 1977), pp. 84-87.

G59   Thomas, Clara. "Feminist or Heroine?" *Essays on Canadian Literature*, No. 6 (Spring 1977), pp. 28-31.

G60   Miller, Jane. "A Pack of Truths." *Times Literary Supplement,* 15 July 1977, p. 872.

Dancing Girls

G61   Hofsess, John. "Atwoodioni Presents . . . a Collection of Unhappy Middle-Class Women, None of Whom Look Like Monica Vitti." *Books in Canada,* 6, No. 9 (Nov. 1977), 27-28.

G62   Hill, Douglas. "Violations." *Canadian Forum,* 57 (Dec.-Jan. 1977-78), 35.

G63   Morley, Patricia. Rev. of *Dancing Girls. World Literature Written in English,* 17, No. 1 (April 1978), 188-90.

G64   Kertzer, Jon. Rev. of *Dancing Girls. Fiddlehead,* No. 117 (Spring 1978), pp. 133-35.

Life Before Man

G65   French, William. "Margaret Atwood, Dinosaurs and Real People. Confusion Amid Tangled Emotions." *The Globe and Mail,* 29 Sept. 1979, p. E10.

G66   Wiseman, Adele. "Readers Can Rejoice, Atwood's in Form." *Toronto Star,* 29 Sept. 1979, p.F7.

G67   Amiel, Barbara. "Life After Surviving." *Maclean's,* 93 (October 15, 1979), 66, 68.

G68   Duffy, Dennis. "Splits Without Spleen." *Books in Canada,* 8, No. 8 (October 1979), 10-11.

G69   Taylor, Michael. Review of *Life Before Man. Fiddlehead,* No. 124 (Winter 1980), pp. 111-12.

G70   French, Marilyn. "Spouses and Lovers." *New York Times Book Review,* 3 February 1980, pp. 1, 26.

G71   Pollitt, Katha. Review of *Life Before Man. Ms.,* 8, No. 9 (March 1980), 27-9.

G72   Sage, Lorna. "The Glacier in the Cupboard." *Times Literary Supplement,* 14 March 1980, p. 289.

Notes

The Where of Here, Sandra Djwa

[1]Milton Wilson, "Klein's Drowned Poet, Canadian Variations on an Old Theme," *Canadian Literature*, No. 6, (Autumn, 1960), p. 14.

[2]Northrop Frye, "Conclusion," *Literary History of Canada*, 2nd edition edited by Carl F. Klinck, Vol 2 (University of Toronto Press, 1965, 1976), p. 342.

[3]Northrop Frye, *The Bush Garden*, (House of Anansi Press Limited, 1971), p. 126.

[4]Northrop Frye, *The Bush Garden*, p. 138.

[5]My sense of Jay Macpherson's iconoclastic use of myth was heightened by remarks made by Jean Mallinson in a PhD dissertation on Canadian women poets now in preparation at Simon Fraser University.

[6]Northrop Frye, "Conclusion," *Literary History of Canada*, Vol. 2, p. 350.

[7]*15 Canadian Poets Plus 5*, edited by Gary Geddes and Phyllis Bruce, (Oxford University Press, 1978), "Notes on the Poets: Margaret Atwood," p. 378. "One way of looking at Margaret Atwood's poetry is to see it as the jottings of a pioneer in the uncharted expanses of consciousness. Her poetry seems to say (to make a variation of the Cartesian *cogito ergo sum*), 'I think, therefore I am in trouble.'"

[8]Atwood, like Pratt, read Conan Doyle's *The Lost World*, but she was also familiar with Pratt's evolutionary world, the description of life before man and the carnivorous dinosaur, Tyrannosaurus Rex, in *The Great Feud*.

[9]Margaret Atwood, *Survival*, (House of Anansi Press Limited, 1972), pp. 59-60. Here Atwood makes a point of noting that Birney transfers images from sea to land.

[10]Birney was not consciously aware of the extent of this influence: "Although I'm not conscious of any direct influence of Pratt on my work, his example had encouraged me to adventure into the writing of a narrative poem with a Canadian wilderness setting." Earle Birney, *The Cow Jumped Over the Moon: the Writing and Reading of Poetry* (Holt, Rinehart & Winston, 1972), p. 35.

[11]Some of the ideas expressed in this essay, especially as they related to Atwood and the Canadian tradition, were developed between 1972 and 1976 for a larger study of Canadian poetry still in preparation. Since that time two essays have appeared which raise some of the issues discussed here. Rosemary Sullivan in "Breaking the Circle" briefly remarks on the relation between Frye's "garrison mentality" and Atwood's nature in *The Journals of Susanna Moodie* and "Progressive Insanities of a Pioneer." Tom Marshall in "Atwood Under and Above Water" remarks that Atwood has worked consciously within the Canadian tradition and that the "under water motif" recurs throughout her work. He associates her notions of inner and outer space, garrison and wilderness, with the poetry of Margaret Avison, P.K. Page and Al Purdy. However these initial remarks are not elaborated. There is no suggestion of a Canadian tradition based on a continuity of poetic myth from Pratt to Birney to Atwood. Both articles appear in *The Malahat Review*, "Margaret Atwood — A Symposium," Number 41, (January, 1977).

Atwood's Haunted Sequences, Judith McCombs

[1]*You Are Happy* (Toronto: Oxford Univ. Press, 1974), pp. 15-16.

[2]*The Circle Game* (Toronto: Anansi, 1966); *The Journals of Susanna Moodie* (Toronto: Oxford Univ. Press, 1970); and *Power Politics* (Toronto: Anansi, 1971). All further references to these works appear in the text.

[3]*The Animals in That Country* (Boston: Little, Brown, 1968), pp. 42-47, 52; *Lady Oracle* (New York: Avon, 1976); Eli Mandel, "Atwood Gothic," *Malahat Review: Margaret Atwood: A Symposium*, ed. Linda Sandler, No. 41 (Jan. 1977), pp. 165-74.

[4]Robert D. Hume, "Gothic vs. Romantic: A Reevaluation of the Gothic Novel," *PMLA*, 84 (1969), 282-90; Peter Haining, "Introduction," in *Gothic Tales of Terror, I, Classic Horror Stories from Great Britain*, ed. Peter Haining (Baltimore, Md.: Penguin, 1972), pp. 11-18; and Ellen Moers, *Literary Women* (Garden City, N.Y.: Anchor Books, 1977), pp. 137-67, 185-213.

Note that Hume, Haining, and Moers all find it necessary to first define, then to justify the merits of, the original British Gothic, for a modern audience that apparently is not familiar with a serious Gothic tradition. Hume's essay dignifies the Gothic by claiming great novels for it. Haining, rescuing Gothic tales that have been out of print one hundred years and more, laments the Gothic's current exile from the general reader, and calls for its rediscovery and reinstatement as honorable literature. Moers' two Gothic chapters, like Hume, claim for the Gothic great works, and, like Haining, seek to rescue particular Gothic works and Gothic elements for our admiration.

[5]My definition of Gothic literature derives in great part from Hume, Haining, and Moers. I am also indebted to Edith Birkhead, *The Tale of Terror: A Study of the Gothic Romance* (New York: Dutton, 1921); Howard Phillips Lovecraft, *Supernatural Horror in Literature* ([c. 1927]; 1945; rpt. New York: Dover, 1973); Montague Summers, *The Gothic Quest: A History of the Gothic Novel* (London: The Fortune Press, 1938); Devendra P. Varma, *The Gothic Flame: Being a History of the Gothic Novel in England* (London: A. Barker, 1957); E.F. Bleiler's "Introduction" to *Three Gothic Novels* (New York: Dover, 1966), esp. p. xvi; and to Margaret Atwood's expert advice on Gothic literature. All errors and opinions are my own.

[6]Moers, p. 139.

[7]Horace Walpole, "Maddelena or The Fate of the Florentines," in Haining, *Gothic Tales*, pp. 21-43; Ann Radcliffe, *The Mysteries of Udolpho* (London: Dent, 1931, rpt. 1973).

[8]*Lady Oracle*, p. 259.

[9]Margaret Atwood, "Afterword," *Journals*, pp. 62-64.

[10]Julia Anne Curtis, "The Unknown! or, The Knight of the Blood-Red Plume," in Haining, *Gothic Tales*, pp. 230-60.

[11]*Survival: A Thematic Guide to Canadian Literature* (Toronto: Anansi, 1972), pp. 45-66. Compare Howard Phillips Lovecraft's tracing of pre-Gothic Western horror-lore back to the "mystic Northern blood" and our "forest-born and ice-fostered whisperings" of hideous boreal rites (in *Supernatural Horror*, p. 19).

[12]Moers, p. 211.

[13]Moers, p. 163.

[14]*Survival*, pp. 36-39.

[15]*Power Politics*, p. 47.

[16]Harold Bloom, "Afterword," in *Frankenstein, or, the Modern Prometheus*, by Mary Shelley (New York: Signet-The New American Library, 1965), pp. 213-15.

[17]Letter received from Margaret Atwood, 1973.

[18]Arthur Edward Waite, *The Pictorial Key to the Tarot, Being Fragments of a Secret Tradition under the Veil of Divination* (New Hyde Park, N.Y.: University Books, 1910 & 1959), p. 116.

[19]Joan Larkin, "Soul Survivor," *Ms.*, May 1973, p. 35; Gloria Onley, "Power Politics in Bluebeard's Castle," *Canadian Literature*, No. 60 (Spring 1974), p. 22; see also my article on *"Power Politics:* The Book & Its Cover," *Moving Out*, 3, No. 2 (1973), 54-69.

[20]Pamela Sargent, "Introduction: Women and Science Fiction," in *Women of Wonder: Science Fiction Stories by Women about Women*, ed. Pamela Sargent (New York: Vintage-Random, 1975), p. xvi: "The story of Frankenstein is a powerful one, mirroring as it does the conflict between growing scientific knowledge and the fear that this knowledge may destroy us, as Frankenstein's monstrous creation destroyed him."

[21]Jean Rhys, *Wide Sargasso Sea* (Markham, Ontario: Penguin Books, 1966).

[22]"Fichter's Bird," *Tales of Grimm and Andersen*, selected by Frederick Jacobi, Jr. (New York: The Modern Library, 1952), pp. 268-71. I am indebted to Margaret Atwood for this and other generous advice on Gothic elements in her work. All errors and opinions are my own.

[23]The phrase "static climax" is, of course, deliberate paradox. In Gothic literature, static is both an inheritance and a virtue. From the very beginning, Gothic literature has emanated from the static surfaces of art, architecture, and dream. Walpole's dream-engendered *Castle of Otranto* is haunted by gigantic hand and helmet and by Gothic structures drawn from Giovanni Battista Piranesi's monumental etchings, *Le Carceri (The Prisons)* as well as by Walpole's own self-designed pseudo-Gothic castle on Strawberry Hill. See A.T. Baker, "Architect for Dreams; Exhibition of Drawings at Manhattan's Morgan Library," *Time*, 18 Sept. 1978, p. 112; and Bleiler (footnote 5 above), esp. pp. viii and xi. Because the Gothic, by definition, seeks to fix, intensify, and prolong its terror and horror, this static, pictorial inheritance becomes a necessary virtue.

[24]The distilling lens and the metamorphosis of something living into something else are both metaphors used by Atwood about her work; see "Karla Hammond: An Interview with Margaret Atwood," *American Poetry Review*, 8, No. 5 (Sept./Oct. 1979), p. 27; and Linda Sandler, "Interview with Margaret Atwood," *Malahat Review: Margaret Atwood: A Symposium*, ed. Linda Sandler, No. 41 (Jan. 1977), pp. 7-27.

Atwood and the Poetics of Duplicity, Sherrill E. Grace

[1]Margaret Atwood, *Lady Oracle* (Toronto: McClelland and Stewart, 1976), p. 246.

[2]Margaret Atwood, *Two-Headed Poems* (Toronto: Oxford University Press, 1978), p. 15. References to the poetry will be included in the text

according to the following key. *DP: Double Persephone* (Toronto: Hawkshead, 1961); *CG: The Circle Game* (Toronto: Contact Press, 1966); *AC: The Animals in that Country* (Toronto: Oxford University Press, 1968); *JSM: The Journals of Susanna Moodie* (Toronto: Oxford University Press, 1970); *PU: Procedures for Underground* (Toronto: Oxford University Press, 1970); *PP: Power Politics* (Toronto: Anansi, 1972); *YAH: You Are Happy* (Toronto: Oxford University Press, 1974); and *THP: Two-Headed Poems* (Toronto: Oxford University Press, 1978).

[3]The double nature of language structure is described by Saussure as the distinction between syntagmatic and paradigmatic relationships and by Jakobson as the poles of metonymy and metaphor. Jakobson's theories are referred to in greater detail below. See Ferdinande de Saussure, *Course in General Linguistics* (New York: McGraw-Hill, 1966), and Roman Jakobson and Morris Halle, *Fundamentals of Language* (The Hague: Janua Linguarum, Mouton, 1956).

[4]See Atwood's interview with Graeme Gibson in *Eleven Canadian Novelists* (Toronto: Anansi, 1973), p. 27.

[5]Atwood discusses her idea of the self on the 60 minute tape made by High Barnett (Toronto, 1973). See also Sherrill E. Grace, *Violent Duality: A Study of Margaret Atwood* (Montreal: Vehicule Press, 1980), chapters I, V, and VI.

[6]See *Violent Duality: A Study of Margaret Atwood,* chapter II.

[7]Claude Lévi-Strauss, *The Raw and the Cooked: Introduction to a Science of Mythology* (New York: Harper & Row, 1969), pp. 6-13 and p. 20.

[8]*The Complete Writings of William Blake,* ed. Geoffrey Keynes (London: Nonesuch Press, 1957), p. 818. Atwood's mistrust of reason and limited vision echoes Blake's; the last stanza of Blake's "Happiness" is as follows:

> Now I a fourfold vision see,
> And a fourfold vision is given to me;
> 'Tis fourfold in my supreme delight
> And threefold in soft Beulah's night
> And twofold Always. May God us keep
> From Single vision and Newton's sleep!

[9]"Margaret Atwood: Poet as Novelist," in *The Canadian Novel in the Twentieth Century,* ed. George Woodcock (Toronto: McClelland and Stewart, 1975), p. 312.

[10]Metaphor and metonymy can be viewed not only in the narrower traditional sense of tropes, but also in terms of association and development in poetic processes. Thus, metaphor refers to the substitution of one word for another on the basis of similarity or analogy; simile, as in this

poem, is a subfigure of metaphor. Metonymy refers to substitution based on contiguity or contextual association; synedoche is a subfigure of metonymy. According to Jakobson, metaphor dominates in poetry and in the romantic and symbolic schools while metonymy dominates in prose and the realistic school. See Roman Jakobson and Morris Halle, *Fundamentals of Language* (1956), pp. 76-82. The heavily metonymic nature of Atwood's poetry accounts, in part, for the apparent 'realism' of her work.

[11]Gerard Genette, *Figures, III* (Paris: Editions du Seuil, 1972), p. 42.

[12]Margaret Atwood, "The Siamese Twins," *The Fiddlehead*, 59 (Winter, 1964), p. 60.

[13]*The Fiddlehead*, 59 (Winter, 1964), pp. 61-62.

[14]"The Witch & the Nightingale" and "The Whore & the Dove" appeared in *Alphabet*, 5 (December, 1962), pp. 44-45 and pp. 48-49.

[15]*Surfacing* (New York: Simon and Schuster, 1972), p. 148.

Meridians of Perception, Lorraine Weir

This paper is indebted to two meticulous critics, Barbara Blakely and Patricia Merivale, who are not responsible for its obscurities.

[1]Margaret Atwood, *The Journals of Susanna Moodie* (Toronto: Oxford University Press, 1970). Although they are structuring devices of central importance, Atwood's collages have not been included in the otherwise complete section of her *Selected Poems* (Toronto: Oxford University Press, 1976) devoted to the *Journals*. Abbreviations used in this paper are as follows: *AC: The Animals in that Country* (Toronto: Oxford University Press, 1968); *CG: The Circle Game* (Toronto: Anansi, 1966); *JSM: The Journals of Susanna Moodie* (Toronto: Oxford University Press, 1970); *PP: Power Politics* (Toronto: Anansi, 1972); *PU: Procedures for Underground* (Toronto: Oxford University Press, 1970); *S: Surfacing* (Don Mills: Paperjacks, 1972); *YAH: You are Happy* (Toronto: Oxford University Press, 1974). Subsequent references will be followed by title abbreviation and page number in parentheses within the paper. Analysis of selections from *Two-Headed Poems and Others* will be found in my essay, "'Fauna of Mirrors': The Poetry of Hébert and Atwood," *ARIEL* 10:3 (July 1979), 99-113.

[2]Collages referred to in this paper are located as follows: one — front cover; two — p. 8; three — p. 18; four — p. 28; five — p. 40; six — p. 44; seven — p. 56; eight — back cover.

[3]Although collage eight is, strictly speaking, a reverse print photograph, I have included it under this heading because of the balancing of collage and photograph in terms of both aesthetic form and perceptual technique which is central to Atwood's concerns in the *Journals*. The

trees in the background of the photograph are said to be "mimetically depicted" bearing in mind the many options available during the "taking" of the photograph and during the initial printing of the negative (as well as during subsequent printings — e.g., the reverse printing technique used in this collage). Both collage and photograph are acts of super/imposition — the collage in an obvious, material way: the photograph in terms of optics as well as processing, and of the perspectival rearrangement of realities implicit within it (photograph as the perpetual tourist's act of memory, surrogate and skewed experience). Collages synthesizing sketch and photograph or engraving mime the puzzlebox inversions of a poem like "This is a Photograph of Me" (*CG*, 11). Or, to use another of Atwood's codes, they are "Tricks with Mirrors" (*YAH*, 24).

⁴See below, p. 79.

⁵Cf. *S*, 187 where the narrator's father, unlike Moodie's husband, does become a shape-shifter in death.

⁶See Paul Schilder, *The Image and Appearance of the Human Body* (N.Y.: International Universities Press, 1950), pp. 85-7 and *passim*. This association of touch with property is transcended in *Two-Headed Poems* (Toronto: Oxford University Press, 1978) in which, through the bond of mother and daughter, flesh is reclaimed. See Adrienne Rich, *Of Woman Born: Motherhood as Experience and Institution* (N.Y.: Bantam, 1977) on the nature of this bond and on patriarchal expropriation.

⁷Cf. Ludwig Wittgenstein: ". . . solipsism, when its implications are followed out strictly, coincides with pure realism. The self of solipsism shrinks to a point without extension, and there remains the reality coordinated with it." (*Tractatus Logico-Philosophicus*, tr. D.F. Pears and B.F. McGuinness. London: Routledge and Kegan Paul, 1961. 5.64.)

⁸Cf. Annette Kolodny's discussion of the conquest of the New World as, first, seduction and ultimately rape of the land in *The Lay of the Land* (Chapel Hill: University of North Carolina Press, 1975).

⁹See Michel Foucault, *The Order of Things* (London: Tavistock, 1970), pp. 21-3, on the ancient concept of analogy, current in European thought until the end of the sixteenth century. Foucault writes that "Man's body is always the possible half of a universal atlas. . . . He is the great fulcrum of proportions — the centre upon which relations are concentrated and from which they are once again reflected." "Upright between the surfaces of the universe, he stands in relation to the firmament (his face is to his body what the face of heaven is to the ether; his pulse beats in his veins as the stars circle the sky according to their own fixed paths; the seven orifices in his head are to his face what the seven planets are to the sky). . . ." This is precisely the tradition which leads Atwood's pioneer to his progressive insanities in the New World.

[10]Other variations on this theme include "A Soul, Geologically" (*PU*, 58), "Axiom" (*AC*, 69), "Journey to the Interior" *(CG*, 57).

[11]Other poems of this type include "Game after Supper" (*PU*, 7), "Girl and Horse, 1920" (*PU*, 10), "Delayed Message" (*PU*, 19), "Woman Skating" (*PU*, 64), and "Younger Sister, Going Swimming" (*PU*, 66).

[12]Cf. Dennis Lee's approach to the strife of "earth" and "world" in his book *Savage Fields — An Essay in Literature and Cosmology* (Toronto: Anansi, 1977).

[13]See Leonard Barkan, *Nature's Work of Art* (New Haven: Yale University Press, 1975) on the melothesia or emblem of Vitruvian man and its literary exfoliations. Note that the cosmology of the seamless universe refers not to an animist world view (in which the European dichotomies of animate/inanimate — and the finality and conclusiveness of the category 'inanimate' — provide an explicit framework for judgement) but to a world in which exists a "basic metaphysical unity in the ground of being," as A. Irving Hallowell states in his study of "Ojibwa World View and Disease" (reprinted in his *Contributions to Anthropology*, Chicago and London: University of Chicago Press, 1976. pp. 391-448). Hallowell notes that the Ojibwa world view (in which interaction of "other-than-human-beings" — including animals, plant life, and so on — and human beings is not only possible but a chief source of dream visions, and disease and cure) "leaves a door open that our orientation on dogmatic grounds keeps shut tight" (Ibid., p. 363). It is to a world view of this sort that Atwood alludes. See also Hallowell's essays "Ojibwa Ontology, Behavior, and World View" (pp. 357-90), and "The Ojibwa Self and Its Behavioral Environment," reprinted in Hallowell's *Culture and Experience* (Philadelphia: University of Pennsylvania Press, 1955), pp. 172-82.

The Making of *Selected Poems*, Linda W. Wagner

[1]Margaret Atwood, *You Are Happy* (New York: Harper and Row, 1974), p. 94.

[2]Margaret Atwood, *Surfacing* (New York: Simon and Schuster, 1972, and Popular Library, 1976), p. 109.

[3]*Surfacing*, p. 127.

[4]*You Are Happy*, p. 10.

[5]*Surfacing*, p. 91.

[6]*You Are Happy*, p. 95.

[7]*Ibid.*, p. 96.

[8]Margaret Atwood, *The Circle Game*, p. 68. In the 1974 collection, she plays with the image of two islands but this time they are not so distinct. References in the next pages refer to poems in this collection and are given in text.

[9]Margaret Atwood, *Selected Poems* (New York: Simon and Schuster, 1976), p. 51. Hereafter cited in text as *SP*.

[10]Margaret Atwood, "Afterword," *The Journals of Susanna Moodie* (Toronto: Oxford University Press, 1970), p. 62.

[11]*Ibid.*, p. 63.

[12]Margaret Atwood, *Power Politics* (Toronto: Anansi Press, 1971), p. 18.

[13]*Ibid.*, p. 56.

One Woman Leads to Another, Lorna Irvine

I would like to thank my student, Melody Ziff, for her assistance in the writing of this paper.

[1]I will refer to the following collections of Margaret Atwood's poetry. Page references and abbreviated titles will be given in the text: *The Circle Game* (Toronto: House of Anansi, 1966), *CG*; *The Animals in That Country* (Toronto: Oxford University Press, 1968), *AC*; *The Journals of Susanna Moodie* (Toronto: Oxford University Press, 1970), *JSM*; *Procedures for Underground* (Toronto: Oxford University Press, 1970), *PU*; *Power Politics* (Toronto: House of Anansi, 1971), *PP*; *You Are Happy* (Toronto: Oxford University Press, 1974), *YAH*; *Two-Headed Poems* (Toronto: Oxford University Press, 1978), *THP*.

[2]In "The Red and Silver Heroes Have Collapsed" *(Concerning Poetry*, in press), a study of Atwood's poetry, I discuss the relationship between the female poet and her male counterpart. In fact, Atwood's poems reveal the poet's altering attitudes to man, alterations that turn the father/god into a human being. Certainly, until the publication of *Two-Headed Poems*, Atwood's poetry has been predominantly dualistic, an analysis of male/female relationships.

[3]Political tensions imaged in the human body are particularly striking in *Power Politics*, for example in the poems beginning "My beautiful wooden leader" (p. 7), "You want to go back" (p. 9), "At first I was given centuries" (p. 28), "You refuse to own yourself" (p. 30) and "You are the sun in reverse" (p. 47).

[4]Until the publication of *Two-Headed Poems*, Atwood's poetry seems to dramatize what Erikson calls the conflict between intimacy and isolation. Hostilities are strong, particularly between male and female, and throughout, the poet betrays a "readiness to isolate and, if necessary, to destroy those forces and people whose essence" seems dangerous to her own. On the other hand, in this volume, the poet seems concerned with generativity, the next of Erikson's stages. See Erik Erikson, *Childhood and Society* (New York: Norton and Norton, 1950), pp. 263-268. The implication of my paper is obvious. I am arguing that the birth of her first child has dramatically changed the focus of Atwood's writing.

Minuets and Madness, Lee Briscoe Thompson

[1]R.P. Bilan, "Letters in Canada 1977: Fiction," *University of Toronto Quarterly*, 47 (Summer 1978), 329-331.

[2]M. Atwood, "What's so funny? Notes on Canadian Humour," *This Magazine*, 8, no. 3 (August-September 1974), 24-27.

[3]Lawrence Fast, "Tripping the Light Fantastic," *Vancouver Sun*, September 16, 1977, p. 33L.

[4]Keith Garebian, "Mediocre clichés from Atwood," *Montreal Star*, March 4, 1978, p. D3.

[5]Sharon Nicoll, "Pirouettes and Falls," *Branching Out*, 5, no. 1 (1978), 44-45.

The Dark Voyage, Catherine McLay

[1]Linda Sandler, Interview with Margaret Atwood, *Malahat Review*, No. 41 (Jan. 1977), p. 10.

[2]For a study of Northrop Frye's theory in relation to *Surfacing* see Arnold E. and Cathy N. Davidson, "The Anatomy of *Surfacing*" in *ARIEL*, 10, No. 3 (July 1979), 38-54.

[3]Northrop Frye, *The Anatomy of Criticism* (Princeton: Princeton University Press, 1957), pp. 163-5.

[4]Graeme Gibson, "Margaret Atwood" in *Eleven Canadian Novelists* (Toronto: Anansi, 1973), pp. 20-1.

[5]Sandler, pp. 13-14.

[6]Northrop Frye, *The Anatomy of Criticism*, pp. 186-206. Also *The Secular Scripture* (Cambridge: Harvard University Press, 1976), pp. 15, 50-8, 102-7, 111, 115, 118 and *passim*.

[7]Sandler, pp. 16, 18.

[8]All quotations in the text refer to Margaret Atwood, *The Edible Woman* (Toronto: McClelland and Stewart, New Canadian Library, 1973).

[9]For a discussion of this, see my article "The Divided Self: Theme and Pattern in Margaret Atwood's *Surfacing*," *Journal of Canadian Fiction*, 4, No. 1 (1975), 82-95.

[10]Linda Chase, *Hyperrealism* (New York: Rizzoli International Publications, 1975), p. 7. The terms New Realism, High Realism, and Hyperrealism seem to be interchangeable.

[11]*The Secular Scripture*, p. 104.

[12]Margaret Atwood, *Dancing Girls* (Toronto: McClelland and Stewart, 1977), p. 117.

[13]*The Secular Scripture*, p. 115.

[14]*The Secular Scripture*, p. 114.

[15]Alan Dawe, Introduction to *The Edible Woman*, n. pag.

[16]Gibson, p. 25.

[17]*The Secular Scripture*, p. 118.

Surfacing and the Rebirth Journey, Annis Pratt

[1]Francine du Plessix Gray, "Nature as Nunnery," *New York Times Book Review*, July 17, 1977, p. 29.

[2]Carol P. Christ, "Margaret Atwood: The Surfacing of Women's Spiritual Quest and Vision," *Signs*, 2, No. 2 (Winter 1976), 330, 317.

[3]See Laurens van der Post, *Jung and the Story of Our Time* (New York: Pantheon, 1975), p. 3.

[4]C.G. Jung, "Concerning Rebirth," *The Archetypes and the Collective Unconscious* (Princeton: Princeton University Press, 1969), p. 114.

[5]C.G. Jung, "The Psychological Aspects of the Kore," *The Archetypes and The Collective Unconscious*, p. 187.

[6]I have written an article on this subject entitled "'Aunt Jennifer's Tigers': Notes Towards a Pre-Literary History of Women's Archetypes," *Feminist Studies*, 4, No. 1 (February 1978), 163-94.

[7]"Sexual Imagery in *To The Lighthouse*," *Modern Fiction Studies*, 18, No. 3 (Autumn 1972), 417-431.

[8]Virginia Woolf, *To The Lighthouse* (London: Hogarth, 1960), p. 95.

[9]C.G. Jung, *Symbols of Transformation* (Princeton: Princeton University Press, 1956), p. 293.

[10]*To The Lighthouse*, pp. 308-9.

[11]Anais Nin, *Cities of the Interior* (Athens, Ohio: Swallow Press, 1974), pp. 531, 540, and from *Ladders to Fire*, p. 58.

[12]*Ibid., Ladders to Fire*, p. 14.

[13]*Ibid.*, p. 18.

[14]*Seduction of the Minotaur*, p. 544.

[15]Margaret Atwood, *Surfacing* (New York: Popular Library, 1972), p. 171.

[16]*Ibid.*, p. 191.

[17]Mary Daly, *Beyond God the Father* (Boston: Beacon Press, 1973), pp. 65-66.

[18]Elaine Showalter, *A Literature of Their Own: British Women Novelists from Brontë to Lessing* (Princeton: Princeton University Press, 1977), p. 297.

[19]Jane Ellen Harrison, *Prolegomena to the Study of Greek Religion*, 3rd ed. (Cambridge: Cambridge University Press, 1922), p. 120.

[20]C.G. Jung and C. Kerenyi, *Essays on a Science of Mythology: The Myth of the Divine Child and the Mysteries of Eleusis*, trans. R.F.C. Hull (Princeton: Princeton University Press, 1950), p. 177, and as quoted in C. Kerenyi, *Eleusis — Archetypal Images of Mother and Daughter*, trans. Ralph Manheim (New York: Schocken, 1971), pp. xxi-xxxii.

[21]"The Psychological Aspects of the Kore," p. 188.

Lady Oracle: The Narrative of a Fool-Heroine, Clara Thomas

[1]Margaret Atwood, *Lady Oracle*, Seal Books, McClelland and Stewart-Bantam, 1977. All references are to this edition of the novel.

[2]Anne, an orphan, and Joan, who feels like an orphan and eventually cuts herself off into virtual orphanhood; Marilla, the adversary, and Joan's mother, the adversary; Matthew, the kindly but ineffectual foster-father, and Joan's father, kindly and ineffectual; Anne's secret fantasy-life and her escape to fantasy places, and Joan's; etc. If Anne is the archetypal girl-child in our literature, Joan Foster is an archetypal case of self-arrested development.

[3]Robert B. Heilman, "Theatre, Self, and Society: Some Analogues," in *A Political Art: Essays and Images in Honour of George Woodcock*, ed. Wm. New, University of British Columbia Press, 1978, p. 44.

Janus Through the Looking Glass, Robert Lecker

[1]Margaret Atwood, *You Are Happy* (Toronto: Oxford University Press, 1974), p. 24 ("Tricks with Mirrors").

[2]Margaret Atwood, *Lady Oracle* (Toronto: McClelland and Stewart, 1976), p. 246. All future references to *Lady Oracle* will be made parenthetically within the text, and will be preceded by the abbreviation *LO*. Future references to *The Edible Woman* (Toronto: McClelland and Stewart, 1969) and *Surfacing* (Toronto: McClelland and Stewart, 1972) will also be made parenthetically within the text, and will be preceded by the abbreviations *EW* and *S* respectively.

[3]Eli Mandel, "Atwood Gothic," *The Malahat Review*, No. 41 (Jan. 1977), pp. 165-74.

[4]Alan Dawe, "Introduction," *The Edible Woman*, New Canadian Library, No. 93 (Toronto: McClelland and Stewart, 1973), n. pag.

[5]Frank Davey, "Atwood Walking Backwards," *Open Letter*, 2nd ser., No. 5 (Spring 1973), p. 79.

[6]T.D. MacLulich, "Atwood's Adult Fairy Tale: Levi-Strauss, Bettelheim, and *The Edible Woman*," *Essays on Canadian Writing*, No. 9 (Summer 1978), p. 122.

[7]Rosemary Sullivan, "Breaking the Circle," *The Malahat Review*, No. 41 (Jan. 1977), p. 40.

[8]Mandel, p. 169.

[9]Sullivan, p. 41.

[10]Mandel, p. 167.

[11]Margaret Atwood, "An Interview with Graeme Gibson," in *Eleven Canadian Novelists* (Toronto: House of Anansi, 1972), p. 20.

[12]Roberta Rubenstein, "*Surfacing*: Margaret Atwood's Journey to the Interior," *Modern Fiction Studies*, 22, No. 3 (Autumn 1976), 396.

[13]Josie P. Campbell, "The Woman as Hero in Margaret Atwood's *Surfacing*," *Mosaic*, 11, No. 3 (Spring 1978), 17-28.

[14]This aspect of *Lady Oracle* has been extensively discussed by Arnold E. and Cathy N. Davidson, "Margaret Atwood's *Lady Oracle*: The Artist as Escapist and Seer," *Studies in Canadian Literature*, 3, No. 2 (Summer 1978), 166-77.

[15]Campbell, p. 19.

[16]As Jerome H. Rosenberg has observed with regard to *Surfacing*, "Atwood truncates the myth — unlike the mythic hero, her protagonist does not return with an elixir that 'restores the world'; hers is not a completed version of the universal myth." ("Woman as Everyman in Atwood's *Surfacing*: Some Observations on the End of the Novel," *Studies in Canadian Literature*, 3, No. 1 [Winter 1978], 128.)

Life Before Man, Cathy N. and Arnold E. Davidson

[1]Joseph Campbell, *The Hero with a Thousand Faces*, 2nd ed. (1949; Princeton: Princeton Univ. Press, 1968), p. 249.

[2]Margaret Atwood, *Life Before Man* (Toronto: McClelland and Stewart, 1979), p. 106. Future references to this edition of the novel will be cited parenthetically within the text.

[3]"Face to Face: Margaret Laurence as Seen by Margaret Atwood," *Maclean's*, 87 (May 1974).

[4]It should be noted, however, that the separate sections of *As I Lay Dying* are narrated in the first person. But Faulkner fully utilizes the full range of his own vocabulary even when "speaking" in the voices of the illiterate Bundren family. Atwood, employing a slightly different technique, achieves a similar effect, and both novels are presented as a series of short, narrative fragments governed by the consciousness of the separate characters portrayed in those separate sections.

[5]Margaret Atwood, *Surfacing* (Toronto: McClelland and Stewart, 1972), p. 191.

[6]Alan Friedman, *The Turn of the Novel* (New York: Oxford Univ. Press, 1966), p. 105. See also Frank Kermode, *The Sense of An Ending: Studies in the Theory of Fiction* (New York: Oxford Univ. Press, 1967), especially chapter 4.

[7]Friedman, p. 182.

[8]Just as the one epigraph, from Björn Kurtén's *The Age of Dinosaurs*, describes how the "behaviour" of extinct animals can persist into the present, the other, from Abram Tertz's "The Icicle," pictures a contemporary fictional character seeing himself reembodied in an envisioned distant future. So even these two epigraphs suggest something of the complex time scheme employed in the novel and the even greater complexity with which "behaviour" wheels therein.

Bashful but Bold, George Woodcock

[1]The address was published in *The Canadian Imagination: Dimensions of a Literary Culture*, ed. David Staines (Cambridge, Mass.: Harvard Univ. Press, 1977), pp. 97-122.

[2]*Poets and Critics: Essays from "Canadian Literature": 1966-74*, ed. George Woodcock (Toronto: Oxford Univ. Press, 1974).

[3]"MacEwen's Muse," *Canadian Literature*, 45 (Summer 1970), 24-32; and "Superwoman Drawn and Quartered: The Early Forms of *She*," *Alphabet*, 10 (July 1965), 65-82.

[4]"Face to Face: Margaret Laurence As Seen By Margaret Atwood," *Maclean's* 87 (May 1974), 38-39, 43-46; and "Marie-Claire Blais Is Not for Burning," *Maclean's* 88 (September 1975), 26-29.

[5]"Paradoxes and Dilemmas: The Woman as Writer," *Woman in the Canadian Mosaic*, ed. Gwen Matheson (Toronto: Peter Martin Associates, 1976), 256-73.

[6]*Malahat Review*, 41 (January 1977), 95-98.

[7]"Eleven Years of *Alphabet*," *Canadian Literature*, 49 (Summer 1971), 60-64.

[8]"Reaney Collected," *Canadian Literature*, 57 (Summer 1973), 113-18.

[9]Malcolm Ross, "Critical Theory: Some Trends," in *Literary History of Canada*, 2nd ed., Carl F. Klinck, ed. (1965; Toronto: Univ. of Toronto Press, 1976), Vol. III, pp. 160-75.

Checklist of Writings, Alan J. Horne

[1]Another version of this bibliography appears as part of the *Annotated Bibliography of Canadian Literature* published by ECW Press. By permission.

Contributors

ARNOLD E. DAVIDSON, an Albertan, wrote his doctoral dissertation under fellow Albertan, Robert Kroetsch, at the State University of New York at Binghamton with the assistance of a Canada Council Fellowship. Currently Associate Professor of English at Elmhurst College, he has numerous essays on British and Canadian literature published or forth-coming in such journals as *Canadian Literature, Studies in Canadian Literature, Philological Quarterly, ARIEL, Nineteenth-Century Fiction,* and others. His book on Mordecai Richler will be published by Frederick Ungar Publishing.

CATHY N. DAVIDSON, Associate Professor of English, teaches in the Canadian Studies Program at Michigan State University. She has pub-lished numerous essays on Canadian and American fiction, as well as women's studies, in journals such as *The American Review of Canadian Studies, Contemporary Literature, Modern Fiction Studies,* and *ARIEL.* She is the co-editor of *The Lost Tradition: Mothers and Daughters in Literature* (1979) and has edited a special issue of the *Journal of American Culture* on "Canada's Women Writers."

SANDRA DJWA is an Associate Professor of English at Simon Fraser University. She has written extensively on Canadian poetry and prose and chairs the National Committee on Research in English-Canadian Litera-ture for the Association of Canadian and Quebec Literatures. She reviews the poetry for the annual "Letters in Canada" section of the *University of Toronto Quarterly* and has written *E.J. Pratt: The Evolutionary Vision* (Copp Clark and McGill-Queen's, 1974), as well as editing the poetry of Charles Heavysege: *Saul and Selected Poems* (University of Toronto Press, 1976). She is currently working on a biography of F.R. Scott.

SHERRILL E. GRACE teaches modern literature at the University of British Columbia. In addition to articles on Canadian fiction and Malcolm Lowry, she is the author of the Introduction to Anansi's 1978 reprint of *The Circle Game* and *Violent Duality: A Study of Margaret Atwood* (Montreal: Véhicule Press, 1980).

ALAN J. HORNE is Assistant Librarian (Reader Services) at the University of Toronto. His publications include *Readers Guide to the Commonwealth* (with C. Simmons), *The Art of W. Heath Robinson,* and *British Book Illustration 1890-1914.* He also compiled "A Preliminary Checklist of Writings By and About Margaret Atwood" for the special Atwood issue of *Malahat Review,* No. 41 (January 1977).

LORNA IRVINE, Assistant Professor of English at George Mason University, formerly taught contemporary literature at Carleton University. Her articles and reviews on Canadian literature have appeared in the *American Review of Canadian Studies, Canadian Literature, Concerning Poetry,* and *Regionalism and the Female Imagination.* Her essay on Canada's women writers appeared in *The Lost Tradition: Mothers and Daughters in Literature,* and she is co-editing *Margaret Drabble: Essays in Criticism.*

ROBERT LECKER teaches at the University of Maine at Orono. He is the co-editor of *Essays on Canadian Writing* and the *Annotated Bibliography of Canada's Major Authors.* Lecker is the editor of the Canadian section of the Twayne World Author series and author of many articles on Canadian literature.

JUDITH McCOMBS has published and presented work on Atwood and on women's concepts of nature in Canada and the U.S. Her poems have appeared in *Aphra, Fiddlehead, Northern Light, Poetry, Prism, Waves,* and in various anthologies, and she has authored two books of poetry, *Sisters and Other Selves* (Glass Bell, 1976) and *Against Nature: Wilderness Poems* (Dustbooks, 1979). She teaches at the Center for Creative Studies College of Art and Design and at Wayne State University.

CATHERINE McLAY teaches Canadian literature at the University of Calgary. She has edited an anthology of nineteenth-century Canadian prose and poetry and has also published articles on Willa Cather, Margaret Laurence, W.O. Mitchell, and Ethel Wilson. She is currently working on a critical biography of W.O. Mitchell.

ANNIS PRATT, Associate Professor of English at the University of Wisconsin, is the author of a book on Dylan Thomas as well as numerous essays on women's literature. She is finishing a ten year study of archetypal patterns in women's fiction based on the examination of recurrent symbols and narrative structures in several hundred novels by British and

North American women. She is also interested in pre-literate archetypes such as those found in women's needlework and in folklore. Her article in this volume is derived from a chapter in *Archetypal Patterns in Women's Fiction*, forthcoming from Indiana University Press.

CLARA THOMAS is Professor of English at York University and a writer of biography and criticism in the fields of Canadian and Commonwealth literature. Her works include *Love and Work Enough: The Life of Anna Jameson, Ryerson of Upper Canada*, and *The Manawaka World of Margaret Laurence*.

LEE BRISCOE THOMPSON teaches Canadian literature in the University of Vermont's Canadian Studies Programme. Raised in Quebec and Manitoba she has presented and published in Canada, the U.S., Europe, and Asia numerous papers, articles, and reviews on Canadian and Commonwealth literature. Her current major work is a book-length study of Dorothy Livesay.

LINDA W. WAGNER, poet and literary critic, is Professor of English and Associate Dean of the College of Arts and Letters at Michigan State University. Although she did postdoctoral work at the University of British Columbia, her twenty books of criticism are mostly on American authors (Faulkner, Hemingway, William Carlos Williams, Eliot, and others). A recent book is *Dos Passos, Artist as American;* her selected essays will appear in 1980. She is currently working on a book on Ellen Glasgow.

LORRAINE WEIR is an Assistant Professor of English at the University of British Columbia. She is author of articles on James Joyce and on Canadian writers (Atwood, Hébert, and Klein). Currently she is working on a book on linguistic modes in Joyce.

GEORGE WOODCOCK edited *Now* in London from 1940 to 1947 and *Canadian Literature* in Vancouver from 1959 to 1977. For a few years, on and off, he taught English at the Universities of Washington and British Columbia. He has written hundreds of radio and television scripts of various kinds, and published fifty books, including *Anarchism, Faces of India,* and *The Crystal Spirit: A Study of George Orwell*. His most recent books include *Peoples of the Coast, Thomas Merton: Monk and Poet,* and *Gabriel Dumont*. His forthcoming books are *The Canadians, The World of Canadian Writing,* and a book of verse, *The Mountain Road*.

Index of Full-Length Works by Margaret Atwood (arranged chronologically)

General Index